PETES
PANDEMIC

---

100 DAYS OF ISOLATED REFLECTION

PETER DAVIDSON

Pete's Pandemic
Copyright © 2020 by Peter Davidson

Tellwell Talent
www.tellwell.ca

ISBN
978-0-2288-4088-6 (Hardcover)
978-0-2288-4087-9 (Paperback)
978-0-2288-4089-3 (eBook)

Contents

In loving memory of Wattie Davidson
(1922 – 1986).

Physician, husband, father, skier, fisherman,
sailor, violinist and polymath.

Introduction

Here in Vancouver on Saturday, 7th March 2020, the two-day World Rugby Sevens took place at BC Place, the covered stadium downtown that has a capacity of about 60,000 people. As ever, many of the crowd were in "fancy dress," the atmosphere was partyish and good humoured. Canada played well and made it through their group to the final day in a good position to progress towards the final. On the Sunday, good friends of ours kindly sponsored a book launch on my behalf. My book, *Kilt in the Closet* was exposed to a wider audience, albeit many of whom I knew well. Canada almost made it to the final, and on the Sunday evening, the crowd dispersed home. On the following day, Monday, 9th March, Italy locked itself down, quarantined itself because of the outbreak of the coronavirus. On that day Collingwood School, where I used to work, finished the term early and closed its doors because a member of the school population had visited the Lynn Valley Care Centre where there had been a COVID-19 fatality.

On Tuesday, 10th March, I flew out to the UK with a return date of April 23rd. I landed on 11th March and immediately took the bus to Bath where I was to visit our daughter, Alison. She met me later that day and we went out to an Italian restaurant for dinner. The waitress confessed that she was Italian and joked that we had nothing to worry about as she had not been home in a long time. Alison and I had breakfast out on the following day, visited the shops and visited the post office where I had to post off a parcel for a friend. We also visited the Roman Baths and a wonderful exhibition of Toulouse Lautrec posters. I was beginning to get excited because my two brothers and I were going to Cardiff to watch Wales v. Scotland in a rugby international along with 80,000 other fans on Saturday, 14th March. Our niece, Rona, was also going to be in Cardiff on Friday night where she and a friend were going to a concert. On Friday afternoon, my brother, George, phoned to say that he felt because of a growing infection rate, that we should cancel our mother's 92nd birthday celebration due to take place on the Sunday. At this point, Rona's concert and our rugby game were still going ahead. Twenty minutes before it was due to start, Rona's concert was cancelled. Around about the same time, the Welsh Rugby Union issued a statement postponing the rugby game.

On Monday, 16th March in the car I had rented from Bristol Airport, I began to drive up to Scotland where I was meeting my friend, Audrey, who had agreed to put me up for a few days in her beautiful flat in Edinburgh. Alison was worried I would drive too far and risk falling asleep at the wheel. She made me promise I would find a place to stay on my first night somewhere in Lancashire. I set off, and the driving was easy. Before I knew it I was in the Scottish borders having left Lancashire in my tailgate many miles before. I settled down into an excellent old-fashioned hotel outside Galashiels. I later discovered that UK traffic was back to 1955 levels.

On the following day, I drove to Edinburgh. I was early so parked in a trading estate and wandered into some of the shops. In one such, three senior citizens were emerging with three new suitcases joking with the security guard that they were going to put them in the corner of their front rooms and place pot plants and family photos on top of them because they knew they were unlikely to be able to use them for travel in the near future. I arrived beneath Arthur's Seat in the dark and the rain in the early evening, and still too early for Audrey who was still at work. I walked up the Royal Mile and entered a Starbucks, which was deserted.

I was worried that Audrey would be so concerned about infection (she works in a care home for the elderly) that she would no longer want to put me up. I need not have worried. On the following two days, we had lovely walks, one on the coast at Aberlady and the other inland in the Pentland Hills.

On Friday, I was due to leave Edinburgh and head for Aberdeenshire. Before I set off, my friends in St. Andrews texted asking me to pick up some child's paracetamol for their son, Harry. Audrey and I found the last two packets on the shelf. I dropped a packet with Jamie on the way north.

I arrived at the village of Tarland and immediately found The Tarland Inn on the main street. I walked through the doors and into the public bar and introduced myself to the barman. I registered for the next twenty-eight days. At that moment Boris Johnson, the British prime minister, was appearing on TV announcing the closure of pubs and hotels! The proprietor, Mrs. Shona Robertson, told me I need not worry as they would not throw me out! For the next five days, like many of us, I felt the world closing around me. I knew by the Monday that I was going to have to cut short my holiday. Alison booked me a flight from Glasgow to London and onward from Heathrow to Vancouver. I drove the three hours to Glasgow the following day, nervously worried that I would be stopped by the police. I arrived at an airport hotel made soulless and dark with almost full closure. I got into my room and was texted by Alison that my flight to London had been cancelled. An hour later she had found me another one. I flew into Heathrow early the next day and spent a fraught day watching flights being cancelled left, right and centre. I was relieved to find myself in the air and on my way with three seats to myself. I was given the quarantine lecture by immigration in Vancouver, caught public transport home and was greeted by Irene, my wife, with a pair of rubber gloves and a bin bag. I was sent upstairs immediately, and there I spent the next two weeks.

I had books to read and the TV to watch, but I needed the discipline of something. So, I decided to write a daily blog on any subject that came to mind. I resolved to send it only to people who were retired or not working. I created a list of eighteen people and, for the next 100 days, for better or worse, most of them received a daily diatribe from me averaging about 1000 words each. My scribblings were ill-disciplined, spontaneous outbursts covering a myriad of differing topics ranging from politics, philosophy, word usage, children, rugby, outdoor experiences and the patently ridiculous.

The following is a collection of my COVID pandemic writings. I have had many second thoughts about putting them into the public domain. I worry about political correctness, virtue signaling and all the current intellectual minefields that have sprouted up over the last few years. So here I feel the need to write something of a disclaimer. I am sixty-eight years old. I have NEVER been a racist, a homophobe or a misogynist. I have always met and treated people as I find them. So, if you find statements or phrases in my writings that you think signal that I am different than I am, then let me assure you that I am not. I may be stupid but I am not dumb. I know one does not have to be a white, privileged, heterosexual male to climb a mountain. A penis is not essential for running a marathon or a business. So please feel free to criticize, to castigate my phraseology, to tear apart my arguments, but know this, Dear Reader, I am accepting of all and dismissive of few, that I like or dislike characters based solely on what we may have in common. I am human, frail and fallible. I have had a wonderful life and I remain grateful for every day. Read on, and I hope you get some pleasure from *Pete's Pandemic*.

*"There is one art of which
people should be masters—
the art of reflection."
Samuel Taylor Coleridge*

CHAPTER 1

THE NEW NORMAL

Sixty-seven years on the planet had not prepared me for this. Suddenly to be confined and restricted hurt immensely. And yet stepping back from the situation and reflecting (and goodness knows there suddenly became plenty of time for that!), it became apparent how lucky Irene and I are. In our time, we travelled the world, had our children, had our careers, bought our house, have a garden, possess our established friendships. To be starting out on life at this time must be a daunting task, one full of uncertainty and hardship. To be in a developing country, already burdened with every day struggles for survival, must be body and soul destroying. If I was not me, I would envy me.

Toilet Rolls and Arse-umptions

A few years ago, a guy wrote in to the *Globe and Mail* advocating the end of toilet rolls. He suggested they were not needed and proceeded to explain why. "Easy," he said, "get up in the morning, do your business and get straight into the shower." All fine and dandy but the assumption is that people's bodily functions work to a timetable. We know this is not true, otherwise we would not need sit-down toilets in our male washrooms at work. Then the pandemic hits and there is a run on toilet rolls. Somebody has yet, after two months, to explain why they were such an essential part of our lives. We probably all saw the Arnie Schwarzenegger picture as he left the store with his horde of thirty-six double ply on his back.

"Where did you get them, Arnie?"

"Aisle B back."

Assumptions are one of life's irritants. I was stopped once on the way to coffee by an elderly couple where the old guy had decided on a short cut to North Vancouver Railway Station. I directed him back to Marine Drive explaining there was no way he could drive through Norgate park. He was insistent there was a way through! I, who had lived here for twenty years, did not know, he who had *never* been here before, did! His wife in the passenger seat was coaching him to turn around and retrace his steps. Now *two* total idiots were giving him the wrong advice!

"A woman can make an average man great or a great man average."

But, dear friends, she cannot change a man who knows it all now and has known it all since he first fell out of his cot. I wish I had had the foresight to say to him, "If I were you I wouldn't try to get there from here," thus throwing another cat amongst the already ruffled pigeons. For this old guy, a toilet roll was indeed essential considering the constant effluent he was spouting!!

Driving back from London to Oxford as a student in the 1970s in George's Morris Woodie Traveler, we were nearly back in town. I was in the front because I was the tallest, Paul and Alan were asleep in the back. We came to a roundabout on the by-pass. No bushes on it, just a kerb and grass. George drove straight over it, a bit of a jolt as we hit the kerb and a rapid slowing as we negotiated the grass. White knuckles from me, another puff on his cigarette from George and we were back on the road.

"George, you really should have gone around the roundabout rather than over it," I stammered when I I was finally capable of words.

"What roundabout, Pete?"

One should never make assumptions, should one!!

My dad owned a sailing boat, a laser, really just a windsurfer in which one or two people could sit. It was a fibreglass body, hollow and buoyant.

"Good idea for you to take the boat out, Peter."

Once when I was on holiday in Cornwall, my father assumed I had a great deal of experience as a yachtsman. Don't know where he heard that from. I had been away when the sailing fad hit the Davidson household. But I rigged it up, sail, tiller, rudder, and I launched onto the water. I should have sailed but I drifted. I should have been able to steer but the beast had a mind of its own. It sluggishly became a victim of the tide, and so I drifted up the tidal reaches of the Camel River towards the town of Wadebridge, eventually finding myself beached on the far bank. You see, Dear Readers, I knew nothing about putting in plugs to stop the hollow hull from filling with water. The boat would never sink, but it floated with the tide and the tide became the boat. Any attempt at control from me was useless. I walked the disused railway line and hitched back from Wadebridge, arriving at our holiday home shivering and in the dark. I had assumed that the boat was seaworthy without plugs. Never had to check the plugs on the ferry from Harwich to Kristiansand in Norway had I? Plugs were always in on the boat from Ullapool to Stornoway, of course they would have been there on my dad's sailing boat! My assumption made an arse out of me.

When I worked in London, my home rugby club in Clevedon from the county of Somerset were coming up for their traditional Easter tour. Couple of games, lot of drinking, off to Twickenham for an international rugby and copious camaraderie. I decided to meet them at their hotel in Kensington. Trundled into reception, smiling and happy, eager to see my mates.

"Yes," an abrupt "Basil Fawlty" leaning over the desk.

"I'm here to meet Clevedon Rugby Club."

"No rugby club will ever, ever be allowed to stay here in *my* hotel."

"But, but this is the hotel, this is the address I was given. May I see the guest book?"

And there they all were, familiar names, "Cruncher" Crane, "Windmill" Parker, "Bootsie," "The Thommer," et al. True, all individuals, but all members of an unmentioned club. Never assume that people who are signing into your hotel do not know each other and are not members of a rugby club. Let us not discuss here how the weekend went with the hotel proprietor and his wise decision never to host a rugby team in his beautiful hotel. From his point of view, it was an assumption too far.

Eleanor, our magnificent Irish renter who is now nursing in Iqaluit, looked after our house while Irene and I were on holiday in the UK a year and a bit ago. More importantly, she looked after our two cats, Angus, the ginger male, and Isobel, his sister. Eleanor was walking down Tatlow Avenue after work one evening and she saw Angus sunning himself on the corner of Sowden Street. She had never seen him so far from home before. She picked him up and gently chastised him as they walked down the street. Angus purred with the phlegmatic insouciance that is the trait of most cats. He did not complain at the loving attention of this warm-hearted young woman. Somehow Eleanor managed to manipulate her key into the lock without putting Angus down. She opened the door and at that moment the real Angus ran down the stairs, hungry for his dinner! We have always assumed that owning cats is easier than owning dogs but maybe that is a wrong assumption as well.

> *"Cats look down on you, dogs look up to you, but pigs treat you as an equal."*
> *Winston S. Churchill*

To end, please, please, please can somebody put me out of my misery and explain why toilet rolls were so, so important two months ago??

Have a great day.

Quarantine Questions: Day 1

Well, actually it is day seven of the Davidson quarantine situation but it has taken that much time for the old fellow to come up with anything. Not so much as a wee toe has nudged over the bottom step, the frontier of my territory. I reside upstairs and am dependent on help from below stairs rather like I am living in "Downton Abbey."

If one lived in Spain or Italy then one would be so happy to be a member of the larger European Union would one not? Aha, my friends, I am sure you can hear and feel the sarcasm dripping from this statement. It would seem to be like any other crisis the world has known; it is human nature to hunker down, to return to the womb of warmth which is our family or, indeed, country. Thus do we see Italian and Spanish borders and, incidentally, help flooding in from that powerhouse of the European Union. I refer, of course, to China. Yes, my friends, just like the USA is receiving equipment and such from that hitherto unknown member of NAFTA—that would be Russia—so Italy and Spain are not alone. Help is coming in from outside, albeit not the "outside" they might have expected. Meanwhile the UK, the island nation, is discovering that it is NOT an island. There are no islands any more. The sea that separates so many countries has, after all, always also been the ocean that links us. COVID-19 is killing Britons.

Is this the end of the globalization experiment? Whither do we go when we are finally allowed local and international social contact again? Do we rush out and rebook that international, that cruise, that we were so looking forward to?

It seems to me we shall remain inextricably linked. We may no longer need to travel for a company meeting now that technology is proving so powerful a tool for us. Not great for those of you who study the nuances of body language; not great if one is a teacher when an absent presence, as opposed to a present presence, will be so, so missed.

A couple of travel experiences that I have read gave me a chuckle.

Back in the 1960s, a media type, Alan Hutchison, decided he wanted to explore Japan. He landed in Tokyo without a word of Japanese. Not being a city type, he could not wait to get out into the country. So he armed himself with a phrase from a friendly Japanese man he met in a bar. He practiced it until he was word perfect. He was now able to ask the following question with impunity:

> *"I'm sorry to bother you, but could you tell*
> *me where I could find accommodation?"*

Soon he found himself on a dark, rainy night, soaked to the skin looking for a place to stay. He arrived at a village street and knocked on a door. A friendly woman answered and he popped his question with precise perfection. She looked confused, said nothing, waved at him and gently closed the door. Similar reaction at other doors until he, more by luck than good management, found himself at the local Youth Hostel. In the communal kitchen he asked a young man why he had received so many strange responses. On repeating his question, he was informed that it was translated thus:

"May I take this opportunity to wish you 'Good night'?"

I challenge the legendary politeness of Canadians to outpolite those wonderful people back in the 1960s. Speaking to people who have lived and worked in Japan and many who attended the recent Rugby World Cup, they are still renowned for their welcoming open-hearted friendliness.

Another incident occurred when a lone English cyclist found himself in a shop in rural Aberdeenshire. Having never heard of the Doric dialect, the patois of the county, he could only make out two words from their brief encounter. They were "Michael" and "Jackson." So, with thumbs up, laughter and smiles, words like "Great" and "Fantastic," he backed out of the shop leaving the proprietor upset and confused at the fact that this heartless stranger had just celebrated the death of a pop icon.

"The gladdest moment in human life, methinks, is a departure into unknown lands." Sir Richard Burton

My recent abbreviated adventure back to the "old country" did not quite become an unknown land, but it was so interesting to be part of a situation that morphed and fluctuated very quickly over a period of a couple of weeks.

It is a fortnight I will reflect upon with pleasure and, I hope, a greater understanding. There was so much on this trip that was an absolute joy. Now in quarantine and you, my friends, being in isolation, I leave you with a Henry Miller quotation:

> *"One's destination is never a place, but a new way of seeing things."*

Bored in Exciting Times

We are all experiencing exciting times, and they will likely become more exciting as things open up again. There is huge uncertainty. Any rate, I was thinking today about how the mundane, which is our lot, can lead to mendacity and to mischief. For example, just as I was going to bed last night I thought, *What a wonderful adventure it would be to take a strong sleeping pill washed down with a bottle of ex-lax.* Now that, my friends, would be a bit of an adventure, don't you know? Of course, there are lots of current videos on social media of things going wrong in our isolated indoor sojourns. Human beings are renowned for great innovations that often go wrong.

I read a wonderful obituary a few years ago about a brigadier general who ordered the use of scaling ladders in an attack on a well-fortified enemy position. Apparently, this was the last time such equipment was used in action. Apparently. "He worked on the basis that he would at least surprise somebody, albeit maybe not the enemy." Who knows the consequences of such a leadership ploy; pretty dire one would have thought.

> *"The mirror is dangerous as a guide of deeds." J.R.R. Tolkien*

Who of us is so wise that we proceed on a new path without running it by somebody first? Without being sexist, there is often an impetuosity about the male of the species that makes him blunder in like a fool where angels fear to tread. A long-dead friend of mine, Andrew MacArthur, had volunteered to help try out new nefarious means of killing the enemy in WWII. He was not accepted and was rather glad he wasn't. One of the experiments was to drop planeloads of troops behind enemy lines with their heavy equipment on the plane with them. In test flights, the plane landed OK, came to a halt OK, but the heavy equipment in the rear did not!

Back in the day in England, some bright spark in the government came up with the idea of raising money by taxing windows, the Fenestration tax. Thus, do we see so many old manorial piles in England that have been de-fenestrated, in other words their windows have been bricked in. Maggie Thatcher came up with the idea of the Poll Tax. Good thing, bad thing, fair way to raise money, unfair on large families, mutterings, murmurings, unease from the Conservative Party and her cabinet.

"Tell you what," she said with starry-eyed enthusiasm (some might say wide-eyed fanaticism), arms raised at her flash of inspiration, "We'll try it in Scotland first."

Oh dear, oh dear, that's chain sawing off the branch upon which one sits if ever anything was. It's hard to be a human being is it not? "There is a wisdom of the head, there is a wisdom of the heart," said Charles Dickens. Leadership, I think, is knowing when and how each is appropriate.

Any rate, I will desist now. I realize that the only way you will ever read this is if you are bored in exciting times!

Statistics and Generalisations

We have probably all heard the story of the guy who drowned because he tried to walk across a lake with an average depth of a metre. We know also the value of statistics as an aid to good government and business management. No point in a supermarket stocking its shelves with tripe and onions if nobody is likely to buy them. Generalisations are risky concepts as well, are they not? Insurance rates for male vehicle drivers over the age of twenty-five years go down significantly, therefore all of that category under that age are bad drivers. Statistically they might be, but generally they are not. Does that seem like a contradiction?

I have been a wee smidge miffed with the COVID-19 TV news recently. They talk about the number of dead from the virus, the numbers tested and the numbers that have recovered. My current bugbear is the report that the United States is the worst hit of the countries because it has over 60,000 dead. That is a sad statistic, it is true, but it doesn't give a true picture. By numbers per head of population, I am informed that Belgium is the worst country hit. Similarly, the UK, France, Spain and Italy would seem to have lost more per head of population than the United States. Of course, numbers are facts—or should be as long as one trusts governments not to lie—but facts can be manipulated like much else in life. Of course, TV news is just a snapshot and one can get details elsewhere, but it is a snapshot to which many of us are exposed. Many more are carried along with the emotive inference of the broadcast.

Such pictures as a young Syrian boy, a boat person who crossed the Mediterranean with his family, lying drowned on a beach are far more meaningful to us as humans than faceless numbers on a page. Similarly, the Khashoggi murder that took place in the Saudi Embassy really hit home because this was a man whose face and opinions were evident and present on our TV screens. That atrocity gave us a more emotional insight into an atrociously misogynistic dictatorship than any generalities about what women can and cannot do in that terrible country. (And we buy oil from them??!!)

Most of us are against generalizations. Opinions about what "drinkers" thought when smoking was first banned in pubs. Who or what is a "drinker"? We all drink otherwise we do not live, do we not?! "Grouse Grinders," "joggers," "commuters," "shoppers" to me conjure up an unfortunate image of some amorphous body that could be you and me. I try not to generalize, but I inevitably do. My current bugbear is cyclists on the Spirit Trail. I have many friends who like to bike, and they are among the most considerate, kind people whom I know. I always feel, however, that if I am walking along that pathway that I am looked down upon by cyclists. I am a lesser being, a member of the "great unwashed," because I am not on a gung-holier-than-thou mission to be ultra fit. There seems to be an unspoken feeling that the Lycra-clad speedsters on a mission have certain rights that I do not have. I am not referring to the lady on an upright bike with panniers, dressed in a floral dress and sun hat gently pressing her pedals on her saddled way to do her grocery shopping. **Generally**, she is smilingly polite, the sweating swathes of grim-faced speedsters are ***generally*** not. Sooo, generalization is not great, yet here I be, guilty as charged, your worship!

Statistically, persistence, practice and experimentation increase the odds of success. We are all encouraged to not give up, to practice our piano playing, our French language classes. Indeed, teachers encourage children along these lines. But there are people and organizations in this world who reinforce failure. The military have been known to do it with a lost cause, and business does it by putting more good money after bad. I do it in the mistaken belief that if I continue to press the button at the pedestrian crossing the light is going to change quicker. As ever it is horses for courses, is it not? It is adapting one's thinking for different circumstances. Generally, however, if at first you don't succeed, don't take up hang-gliding. I am trying to be more discerning in what I believe and how I use information. I have several friends who can read a book or newspaper article and can immediately come up with a wise synopsis of its inferences. To my eternal chagrin, I cannot. It's not all my fault. I ate boarding school food for five years. I did, however, have an inspired moment many years ago when I asked Irene to marry me. That was wise discernment and perception that has lain dormant since 1982. I like the quotation that goes something like this:

"There are lies, damned lies and statistics."

I suppose that what I am saying in my rambling way is that stats and generalizations can form a good starting point for a chat. They can lead from ideas that may be as shallow as a bird bath to ones of oceanic depths.

> *"We must all move with the times or the times will move without us." Theodore Dalrymple*

In this pandemic it seems to me that the world is working in parallel but not yet as a team.

Enjoy the sun.

Locality and Globality!

Yes, I know there is no such word as "globality," but it just seemed to fit!! Just after completing yesterday's contribution to the landfill of your technological trash, I came across this Shakespearean quotation:

> *"I could be bounded in a nutshell and count myself a king of infinite space," from* **Hamlet.**

I don't know how many of you, my fellow isolates, feel like the Prince of Denmark did. Most of the time, I am pretty much fine with it. Irene seems the most content. She is always plucking the occasional weed here, dabbling with our finances and taxes there, Zooming with her friends, reading her John Cleese autobiography, picking forth interesting articles in the media. She walks around the block, pauses by Mackay Creek in hopes of seeing the ducks, moans about the cyclists on the Spirit Trail and gives a piece of her mind when a passing dog does its business on or near her beloved hedge.

As I was brewing a cuppa Joe today, I watched a solitary crow walking around the garden picking at the scattered eggshells Irene spreads over her seedlings to keep away the bugs. Crows seem to walk with fluency. They are not penguins, for whom walking is such an awkward process. They are, however, unable to take a step without thrusting their heads forward at the same time, as if always searching, always on guard, always at the ready. A friend of mine who used to live near the highway just off Lonsdale was always dive bombed by the same crow on his way to his car in the morning. I read afterwards that not only was he destined to be treated this way forever by this same crow but that crow parents hand an inherited antipathy on to their offspring. Thus, my pal was doomed to suffer not only the sins of the father and mother but also the generational bombing of their children. What's the point here? Well, everywhere I have lived there have been crows. But I never gave them an ounce of my attention before, so I guess that the slowing down of our lives has given us time to notice such things. If we look closely enough there are "infinite niches in a little room" as Marlowe said.

My father was a wise man. He warned me early in life not to pass judgment early on people because they may not have been enriched as I had been enriched. It is very possible, he would have said, to be a shrewd judge of character with no foreign travel and very little experience of movement within one's own country or region. Of course, travel and experiences enrich us, change our perspectives and widen our views. Yet, last year I spent eleven days on a Norwegian ferry accompanied by a wonderfully eclectic group of people. However, there was a couple from London who boasted that they never left the boat. If you were to run into them tomorrow, they would tell you they have been to Norway. But but they talked up a storm, they shared stories of this and that—but did they notice, did they listen, did they learn? Hmmm. I spent one night at their dinner table and then managed a transfer to a table with three delightful

Norwegians, a couple and a wonderful retired teacher. For the rest of the trip I was always on a rushed mission when I passed the London couple's table which, as the trip progressed, always seemed to have space! They were probably grateful I had ceased being part of *their* company. There is always room for different types of people in this world and a ready acceptance of all is part of civilized behaviour—as long as one doesn't have to have dinner with them! We could have chatted and reminisced about London. My first job was in the "Big Smoke" back in the day, and I could have been at home with the locals and the locality, if you like. But we were off the coast of Norway, for Pete's sake. I wanted to talk to Norwegians, enjoy my time ashore in a different culture, sample its history and geography. If a crow had walked across the deck of the ship, I would not have noticed it, let alone its style of walking. My senses were being stimulated—over-stimulated if you like—by so much that was new and wonderful. My point is that there is merit in the time we spend isolated in our locality at the moment. There is much to learn about life at home, as there is much to learn about life when we travel. As Blake would have it:

> *"To see a World in a grain of sand,*
> *And Heaven in a Wild Flower,*
> *Hold Infinity in the palm of your hand,*
> *And Eternity in a hour."*

"Helt Nydelig!" (Quite fantastic!) as Frodo Keyser, my Norwegian dinner companion, would have said.

The great writer Thomas Hardy (1840-1928) wrote so well about the hardships in rural Wessex in the 1800s, but with much more relevancy about the poignant, tragic struggles of womanhood at the time. Unwanted pregnancies, terrible marriages, the poorhouse and death, they all sound wrist-slashingly morbid, do they not? And yet their message is so well written and strong that they were turned into movies and TV series. *Far from the Madding Crowd*, *Tess of the d'Urbervilles* and *Jude the Obscure* all have the power to move us and cause us to think. (Of course, I, like one other of my male friends, remembers Julie Christie as Bathsheba Everdene, but that is a wee bit different!) Point here is that Hardy was writing about rural England where people lived their lives almost exclusively in the same place. In that microcosm there was wisdom, foolishness, love, folly, accident, plot, murder and a real understanding of the world that could equally have been found in isolated tribes in the Brazilian rainforest. Peter Ackroyd, much respected biographer, tellingly quoted Hardy:

> *"It is better for a writer to know a little bit of the world remarkably well, than to know a great part of the world remarkably little. In England, it is believed that to know one's locale thoroughly is to understand the forces of the world, or even, of the universe."*

So, for the moment, I will look out of the window at that crow again and try to convince myself that I can learn as much from that bird as cruising up a Norwegian fjord!?

Have a good day, my friends.

The Number Seven

The resolution to get some exercise yesterday lead me, as it frequently does these days, to the foot of Pemberton Heights and the stairs leading up thereof. One set works out as roughly fourteen floors according to my Fitbit. I had resolved to improve on my last effort by completing seven sets. I was trundling and struggling along through my work. They were, of course, getting harder and harder. I had sprung a leak and was fast running out of "pech." Would I make the seven? Somewhere around about the fourth set I decided to avert my mind from the effort by thinking of other things. I settled on the number seven. You see, friends, I don't hate much with a passion, but I have always detested this particular number. A psychoanalyst would somehow decipher that I had been traumatized at the age of seven, but he or she would be wrong. The seven deadly sins are merely a starting point if one has my heritage where there are, at least, eight. Here am I committing the eighth deadly sin, which in Scotland is talking about yourself in a boastful manner. Perhaps we all may be forgiven for this at this time because we are so isolated from other people that talking about others is difficult. But the fact is that there are supposed to be seven deadly sins. I, however, can think of other reasons why seven is such a deadly number.

Film and TV are to blame to some degree. *77 Sunset Strip* is a double whammy, is it not? *Seven Brides for Seven Brothers*!!

How does one make a movie, let alone a musical, out of such drivel? The *Seven Samurai* is iconic. I do not know what the Japanese is for the number seven, but maybe if I did, I would like it. Of course, it spawned *The Magnificent Seven*, and worse, *Return of the Seven*. I love *M*A*S*H*, the TV series not the movie, but the 4077 sets the Davidson eye twitch speeding up to a terrifying rate.

How many judges are there in the supreme courts around the world? I understand that they should have an odd number for a deciding vote. Britain, therefore, has twelve?? The States has, sensibly, nine as does Canada. Thank goodness for that. Back in the day in England, there was one and he was the king and he had what was called the "divine right." The 'Divine Right' of kings and queens is a patently ridiculous idea, given that people make mistakes, except those of us who are sixty years old or older, of course! Two judges causes a possible difference of opinion with no solution, so they need a third to sort things out but, then, three is a crowd. Four is often two against two, duets of cliques in corners bad-mouthing the other pair. Five might work. Davidson likes five possibly because it is easy mathematically. Six, however, is the loveliest of numbers. Why? Well, I guess that I grew up with the duodecimal system, twelve pennies to the shilling in the old Brit coinage. And "dozen" is such a lovely word. So much better to ask a baker for a dozen rolls than for twelve, is it not? But then the old baker is likely to give you thirteen, which evokes a smile at her generosity, a feeling of the customer pulling one over on the vendor. Twelve years of age is the last year when parents can speak to their child as a child as the impending doom of teenage-hood rears its ugly head. Twelve isn't a bad number 'cos it stems from six and eventually will morph into a "gross." To me, 144 is anything but gross. As a child, it signaled a happy end to the learning of my multiplication tables. It was a triumphant full stop on the whole process, and it all stemmed from that wee, wee six, the mother of so many other worthy numbers. Yes, my friends, six is the happiest of numbers for me.

Back to those stairs. So annoyed was I that I had set off with the hope of accomplishing seven flights that I resolved to stop at six. But then, an obnoxious runner on a mission refused to social distance properly despite my efforts to give him room and space. So, I diverted my anger and actually managed eight flights. Ha! Thank you so much, oh Selfish Strider; you pushed me farther. Or was it the impending doom of the number seven?

Self-Made Men and Women

With the current batch of some Americans (and some foolish Vancouverites as well) who take it upon themselves to gather maskless to demand that the government allow them back to work, one is left with an understanding of the ridiculous belief in rugged individualism. It would seem that fending for oneself, making one's own way in the world successfully or otherwise, is an ethos that cannot be shifted from the psyche of many. To me, nobody makes their way in the world alone. There is no such thing as a motherless child, last time I looked. Admittedly, there are parents out there who shouldn't be. But even without them, there are societal influences, sometimes subtle, sometimes blunt, which colour the way we act, the way we do things.

To me, rugged individualism is a smack in the face for every mental patient, every disabled person, every ethnic minority for whom success needs them to somehow escape from behind the restrictive eight ball. To me, the current crisis proves, if nothing else, people need big government, centralized Medicare for all and so on. Nobody is suggesting that countries nationalize everything, that was a failed experiment in the old Soviet Union. But, my friends, some things—some things—just need to emanate from a central control. Listen to good old John Donne:

> *"No man is an island entire of itself;*
> *every man is a piece of the continent, a part*
> *of the main."*

And his ending:

> *"Any man's death diminishes me,*
> *because I am involved in mankind.*
> *And therefore never send to know for whom*
> *the bell tolls; it tolls for thee."*

Thank goodness I am not putting this out there for general consumption 'cos somebody would tell me that I am being sexist. Trudeau would preach me towards "humankind," but I didn't write it and it wasn't written yesterday, and it is about women and many other genders as well. Donne's message is clear: we are in a time of national borders again, statistics that preach about "our" success controlling the virus and "their" mistakes and other playground blame games aimed at diverting things from my country to yours. Some pundits see this crisis as the end of globalization, which seems to me to be another ridiculous argument because, since Marco Polo trekked off to China from Venice or European fishermen harvested cod off the coast of Newfoundland, there has always been globalization. The sea that separates us also joins us. When the economy restarts, Scotch whisky will be exported, oil will move from one region of the world to another and we will trade with others like we have done for thousands of years. So, the foolishness of the few, the selfishness of the individuals who are exercising their freedom of demonstration, are not, in my opinion, operating in the best interests of anybody at this moment.

On a lighter note but on the same topic, I found a couple of quotes from Joseph Heller's novel *Catch 22*, one of my favourite books of all time:

> **"Nately had a bad start. He came from a good family."**

And:

> **"He was a self-made man who owed his lack of success to nobody."**

Ha! I love it! Apparently, Joseph Heller was notoriously immodest as proved by a TV interview a few years ago.

"So, Mr. Heller, for the past twenty years you have written nothing to match *Catch 22*."

"Who has?"

Ha! I love it more!

Have a good day, my friends.

Day 15: Daylight Come and I Wanna Go Out!

Quarantine was an easy fortnight for me and a difficult one for Irene. Although I try not to be a nuisance, I am a man, which, by definition, makes that impossible. I was, however, up a tree with a saw, a hammer, a nail and direction from below. I was then in a plant bed with a spade, a fork and direction from the side. Tomorrow I am to be allowed out with a list of instructions, a plethora of advice and a face mask, all delivered with forceful intent. I came across this advice yesterday from Tibullus:

> *"When you are lonely, become your own crowd."*

I suppose that means one can talk to oneself with impunity, ruminate aloud and verbalise sonorously.

I also read this highly appropriate Shakespearean quote from Susan Hill writing in *The Spectator*:

> *"Now I am cabined, cribbed, confined, bound in*
>
> *To saucy doubts and fears."*

How many times has a Shakespeare, a Dickens, a Burns or another literary giant said with so much clarity what we have felt?

> *"One must make friends of apartness."*
> **Charles Moore** (The Spectator)

So, morning dawned, and Davidson walked up to get some groceries. Wore his underwear bandana. It was a frisson of freedom as you all know too well. But it did feel strange to be out and about. Passed and briefly chatted with six people I knew, staff at Bean Around the World, Dermot, Ron and Gail outside of Timmy's. Even those brief but distant contacts were very pleasant. The old underwear makes a fantastic face mask, by the way, although I would not want to wear it for too long. Far too tight and restrictive, I removed it after I had bought my groceries.

Never the most practically creative of people myself, I am amazed at the innovation and initiatives I am seeing on social media. Loved seeing the Russian Ballet dancing at home, hearing about the use of 3D printers and the creative ways people are teaching and entertaining their children. I have the feeling that I am a bit of a neighbourhood joke 'cos my wonderful wife does all of the yard-work, the taxes, the painting and much more. Occasionally I do get involved, however, and not always with totally catastrophic consequences. John Angus was a witness to the raising of the couches to the outside balcony to get them upstairs, using a rope over the roof attached to the car and so forth. Could not have done it without him to negotiate them over the edge. Rob next door was a great help when I tried to unblock the drain in front of the garage using Irene's hoe, which went in with difficulty yet was jammed tight and impossible to get out by hand. We rigged up ropes and such, attached it to the back of the car. I drove onto the lawn, and with much revving and jerking the thing finally was released. We had to get the plumber along to unblock the drain. Admittedly there is a Darwinian element to my attempts at practicality. Had I been alone with the hoe removal, it could possibly have come through the back of the car doing damage to vehicle and driver. We shall not mention the very silly attempt to burn important papers in our plastic composter, which really did destroy the paper but melted a large part of the composter in the process. Needless to say, Irene was not at home for all three of these magnificently innovative, outside-of-the-box solutions. Now there is talk of me painting a small section at the side of the house and cutting up some branches for the garbage pick up. This I can do. I think. The woodcutter says that:

"Life is fuller of surprises than certainties."

The continuous source of surprise and delight to me is the string of resilience and initiative of human beings, present so evidently in the past but still with us today.

Enjoy the sun, my friends.

Questions but No Answers?!

Since I arrived back in this country four weeks ago, I have been without a cell phone. Now for somebody who did not own one for all of his working life, this would seem to be no big deal. However, it was. Somehow habits change very quickly, and one becomes reliant. When I landed in the UK, I trekked into a cell phone store in the city of Bath and availed myself of a British SIM card, putting my Canadian one in a safe place. The world is full of Davidson "safe places," so sometime five years from now there will be an "Aha!" moment when it appears again.

So *Gullible* returns home, discovers that Koodo, his provider, has all of its stores closed. No SIM card, so shrug the shoulders, be philosophical and do something else. Then our wonderful neighbour, Rob, has a friend who will get me a SIM card. Being a man of his word and the most kind and generous neighbour one could wish for, SIM card arrives. So, I slot it in and proceed to the Koodo website and helpline, having made a conscious effort to not get frustrated, and to put a perspective on my First World problem.

So, I arrive at the helpline. Rather nervous, like Usain Bolt in an Olympic 100-metre dash, I wave to the crowd, I limber and shake, I cross himself, I put my finger to my lips, turn my eyes to heaven, I take my marks, get set and—bang!— I'm off. Alack a day, I pull up in the first ten metres, false start. This seems to be an *unhelpline.* You see, friends, my poorly-worded question was too long. Restart, scribble a shorter question in preparation. Begin again. Nope, this was not a question that they were equipped to answer. After much banging and clanging in the Davidson head, I start again with the crowd leaving their seats with the better realization that they are not to see a gold medal run this day; I decide on one final try. I manage to get to the point where I enter the long code on my new SIM card. Now "Unlock your phone." Hands in the air, jump up, run around the room hollering—almost shouting—over to next door for a trumpet celebration from Richard, Rob and Carol's son, at my success. "Enter the three-digit number to unlock your phone. You have only three attempts at this before the phone buggers off and abandons you for good," or some such statement. What three-figure number? I have no three-figure number? Where the foundation skills is the three-figure number? I surrender and clear off to cut the grass, saw the branches, dig the garden—honey-do jobs that had stayed on the back burner for days.

Of course, I could have asked friends who would have said, "You did what? No, no, no, Pete, this is what you should have done." Or kindly but worse, "First you should have connected the flibbety gibbet to the thingimebob, using the bummblethorpe protraction tool with the three-pronged bastelthwaite schnapdorker." Or something equally confusing.

So, I did what I have done so well over the years: I gave up. But I have never fully been able to set aside failures completely, as bits remained gnawing away at the Davidson ego, chipping pieces out of the Davidson confidence. So, I tried again. Were there any Koodo stores open anywhere on the Lower Mainland? Nope. OK, get on the phone. Made myself comfortable on the landline, expecting an hour or so of the well-intentioned at the other end of the line talking me through the process with baby steps and infinite patience.

"Should you wish to pay your bill, press 1."

Why would I want to pay my bill for a service I hadn't had? Press 2, 3, 4, 5. Eventually get to the number for a live operator.

"Due to the current pandemic and in the interests of the safety and health of our staff etc., etc."

OK, of course, this is the right thing to do. So now I can really, really give up with impunity, after all my cell phone issue is a "mote to trouble the mind's eye" compared with all that is going on in the world, is it not? But that damned rodent is gnawing away in Davidson's head and there are no longer venting jobs to be done in Irene's magnificent garden.

I return to the computer to Google Koodo stores on the North Shore and write down telephone numbers with no hope that anybody will be working in an office, let alone that one may be open. So, I call, and to my surprise, I receive a live person straight away.

"We are at 18th and Lonsdale, and we are open until 6:00 p.m., and we can fix your phone."

Stunned silence from me, eventually a nervous, "You can?!" So, I grab the necessaries, put on my boots and begin to walk along Marine Drive up to Lonsdale, having texted our son asking for our car back so I can get there quicker. So, I am opposite St. Thomas Aquinas School when Grant pulls up, gives me my car keys and walks off through the woods to walk his dog. After my walk, I have resolved to be calm and phlegmatic if they cannot fix the thing—no childish tantrums from me, just a final acceptance and a philosophical determination to not let it get to me any longer.

So, I enter the Telus office, observing with cynicism that this has nothing to do with Koodo. The young techie is there, I give him my details, I disinfect my phone, I hand it over, I pay my money, and it is fixed! I test it. It works. It has unrequited messages on it from the last month or so. I phone Irene. She answers. I am ecstatic. I walk to the door. I open it. I expect to be greeted by a brass band with celebratory bunting. I expect the *North Shore News* roving reporter to be there to ask how I am feeling now that I have a working cell phone. I hope for a police escort home. I expect Tatlow to be out in force, rattling pots and pans, Richard on his trumpet. But the streets are almost deserted. There is an eerie quiet. I drive home and Irene greets me with a smile. I once more have a working cell phone after four weeks of wondering and wandering.

Time to contact "Dear Mary"* on her problem page and ask her advice. I should and would expect a reply something like this:

Dear Peter,

Regarding your problem with reconnecting your cell phone. Get a life.

Yours sincerely, Mary

Dear friends, I can now be called on my phone again. Would love to have a chat.

Have a great day. Pete

*"Dear Mary" writes in *The Spectator* magazine. The problems she solves are often related to the well-off and upper middle class. Most are problems of etiquette.

Social Distancing 101

I was thinking last night what a huge relief this social distancing protocol is to Irene and me. Before you scream "Unsocial bastard!" at me, let me give the full perspective. I love get-togethers over coffee or worse. I love listening to you setting the world to rights with experience and sound common sense, I love hearing your news and views, I love listening to your politics, your thoughts, your lives. Most of all, I love your humour and banter. And, as a bonus, we can do all of this now without the shaking of the hands or, worse, the now common hug, which has made its way into social etiquette. Irene and I are not huggers. Indeed, we only ever hug each other when we go our separate ways at YVR. I can't ever remember hugging my mother and, to this day, I give her a peck on the top of the head on arrival and departure. My Dad always shook my hand when he dropped me off at boarding school, usually with some pithy advice:

"Don't do anything stupid, and I'll see you in a few weeks."

When I worked at school, effusive parents occasionally approached me with hug-intent, and generally I managed to head them off at the pass with an outstretched hand and a vigorous shaking of their equivalent. So whenever greeting friends or family I have to do a mental recap. Does this person hug and if he/she does is it a bent-at-the-waist, hands-on-the-shoulder, barely-touching, speedy-break-away one or is the full-frontal slap on the back thingee? Rarely have I initiated hugs in my life, but I will follow other people's protocols and fit in with what makes them most comfortable.

I was taught at school when receiving an award to march up, look the giver in the eye and shake her firmly by the hand. Thus did I occasionally teach my nine-year-olds at school when award ceremonies came around.

Shaking of hands is still not a comfort zone for me. Irene remembers ancient aunties who only shook hands if they had their gloves on. When I had to do so as a child, there was to be no cold wet fish, no limp effete whimpiness allowed. It was to be a firm grip, a couple of vigorous shakes and then let go and step back. Effusive hail-fellow-well-met-edness was to be discouraged. There were always those who took it too far, they shook for too long and too vigorously. Worse still, they grabbed your elbow with their other hand. There was no escape from this except a vigorous left hook to the jaw, which sort of defeated the purpose of the handshake in the first place, I think.

The continental habit of lightly brushed kisses on the cheeks filled us with disgust as children in the UK. But then we discovered in our history lessons that Mussolini had outlawed the handshake as being unhygienic, leaving the Italians with a fascist salute as a greeting. No wonder they eventually strung him up! We did think that that was against all we had read about Italians, particularly after studying *Romeo and Juliet*.

Bringing a bottle of wine or a bunch of flowers to a gathering is a great ploy for avoiding social contact. Giving over the gift while reaching to take off one's coat is a great move. I think "Dear Mary" would approve. Ushering—showing people where to leave their coats, drop their dishes and so forth— is also a good move. Rod Liddle writes amusingly in *The Spectator* that his own personal lockdown is something he has longed for for years. I have heard from an ex-colleague, now teaching online from home, that this is the way he always wants to work in the future.

When I returned prematurely from the UK four weeks ago, I knocked on the door here at Tatlow. Irene greeted me with rubber gloves and black garbage bags. From two metres distance, she smiled and said, "You're back?" I grinned back and said, "Yep." Her next move was to step back even farther and point me upstairs where I was to serve my quarantine with orders to shower, bag my washing and throw it downstairs. All welcome homes should be as simple as that, I feel.

Maybe on Burns Nights of the future, we rig up a spray tent outside, take people's temperature, disinfect and issue face masks, some with special adaptations for those of you who smoke, and a hole for your straw so that you can drink. I do not know whether haggis works intravenously but, hey, there's a lot of innovation out there, and we have over nine months afore the event.

Have a great day, mes amis.

Beyond Canada Day

T he Borders area of Scotland, just north of Hadrian's Wall and south of the metropolises of Glasgow and Edinburgh, is an area of rolling hills, narrow roads, farms and small towns. It is Sir Walter Scott country, whose ancient pile at Abbotsford has a long sloping vista at the back that leads down to the River Tweed. An ailing Scott asked to be moved from his sick bed so that he could look out with ease on his beloved river. Towns like Melrose, Galashiels, Hawick, Peebles are dotted here and there about this cosy, quaint countryside. One such town is Selkirk. Its rugby club takes up room at the bottom of the valley. A steep drive up the hill takes one into the village square, which has its share of shops and pubs and, of course, the kirk. Back when Robbie Burns was scribbling his rhyme in the late 1700s, these towns had come through the border wars, the reivers and drovers were able to mind their cattle without raiders from the south and vice versa. The area was finally coming to some form of peaceful co-existence. Burns remembers hearing a local expressing the view proudly:

"A day spent oot o' Selkirk is a day wasted."

Now that, Dear Reader, is jingoism, almost, and patriotism, certainly. It is a giant, biased belief in a wee corner of the world.

Patriotism is recognized as a quality, seemingly without question, although Samuel Johnson would have it "as the last refuge of the coward." Loyalty to the place where one pays ones taxes, where one respects its laws, where one is part of its culture is perhaps laudable. But, of course, the other side of this is that the patriot can become one-eyed, developing a blinkered view of the world, shutting out so many wonderful opportunities and differing points of view. Our country should be our comfort zone but we all know we become better people if we step outside our area of peace.

> *"A ship is always safe at shore but that is not what it's built for." Einstein*

I am *not* proud of the fact that in twenty-nine years of living here, in Vancouver, I have only been into the USA three times. I have never been to Seattle or California. It is true that I Greyhounded around Wisconsin in my teacher's holidays in 1979. But it is almost a quarter of a century since I crossed the line. There is much I want to see down there. Mt. St. Helens, the Oregon coast and Boston all have an appeal. Irene, incidentally, has only been down there once since we have lived here. I don't know why we have not visited. It is certainly not based on any antipathy towards the place, more likely I suspect it is because it is always available, always in our back yard, something we will get around to sometime.

But, Dear Reader, on the occasions I have visited it is true to say that I don't really feel at ease. The people have been very friendly and exceedingly generous but—but—there is something within me or something underpinning the façade that makes me wary. I felt very at home in Australia when I lived there. I loved my time in India and Nepal. The Scandinavian countries I adore. Central Europe was where I hitched and journeyed and skied in my youth, and those countries were havens of relaxed enjoyment. I guess what I am saying is that I am conscious and careful about how I act and what I say around Americans. My young nephew, Seumas, was over here for a couple of years from the UK on a working visa. An articulate, hail-fellow-well-met kind of character, he will talk to anybody. In his early days here he found himself on a ski lift at Whistler with three members of an American family. It was halfway through the ascent when Seumas found out that they were from Washington State.

"Hmm, Americans? So, what's your favourite type of gun?"

Silence for the rest of the ride upwards. Aghast looks from Irene and me when he told us this story. I guess we are all influenced by where we grew up and where we now live. (I always thought that everybody understood the British sense of humour but that is not the case, and why should it be?) But I think that powerful people, strong, privileged nations, countries that have great influence in the world, need to have some humility, some periphery that allows for differences in other nations and diverse peoples, some understanding that what is suited to one nation may not work for another. Rightly or wrongly, I do not feel that this is the case in the U.S. at the moment. There is the complaint down there that Russia has interfered in the election process and presumably will try to do so again. This may be a legitimate complaint indeed, but please don't let us pretend that the USA doesn't behave in the same way. Italy in 1948 may well have gone communist were it not for American power and money. The Shah of Iran may well have been a western installation. Allende's Chile was democratically elected, but American money and power pedalling overthrew him and gave Pinochet's army seventeen years of dictatorial rule. Vietnam, a nation that wanted to decide its own fate, was not allowed to do so. Iraq was going to suddenly be opened up for KFC and Baskin-Robbins. Afghanistan was going to become a world leader in women's rights. Pride parades were going to be an annual event on Kabul's high street!? Don't get me wrong, there seems to be much that is praiseworthy in the American democratic system. There is cutting-edge research and development in U.S. places of higher learning. But loyalty to a flag and standing for a national anthem omits the fact that loyalty is a two-way deal, and for so many Americans deprived of healthcare, decent wages and the chance of advancement this does not seem to be the case at the moment. I do not think I would be standing for the national anthem if I was American during this time.

"My country right or wrong," or the even more appalling statement, "Love it or leave it," are not the pleas for patriotism that should be listened to in my opinion. Indeed, one might ask when patriotism morphs into nationalism. That is something that one could also debate long and hard.

So, on this Canada Day where does the graph of my level of patriotism sit at the moment? I am pretty proud of Dr. Bonnie Henry (but that is provincial). I am pretty ashamed of the poverty on First Nations reserves. I don't care one jot about the fact that Canada did not make it on to the UN Security Council. I am a liberal, but I don't much care for the Liberal leadership. However, if one is to make the mistake of comparing Trudeau to certain other world leaders then I would rather have him. Sadly, Nicola Sturgeon, Angela Merkel and Jacinda Ardern are ineligible to lead us. I think I can be proud, at least grateful, of our healthcare system. I am not sure how to solve the homeless crisis but then nobody else is. I don't like the way we treat our mental patients. I think that our environment and green policies could be stronger. By and large, I can still stand and sing our national anthem lustily, and, despite Quebec politics, will sing it, albeit with a little less vigour, in French. On the whole, I feel that a day spent outside of Canada is *not* a day wasted, unless perhaps it is spent in the United States!

Hubris and Humility

OK, so we all know what both these two characteristics are, do we not? "Hubris" ensured there were never going to be enough lifeboats on board the unsinkable *Titanic*. "Hubris" prompted Hitler to declare war on the United States after Pearl Harbour. "Hubris" told we occidentals we could go to war in the Middle East and create countries in our own image. We have read about the Emperor Caligula who made his horse a consul, King Canute who ordered his throne to be set on a beach so that could command the tide not to come in (OK, so I do not really believe that Canute really anticipated that putting up a stopping hand up to a retreating tide that was about to lap his royal feet would work. I believe he was making the point that he was as human as the rest of us), and King Charles I who was executed by Cromwell and his republicans because he believed he had a "divine right." Maybe Charles Stuart should have re-read that story before he affirmed his ridiculous "right of kings." The dictionary lists "hubris" as "excessive pride or self-confidence." The word is Greek and, of course, in a human being it would make the Greek pantheon on Mount Olympus angry because the gods believed they should have a monopoly on that particular trait. Any jumped-up little human was destined to suffer their wrath if she got above herself or he assumed victory and strutted into battle with consummate arrogance.

"Humility," however, is disarming, is it not? When we pose questions to others, we are involving them in a decision, we are not taking all of life's burdens on ourselves, we are giving them respect. Don't we all respond well when we are asked for our opinions, when somebody calls us for advice, when we ask for help to complete a task? "Humus" in Latin means "low." When we are humbled, our bodies seem to shrink, our heads bow, our shoulders slump, we want the ground to swallow us up. Not for nothing does "humus" also refer to qualities in the soil. It's where we want to be when the "world has become too much with us, late and soon." Humility should teach us when to give but it should also teach us when to receive, should it not?

"What's his point?" I hear the cry.

I guess a great number of us are watching the "news" more than usual. I can't remember when the nightly news was so very personal. We hang on every word, seek out every glimmer of hope, clutch at every straw of an exit strategy. There is humility in our politicians and leaders although they may be more renowned for their hubristic tendencies. Many will argue that it takes a huge ego, a bulky mass of self-esteem, to want to be a leader in the first place. I always tend to listen to ex-leaders more, so many of them are now entitled and more liable to be honest and truthful. They seem to acquire humility having realized the fickleness and fleetness of fame. Daedalus warned his son, Icarus, not to fly too close to the sun and not to drop dangerously low to the sea. He ignored his father and the sun melted his wings and he fell to his death. I have never met the British prime minister. I hear he was a wonderful mayor of London but not such a great foreign secretary. I have read many of his articles and enjoyed them. My friend, Jamie, reminded me what a very fine journalist he was and is. He is now a father. He has suffered a life-threatening illness. Both events should mitigate the hubris and bring a more humble side to the fore. The current president of the United States is unlikely ever to fly too close to the sun, partly because he believes he is his own light, he is the sun.

Finally, the point!!

I watched the VP of the U.S., Mike Pence, visit the prestigious Mayo Clinic last night. Everybody else was wearing a face mask. He was not. His argument was that he was tested for COVID-19 every day so did not need one! He just doesn't get it, does he? The rule is that ***everybody*** who steps over the threshold of that institution has to wear a mask. Even if you did not see the need, even if you wanted your face to be seen on TV, even if you could produce every reasoned argument for not so doing, if you are a leader, you obey the rules, you wear a mask. You arrogant bastard, Mr. Pence. You thoughtless, inconsiderate, dishonourable apology for a man. You live in a country that eschewed monarchy for a more democratic way. Last time I looked there was no "Divine Right of Pence," although you very clearly think there should be. I knew very little about you before, but if I was American and you were the candidate for the presidency then that one act yesterday has cooked your goose as far as I am concerned.

A BCAA employee arrives to help a motorist who has a flat tyre.

"But you're blowing up the wrong tyre, sir, it's the back one that's flat."

"Goodness me! You mean the two of them are not connected?"

Aaaah, but if one is talking about leaders in government then they very much are connected. If one lives in the United States, then surely "we the people" are connected to "I, the vice president," and, if not, then what is the point of an election?

Have a good day, mes amis.

Full Circle

Being of a bit of a strange frame of mind, somewhat outré, I have a terrible penchant for taking an interest in things that most people find, at best, boring and, at worst, irrelevant. Driving out of Edinburgh with my good friend, Audrey, last month on the way to the beautiful walk across the dunes to Aberlady looking out into the North Sea, we passed a large country estate. Probably a pile manufactured in the nineteenth or eighteenth century by some guy who made money by exploiting the natives in some far-reaching outpost of empire. Surrounding the grounds of this pile was a wall between eight and ten feet high. It seemed interminable. It was obviously built to last. It occurred to me that *somebody* must have built it (wondrous thoughts like that do pass through the Davidson mind!). Maybe wrongly, I saw it as a massive job-creation scheme at the time for the out of season farm workers. Lord Cecil Full-Hamper could not have his workforce sitting idle during the off season because the devil and idle hands are not a good combination, don't you know? Get the peasantry to build a wall. The ***noblesse oblige***, so keenly preached as a sort of quid pro quo for the life of lavish leisure that the aristocracy enjoyed while exploiting the great unwashed, was a propagandist coup that lasted a long time. Any rate, where am I going with this?

Back in the day, most people did not wonder or wander too far from home. Indeed, my GP father attended the deathbed of an eighty-something who had lived in the village all of her life and had never been to the city six miles down the road. Home was bounded by a parochial locale. Before the Industrial Revolution took people off the land to the factories in the cities, there were things called cottage industries. People sewed and knitted and grew things at home, and if they didn't, they worked the land of the local lord of the manor. Many shared their houses with their beasts, cattle mooing and baying just a wall away. In fact, they worked from home. Aha, dear friends, so you see where I am going with this.

Because of the current situation, so many people who are still in the workforce are being encouraged to work from home. For our daughter, the library computer technologist, this is indeed possible; for my teacher friends, it is indeed possible; for my friend, Audrey, in Edinburgh it is *not.* She works in a care home for the elderly.

It is always a surprise to me that it seems a surprise to the media that the poor should be taking the main brunt of any epidemic, be it a pandemic or otherwise. We hear about the impact on the African American communities throughout the USA wholly out of proportion in deaths and suffering compared to their white, rich, privileged countrymen on the other side of the river. One thing this pandemic has reminded us of again, as if we needed any reminding, is that there are too many "other sides of the rivers" throughout the world. The poor and underprivileged are more likely to die in this pandemic. When it is over, the poor and underprivileged are more likely to suffer starvation and famine.

The solution? Who knows, but history tells us there have been solutions in the past. After the Second World War, the

Marshall Plan saved Europe. In the 1930s, FDR's New Deal built dams and roads and put Americans back to work. Dr. Gorgas "solved" the malarial problem in Panama that de Lesseps and the French couldn't, which allowed the canal to be built. It has not escaped my notice that these three "solutions" have emanated from the United States of America. It seems likely that a solution to our current crises, and there *are* more than one, lies in the democracies of the western world where sixteen year olds can use three dimensional printers to facilitate better designs of PPE; where face masks for divers can be converted to making face masks for hospital workers; where large and local factories can quickly adapt their equipment; and where Josephine Blow on the shop floor has the confidence to approach the boss with her innovative idea and not be shot down—figuratively or literally.

It seems axiomatic that so many issues throughout history have been solved by statesmanlike leadership where the leader sets his or her ego on the back burner; gives credit where credit is due; is not threatened by those who speak truth to power; is shrewd, hard-working, forward thinking, adaptable; harbours no grudges or bitterness; is selfless, humble and works "pro bono publico." In short, as Abraham Lincoln would have it: when situations bring out "the better angels of our nature."

Dermot, I know, has read James Kerr's book. *Legacy*, about the phenomenon that is the New Zealand All Blacks rugby team. It is full of useful quotes. One that strikes home is the following:

> *"The idea of humility as a central value grounds the team, creates respect,*

encourages curiosity and generates bonds
that sustain them."

There is another great leadership book, called *Extreme Ownership*, by Willink and Babin. It hits the mark right in its first chapter when an incident in the Iraq War could have resulted in U.S. soldiers being killed accidentally by their own troops, so-called "friendly fire." There had to be an inquiry. It could have been a blame game, a passing of the buck, a scapegoating "not-my-fault" scenario. The local commander called his team together, explained that they all had to get to the bottom of the incident to avoid a repeat. He then reiterated the statement that all great leaders have done through the ages and said that whatever the outcome, "I am to blame." There would be no recriminations or sanctions on anybody else because he was in charge and the buck stopped with him. The outcome was that everybody else was relieved, put their shoulders to the wheel and worked to find the truth and to prevent a reoccurrence.

Winston Churchill said that one should never waste a good crisis. He also once asked one of his underlings quizzically, "Are you not enjoying the war?" Going back to the Greeks and their creation of the word "crisis," it is important to note that this almost doubled for the word "opportunity."

Now about that wall in Scotland!!?? Well, walls are a bit of a barrier, are they not? Let us hope that the solution to our problem is not lost 'cos some clown has blocked it for all the wrong reasons.

> *"Cluster the branches of the magnolia so*
> *they will not break." Maori proverb*

Baby Boomers

Having arrived in Canada from the UK in 1991, I had never heard of the term "baby boomer." Talking about this and thinking about it, it seems that it may well have been a term exclusively applied to North America. My father-in-law, Gordon Pennicuick, was away serving in World War II for five years and ten months. He was a Canadian soldier. Unlike European soldiers who served, there was no home leave. Presumably, home leave in European countries or among civilians there meant opportunities to procreate within the institution of marriage and thus the arrival of babies was not such a rush of numbers when the war ended. Any rate, it is a theory. I know enough about the male gender to agree with author Martin Amis, who said that the male libido was "like being chained to an idiot for fifty years." Of course, the returning military personnel would likely have had enough of the exciting abnormality of war and would want to settle down to a "normal" life, which would likely include marriage and children.

So I, like so many of you, are a part of that generation that was born between 1946 and 1964.* It also means that we are a part of something of a generalization, and you will know my views on that concept from other writings. So, the pandemic is also being labelled a "boomer remover." Apparently, we are also to assume some level of guilt for our impact on the planet and climate change. Some would say we grew up as the spoilt brats of millennia of previous generations. Indeed, Harold Macmillan, the British prime minister in the early 1960s, famously said:

"You've never had it so good."

I was thinking about his statement yesterday. Irene and I are in our late sixties, and seventy years of age is not such a distant horizon. I am inclined to agree with Macmillan's statement. It is true that I grew up in the British middle class; that I enjoyed democracy and a certain freedom of speech; that I had a good education; that I never went hungry, always had a roof over my head and could always rattle a pocketful of change or better. It is also true that I am white and male and have enjoyed the benefits of health from an NHS, which, for all its faults, has never prohibited me from seeking better health because I could not afford so to do. At nearly sixty-eight years of age, unlike my parents and grandparents, I have never had to go to war, nor have I seen our children have to defend their country. When I settled into the job market after my schooling, it was unlikely I would ever have had to change jobs. I know that, barring an act of Davidson foolishness, I could have completed my whole teaching career from 1976 to 2018 in the same school, had I so wished. Yes, I have been very, very lucky.

How should I feel about my luck? Should I feel guilty in light of what has happened to Generation X, the Millennials, and now Generations Z and Alpha? Certainly, many of my attitudes growing up are rightly unacceptable today. And that leads me into an historical perspective, I suppose. Every year in this country we "celebrate" Remembrance Day. Solemn assemblies at school. Irene and I attend on the day at the

Victoria Park Cenotaph in North Vancouver; we never miss. Indeed, our adult children attend with us when they are both in town. I think that it is important that we continue to do this, that youth has some sense of history, that I reflect on my family. Indeed, that twenty-year-old Uncle Billy, who sits above my desk as I type with not a wrinkle on his fresh, boyish face, who was shot down and killed on December 17, 1944, has a nod of appreciation every day from a relative he never knew. Occasionally, however, I am of a semantic frame of mind. So, I ponder the term "Remembrance." To me, if one uses this word then it suggests an experience of an event or a person, it suggests a memory. I can certainly remember, but can a Millennial or someone from a later generation? Well, I guess they can. There have been enough wars since 1945 for young people to know somebody who has been involved. All, I think, that I am suggesting is that the tradition continue but with thoughts about its title.

In the current situation,

> **"The sense of changelessness only magnifies the change." Ben Gurion**

We have been used to doing things the same way for so long that it has come as a shock to us to have to do things differently. By and large, individuals have reacted with varying degrees of success. Societies as a whole have done so by embracing the rules because the alternative, if not lethally dangerous, is certainly unknown. Traffic in the UK is back to the level it was in 1955, CO_2 emissions worldwide have been cut by 8%, and, unless we are still at work, there are more roses being smelled and more decisions being given more careful thought. It is easy to be mortified by the negatives where we sit but better to be fortified and see the positives. And there are so many, are there not? I am discovering there are no strangers in the world, just friends I haven't met yet. I like this Italian proverb:

> *"Once the chess game is over, the king and pawn go back in the same box."*

I am hopeful that the rich and powerful come to a realization that if one doesn't take care of the problems in the back yard then they have a tendency to appear in the front. The U.S. desperately needs to socialize its medical system once and for all. If you are a world leader, you should understand that you can become just as much a victim of this virus as anybody else, and if you recover you should be humble enough to wash the feet of the poorest in society. Bill Gates should push his fellow billionaires to act as he does; nobody needs that much money. We should all adopt "nasake," the Japanese quality of compassion for the swordless. We should, as Einstein said,

> *"Try not to become a person of success rather than a person of value."*

There are many worthy and worthless baby boomers just as there are in every generation. Let us not be guilty of generalizing generations because such behaviour falls short of taking an individual as we find him or her.

All of this is easier said than done, eh?

Sun shining, temperature up, have a good day.

*Most of the recipients of my daily writings are retired.

Trouble is—?

Trouble is, Dear Friends, that I am not a great isolate. Being insular is not in my nature. I understand the importance of it, and I will not take risks. But I grew up as a roamer. From a young age I was expected to be out of the house. No adult was in the slightest bit interested what I and my mates were up to when we were out and about, what we were doing, no matter what level of rascality, as long as we came in when we were supposed to. Then there was the routine of boarding school, a timetabling of life that encroached on roaming. But, readers, it produced a new kind of freedom, a new kind of wander, and that was the wondering of the mind. If there was not the freedom to roam physically, then we could still have the freedom of dreaming. I became a master of the inward journey with the ability to be in a crowd or a class or a raucous dormitory and be free.

I am not a hugger or a close talker or an easy handshaker, but I do like to hear what people say and engage in chat. Don't get me wrong, I am quite happy with my own company. Alone, to me, does not mean lonely, but the trouble is, friends, I like the freedom of choice. The trouble is that none of us have that at the moment. We are missing activities that are good for our soul, good for our bodies and good for our mental health. Scottish dancing, cribbage and bridge, drinks with friends, work with friends, sport and such are on hold. One word that sums up our loss seems to be "camaraderie." Sure, we still get it, but it is not the same. It lacks the warmth of before, lacks the closeness of before and lacks the freedom of before. Trouble is that this is good for our physical protection but not good for our mental health.

We all mitigate and ameliorate in our own ways. I walk a great deal. Irene gardens and paints and tries to perfect my imperfections. (She succeeds with two out of the three). I have a domestic early morning regime: make the bed, make a mess, tidy the mess, and I write this blog. All of this works for Irene and me. We can pretend we are fine, smile that we are OK, brave-face that there is nothing wrong. Trouble is, of course, that, at the moment, we are subject to great uncertainty. Our futures hang in the economic and health balance. Our families are always a worry.

I guess we have to sit back and try to philosophize. We have to take stock of our lives and realize that, certainly, this world event is extremely serious and killing many, but no matter how you look at civilization and life, they have **always** been bloody dangerous. Rogue busses and diseases are always just around the next corner. Strokes, heart attacks and Devonshire cream teas are dangers we face every day and do so with panache and aplomb. There are chain-smokers out there who are frightened of terrorist attacks, alcoholics who are terrified of flying. Trouble is that times of crises skew our perspectives, warp our logic, over-focus our concerns. I guess that what we really need to do is simply put one foot in front of the other, live each day fully, enjoy that sinful chocolate bar, sip that gentle glass and give those in our bubble that extra hug. We need to dwell on the birds that sing, the plants that grow, the smiles that gladden; we need to pat that dog, wave and smile at that baby, engage in a brief moment of chat with that stranger, hold our heads up high and never forget that the world is our oyster and every day is too valuable and precious to be wasted on something that may or may not happen.

I remember a friend telling me that "he had never been to the other side of anything," and he wanted to go, he wanted to see for himself, he wanted to explore. There had been restrictions to his movement, not least his education, but more his lack of money and growing up with a family for whom an adventure was finding a bone in one's soup. He found a way. He flew for the first time, he travelled abroad for the first time, he went from the local to the global in an easy leap. Let's face it: his inner adventurous soul was there way before he ever boarded the plane. The smile that was always his, the eyes that always shone, were wider and brighter with every new experience and excursion. He always knew there was a broader world out there, and as soon as he experienced it there was no going back. He never forgot his poverty, the mind-numbing restrictions on his expectations from his family. He realized he had to step away from his family's traditional way of being. Having done so, nothing was hard for him ever again, let alone a simple world crisis like a pandemic. When the world came knocking, he welcomed it in no matter how imperfect it was.

Trouble is, friends, that I have had a very good life, yet there is much I still want to do and see. I want more of Scandinavia, more of Six Nations Rugby, more of different cultures. Trouble is I feel guilty wanting it. For millions of people in the world, the trouble is fresh water, lack of food, lack of healthy shelter, lack of the ability to get ahead. So, my "trouble is" is pretty selfish, pretty pathetic, pretty wildly above and beyond what most people in the world can hope for. So, tomorrow the sun will shine or the rain will fall, and Irene and I can walk out in both, can put food on the table, can be warm, can be entertained, can read, can write and, surely to goodness, can get a more reasoned perspective on our minor "trouble is-es."

A Paucity of Purpose

L ife is like two pieces of string: just as one thinks one can make both ends meet, somebody moves the ends! How many of us have sworn to read *War and Peace*? There is so much out there that we keep meaning to do either for pleasure or out of necessity. Now that we have the luxury of time many of those things become possible. Well, one cannot hang-glide off Mont Blanc or visit the Louvre at the moment, but one could read that long-promised book if one had a mind to. Michael Harris is the acclaimed Vancouver-based author of a wonderful little book called *The End of Absence*. He had intended to read *War and Peace* for many years. So, when his partner left the city for three weeks, he set his stall out and began reading. But, the tyranny of technology kept interfering. He read the first paragraph and then checked his phone, he forced his way through a page and looked at his email, he battled through the first chapter then surfed the web. But then there was a tipping point. The novel gripped him. Soon he was ignoring all of his devices as he could not wait for the adventure of turning that next page. He rattled through the 1,000 plus pages and was saddened when it came to an end. On another occasion he found himself on the top of the Eiffel Tower as the sun was setting over the city of Paris. It was a magnificent moment in his life, almost an epiphany. He took a selfie and sent it to his friends. He received comments back: "Wow," "Wonderful." "Great." He wished he had never taken the picture, and he heartily wished he had never shared it. It had been **his** moment. To share it was watering down milk, a sullying of the experience. It was impossible for anybody else to share his awe, his wonder, his sheer joy. The connection between these two vignettes is that they are part and parcel of the same person, but reading the novel was one of careful focus and considered planning. We have this luxury in a pandemic. The experience on the Eiffel Tower was an unplanned moment of madness, a blundering in where angels fear to tread. Maybe a pandemic shows its benefit not only in reading *War and Peace* but also in the prevention of mistaken spontaneity.

As we have discovered, a lockdown can be a lowdown. Suddenly the little things assume size and importance way beyond what they should. In our house, last night's dirty dishes have become a thing of the past. They are washed and dried almost immediately after use. One singular pathetic little weed is discovered early in the morning and Irene is out there before breakfast and it is gone. Outside tasks that would normally involve a drive are now a walk. But, Dear Reader, it has been difficult for me to find a purpose. But then along came Leigh from Collingwood School who kindly offered me work for the first two weeks in June when Collingwood opens up for Grades K to V. I was ecstatic. What did I want to do? I didn't care.

"Unsure of the safety protocols at the moment," she said, "but we are working through them."

"I trust you," I said.

We went from email to a chat on the phone to me skipping along on my walk with a big smile on my face. I was eager to work with children, delighted to meet and chat with my former colleagues. But I was mostly over the moon to be part of a bigger whole, to have a purpose that was not a solipsism, a chance to give something back.

Then two days ago, Leigh contacted me to say I would not be allowed to work because of Ministry advice for those of us over the age of sixty-five. She was so apologetic but, of course, it was not her fault. I did my best to mitigate her guilt.

"No big deal."

"I understand completely."

"Really nice to be considered in the first place."

"Thanks so much for taking the time."

Then I put the phone down and took myself for a different sort of walk—a head-down, self-pitying, gloomy trundle and a real mental struggle to get a proper perspective. It's OK to say that I am the luckiest of men. I live with Irene in a detached house with a garden. I do not have to worry about work. I am not starving. I am not living in the USA or Brazil or a Third World country where people cannot socially distance or have lost their jobs or are worried about where their next meal is coming from. Get your pathetic head up, Davidson. You are the luckiest of guys. Why would you worry about a measly fortnight of work that you do not need financially, and that will be stressful and tiring? Talk it through with friends and family and come out the other side of this so you do not come across as a self-centred, selfish, "woe is me," pathetic apology of a man. Go back to your lockdown routine, fall back on the book you are reading, believe—please believe—that mowing the lawn is a most pleasurable thing, make your bed, cook the supper, vacuum, vacuum, vacuum, change the sheets, climb the C-Lovers stairs until the sweat and breath have left your body, until your legs are quivering, your muscles are screaming, your thoughts and focus are on the bodily challenge; wimp not away from the confrontation of self, sacrifice your pathetic pride by sharing your woes with friends and family again, selfish though that may be. Pour your heart out in this blog and get back to where life and thought and hope and care are in a better place. Then it was my birthday, so for the second time in ten weeks I have some alcohol and use the wisdom of Robbie Burns to mitigate and ameliorate my paucity of purpose:

> *"Gie him strong drink until he wink,*
> *That's sinking in despair;*
> *An liquor guid to fire his bluid,*
> *That's prest wi' grief and care:*
> *There let him bouse, an deep carouse,*
> *Wi' bumpers flowing o'er,*
> *Till he forgets his loves or debts,*
> *An' minds his griefs no more."*

So, Dear Reader, there is solace and calm, a deep joy in the rhythm of the words from 200 years ago. Enjoy the day, my friends.

Arrogance and Ignorance

Much has been written about this most deadly of combinations. "Fools rush in where angels fear to tread"; acting "like a bull in a china shop." Even those of us who have a smattering of knowledge, who never act without forethought and preparation, still have moments of madness, an idiocy of folly, a "What was I thinking?" moment when the wisest decision was patience and no decision. Then there are moments of distraction. Putting my school laptop in the back of my son's truck on a showery day, thus ensuring it of a watery death, a premature demise, was not a stellar moment in my teaching career. Nor was it the wisest decision in my life to fling ropes over the roof of the house, attach one end to a couch and the other end to the tow hitch on my car. These were moments of confidence given to me by a good night's sleep, a full belly, because somebody had said something nice to me at work or play, because the school rugby team had just won a championship. These actions were the product of boyish exuberance, elation, a sunny day, an upcoming holiday, the beginning of a weekend after a hard week. They were careless, spontaneous acts of blithe unthinking stupidity, and thank goodness they caused no lasting harm to roof or car or accident or hurt to other people.

So, while on another camping holiday or maybe the same trip as the "sheetie" incident,* the Davidson family were camping in the little village of Ullapool, which is also a ferry port for the Isle of Lewis. As so often on our camping trips, the wind and rain were driving off the sea. It was early evening, but we were already in our tents taking shelter when two or three cars arrived far too quickly on the grassy pitch next to us. Out piled two families who seemed in some way to be related to each other. A "smytrie o' wee duddie weans" varying in age from the very little to the early teens, bundled out of the vehicles, were bundled into waterproofs and proceeded to vent their car-cramped energy on the nearby playground. The mothers found the wash and shower block, pulled out a couple of fold-up chairs, sat down in the paltry shelter of the entryway, lit up a cigarette each and supervised the children from the relative dry. Meanwhile, the waterproofed husbands pulled out the tent bags and did a pretty good job of protecting them from the elements prior to putting them up. The beginning of the process looked to be proceeding with efficiency and calm. But suddenly the slow, calm movements became fraught and more vigorous. Brows became furrowed, happy hoots and hollers disappeared into a changing mood of brood and frustration. I watched with increasing interest from the shelter of my open-flapped tent. The two men eventually stopped and went and sat in the front of one of the vehicles. They must have drawn straws, for eventually one of them appeared out of the driver's seat and approached their partners, the other following a step behind. I craned my ears to hear what was about to be said:

"We forgot the poles; we left them in Inverness."

Hearing that, I retreated farther into my tent but enough to hear the suggestion that the two guys leave the family and drive the couple of hours back to Inverness to pick up the poles. That was never going to wash! Eventually a solution was reached, and the two women were going to leave the men with the children, and they were going to make the drive. They pulled off and the two guys gathered up the children and took them to the pub. I am, Dear Reader, unsure whether that is an example of arrogance or ignorance or really just an example of guys being guys.

There would seem to be innocent ignorance of the willful variety. The innocent occurs when a Huron from Canada sees Paris for the first time or a native from the island of St. Kilda is introduced to Glasgow. The experience is so new to them both that they leave believing that the buildings are carved out of the native rock. There is no understanding that rock would be imported for the purpose. Then there is the ignorance that is deep but is matched by an amazing self-confidence, which suborns all the evidence towards an unfounded belief. Lord Cardigan, leading the Light Brigade into the valley of death, charging on horseback the Russian guns which, of course, caused havoc on his own men, was foolhardy. Defying reason, ignoring the experts, failing to prepare, doing no background research, no pausing before action, allowing self-belief to be one's guiding light; all of these lead us into situations that are often likely to go wrong. Sometimes we find ourselves with a storm in a teacup and can extricate our folly with minimum consequences, on other occasions we find ourselves in a teacup in a storm.

Please, please save us all from the celibate, unmarried priest who is giving out advice to a young couple about to be married. Please, please keep me away from the single man who gives me parental advice. Please don't tell me about the terrible waste of time it is to go to a doctor; that western medicine is local hocus pocus when western medicine has saved the lives of three of my family.

Peter Newman, the acclaimed author and journalist, was at a cocktail party. He happened to run into a neurosurgeon who asked him what he did for a living. He explained that he was a writer. The medical man smiled knowingly and said, "You know, when I retire, I am going to write."

"Hmmm, when I retire, I am going to be a brain surgeon."

Before we pontificate about the rights and wrongs of a situation, we need to establish the credentials of whom we are listening to. We need to be critically aware that an expert could be wrong but also aware that he or she could be right. We can have opinions and we can pontificate as long as we recognize that we don't have the knowledge and adapt our opinions when different evidence becomes available.

As you know, Dear Reader, I write frequently, but I am *not* a writer. It is a hobby, a pastime, a relaxation. I enjoy reading good writing and listening to good writers when they speak about their art. The more that I read, the more ignorant I think I am. I hope it causes me to step back from any arrogant pontification, any pretension. It would be a help in this world if those in power listened to the experts and attached that listening to some background reading. Then maybe difficult solutions might be easier to find. But, my cynicism at the ability of world leaders at the moment suggests to me that most of them have forgotten the tent poles.

Sun is shining.

*See other blog.

Leadership

There is a plant falsely rumoured to have been named after Prince William, Duke of Cumberland, who won the last land battle fought on British soil at Culloden in 1746. It is called "Sweet William" or "Stinkin' Billy" depending on what particular side of the political divide one leans towards. Thereby lies the dilemma of leadership, does it not? One woman's hero is another man's villain. It is impossible to placate and please all of the citizens of a nation-state all of the time. One cannot praise diversity with one hand and expect unity with the other, can one? In western democracies we always elect a representative to parliament, but do we also delegate the power to them to make decisions without consultations? Common sense would suggest that running a country through a morass of constant referenda would be an awful, time-consuming, expensive waste. It is impossible for us to live by the Roman maxim:

"What touches all must be approved by all."

If, for example, we on Tatlow Avenue were to petition for speed bumps at intervals on the street, it is unlikely that we would be supported 100%, sensible though many of us think the initiative to be. Charles the Bold of France described the eight pillars of leadership as follows:

"Truth, patience, generosity, powers of persuasion, punishment of evil, friendship,

lightness of tribute and equality of justice between rich and poor."

There are two that seem to stand out in the current crisis: "truth" and "equality of justice." Inevitably, when the world is dealing with an unknown, the truth of a solution is going to take many forms. Maybe a better word here is "honesty." What is wrong with a world leader saying that they honestly don't know the answer but are working on finding it? An honest, heartfelt answer or apology can go a long way to diffusing a situation. An acceptance of "buck stopping" rather than "blame gaming" would be a good start, don't you think? Certain leaders need to read a bit more Confucian philosophy:

"When you see a worthy person, endeavour to emulate him. When you see an unworthy person, then examine your inner self."

Trouble is that leadership requires a certain amount of ego, which begats self-conceit, which then allows for the fact that the only "worthy person" is him or herself.

"Power corrupts. Absolute power corrupts absolutely."

One cannot go to a place of work without recognizing who is a good leader and who is not. I have worked for and with many outstanding leaders in my career. The best ones genuinely liked people and really loved working with children. They listened rather than talked. They had humour. Most importantly, they had a hinterland, a place outside of work that was another passion. Winston Churchill re-read the works of Jane Austen during World War II. Ted

Heath, another British prime minister, was a yachtsman and an organ player. Harold Wilson loved the Scilly Isles. Boris Johnson has made lots of babies, Donald Trump has made lots of ummmm, likes to ummmm, has ummm, well at least he's made America grate again. It is so important, is it not, to be able—especially at a time of a crisis—to step back from a problem, rise above it and look at it with fresh eyes.

> *"One moment of patience may ward off great disaster. One moment of impatience may ruin a whole life." Chinese Proverb*

I love the movie *The Hunt for Red October*. There is a scene when the captain of the Russian submarine, Sean Connery, turned to the American on the ship and asked him what he did in the CIA. He said that he wrote books and analysed foreign documents. Connery pauses for a moment and says that he knows these books and that the conclusions are all wrong. Nothing wrong in this except that in seconds they all know they are going to be blown up by a torpedo. Seconds pass and all are sweating on a decision. At the last moment Connery moves, and the sub avoids destruction. He knew his enemy. He knew what he was going to do way before the decision had to be made. The plan was well thought out. He was ready to lead. Throughout the whole movie, the Russian captain comes across as a well-read, pragmatic, commander respected by his men and respectful of them. There are certain things leaders do not want on their gravestones. Tony Abbott, one of many recent Australian prime ministers, has been described as "The suppository of all wisdom"; not something he would want on his resting place. "He learned so much from his mistakes that he thought that he would make a few more" would not be a great epitaph for a king or a queen. King Henry VIII possibly thought that five of his six wives were mistakes. How about this for a good leader's grave: "She dreamed of a society where a chicken could cross the road without its motives being questioned." Not a bad one, one thinks. Then there is the arrogance of power: "He knew the scenery so well, he no longer saw it."

Leaders need to accept the Finnish model. The belief that it is good to sit in silence as the sun goes down, to contemplate nightfall. "Keeping the twilight" it is called. Not a bad engraving for a great leader.

"She kept the twilight."

Leader may make better decisions if the people of the world all "kept the twilight."

For the moment, friends, as countries start the experiment of opening up their societies yet again, the days ahead continue to be uncertain. We are all taking a deep breath and tiptoeing out into the world. The following T-shirt slogan seems to sum it up:

"The past, the present and the future walked into a bar. It was tense."

The past is over and it now looks like a sunny upland to a large number of us. The present is a constant concern, and the future is a minefield of uncertainty. We need true statesmanlike leadership for the present and the future.

Sun is shining. Nature is blue, green, bright and chirping. Off for porridge and coffee in the back garden.

Have a great day.

Life's Little Luxuries

It came home to me yesterday that we have all—those of us who who have the luxury of living in the First World, of course—had to curtail so many of our Epicurean delights. Staying with my friend, Audrey, on March 19, we had a glass or two of red wine. I haven't had any alcohol since. This has not been a deliberate act on my part. Indeed, until last week I hadn't thought about it at all. I have no idea why I have not had a drink. I do know that when I worked for a living, I used to open a bottle of red wine on a Friday night. Other than that, I would have a social drink when out for dinner or at a pub with friends. It seems that, therefore, alcohol for me is something celebratory. This, however, does *not* mean I am living a spartan lifestyle; stoicism is not a Davidson trait! Why, therefore, did it suddenly hit me yesterday? Well, I was at VGH for my annual visit with a specialist doctor, a wonderful woman called Dr. Katherine Paton.

Two years ago, I was reading a wonderful book in the waiting room called *The Old Ways* by Robert MacFarlane. She took an interest. I had two copies, so I gave her that one. I forgot about it at last year's visit but yesterday I asked her if she had read it. She said she had, and it was obvious she had enjoyed it. No big deal, you may say. But, dear friends, to me at that moment and in this period in our lives, that news was a little luxury that gave me an unreasonably buoyant gladness on the way home.

So, I decided to carry on the feeling of uplifted cheer by taking my daily walk past The Cheese Man shop, which sits on the little trading estate south of the Capilano Mall car park. I have told many that Bulk Barn is my favourite shop, but it is so no longer. Doug Martin and his small cheesy business have usurped the bulk buying experience. Because of social distancing, only one person is allowed into his shop at any one time. There is a ribbon behind which we have to stand. There are jars of hot and less hot peppery preserves to choose from, packets of oat cakes, crackers, accoutrements to accompany his large and tasty variety of cheeses. I have white cheese with pieces of orange dotting its tempting interior, I have crimson, fruity slabs, blue-veined electricity flowing through stilton and Danish, Red Leicester, edible Edam, brilliant brie and—my absolute favourite—the Norwegian Gjetost, a fine blend of goat's and cow's milk, savoury but sweet, sweet but savoury. I love it dearly. With the current crisis, Doug has cut a deal with a baked goods company that used to sell to restaurants. So, one can order bread, bagels, croissants, desserts and spicy beef and chicken rolls online. The prices are phenomenal. Doug is open from 10:00 a.m. to 6.00 p.m. every day except Sunday and Monday. He accepts cash only. It is a delight to shop there, not least because I have started to enjoy my brief interactions with Doug outside of the act of buying. Oh yes, I forgot to mention the cheese recipe book that mine host has written. I have resisted the temptation to purchase this yet as I fear it may be a waistline too far!

Abraham Lincoln said, *"The dogmas of the quiet past are inadequate for the stormy present."*

I feel the same about past luxuries. The sybaritic therapy of a hike up the Grouse Grind; the swish of snow on a ski run; a little dip in sea or lake—they are not there at the moment. But walking with Irene, we have stopped and looked at plants, many of which I recognize but do not know the names of. She is a mine of information. Thus, I am getting to know my laburnums, the different variety of dogwood and various types of flowers. Thus, I am reading a lot more. Thus, I am writing, poor readers, a lot more nonsense than usual. There is even a subtle pleasure in cutting the grass, digging over a border, cutting a branch off a tree. One wouldn't describe these activities as examples of overindulgent hedonism. They are hardly that but in these isolating times they are little pleasures. After all, friends,

"Normal is just a setting on the dryer."

Buckets of substantially juicy rain during the night wasn't there, a pleasant gentle mizzle at the moment. Good day to toddle off to Doug's emporium for a nibble of cheese and the luxury of an experience.

Conventions and Contradictions

T rundling out for a wee dander along the Spirit Trail yesterday afternoon, I saw many users. Joggers, cyclists on a mission, cyclists on family outings, dog owners and walkers were all out enjoying the weather. The rules of social distancing seemed to be working well. On Friday night when I walked through the strip park to pick up our Cactus Club order. Halfway down the strip park were a couple of young families standing a safe distance apart, having a beer. On the way back, I cut up the road between the fire hall and Shaw. There was a large group of about ten guys looking like they had just finished work. They, too, were supping the odd beer from a respectful distance and winding down after work. It occurred to me that a few years ago I read an excellent book about habit forming. If I remember rightly, it takes about six weeks to form a habit for good or bad. Therefore, with social distancing having been in force now for about seven weeks, I guess the habit should now be ours.

Of course, if one is trying to form a habit, one lapse after the beginning means that one has to begin the timeline again. The habit is broken before it becomes an habit. Brian Burke of Canucks and Leafs fame, and who is now a hockey pundit and so forth, once came to speak to Collingwood senior school students. I did not hear him but heard his message. He grew up in a large family. Right from the arrival of the first born, Mr. and Mrs. Burke set out the rule that every night between 7:00 p.m. and 8:00 p.m., the whole family had a reading hour. Nobody dictated what had to be read, but Mum, Dad and all of the children were reading for pleasure for that one hour. Nothing else was allowed. Of course, as babies they would need to be read to, but what a wonderful experience to be a fly on the wall when they were all teenagers and lounging and draped about immersed in a book. No phone could be answered, no radio or TV were on, nobody spoke; just silent submersion in their book of choice. What a wonderful convention, what an incredible tradition to give one's children. Where is the contradiction here? Well, I have to say that I cannot find one.

The contradiction came from another source. A mum and dad had taught their children well. They had told them that lying was never the right thing to do. If they had hurled that rock at that child in the playground, they were to put their hand up and admit they were responsible. The dog did not eat the homework, you just didn't do it. So, Mum and dad had taught their children **never** to lie. Day came when the family decided to go on an outing to the movies. As they lined up, Dad noticed they could get in cheaper if the children were under a certain age. Therefore, when he went to pay at the booth, he lied. At that moment, **all** of their hitherto excellent parenting, their chats about the moral turpitude of telling a lie—**all** of that—was as nought from that instant. Great convention, terrible contradiction.

In case I am coming across as a haloed member of an elite sainthood here, please read on. When our son, Grant, was in Grade VIII at Collingwood School, he was playing football at recess with his mates. An altercation occurred and he knocked out a Grade IX boy who was giving him some lip. Ambulance called, Grant to the office, Irene called to the school, son rightly suspended for three days. Dad read the Riot Act and lectured him when he returned home—self-righteous lecture, forceful finger waving. In the midst of this suspension, he had to accompany me grocery shopping, after which we popped into Starbucks so I could buy a coffee. There was an incident in the coffee shop with a complete stranger who started asking me about the price to send a child to Collingwood School. We had a Collingwood teacher discount, and I had no idea of the price for other students. I was their teacher, and I had no interest in how much other parents paid. This stranger, however, was a dog on a bone. Normally, I would turn on my heel and leave, but there was something about this clown that really, really irritated me. I felt my blood rise and I clenched my fists when suddenly my son was pulling me away with his surprisingly strong arms. The irony of my forceful teenager escorting me from the building was not lost on either of us. He had cut away the moral high ground from underneath my feet. Grant knew it and so did I. The previous day's preaching was now so much hypocrisy. Philip Larkin was right:

> *"They fuck you up, your mum and dad.*
> *They may not mean to, but they do.*
> *They fill you with the faults they had*
> *And add some extra, just for you."*

That poem has as much subtlety as a stain, does it not?! New conventions have been thrust upon us during the past couple of months and they look to be habit forming. But, as with all crises, where society is flying by the seat of its pants and governments are searching for the right thing to do, there will inevitably be contradictions locally and globally. Things change on a daily basis but, if history proves nothing else, humanity always bobs to the surface again like a cork after immersion. As John Keats would have it, we may, at times, be "mantled before in darkness and huge shade," but he also said we shall enjoy "the calm luxuriance of blissful light."

Sun is shining, breakfast and walk beckons. Pete.

"We have sunk to a depth in which restatement of the obvious is the first duty of intelligent men."
George Orwell

CHAPTER 2

THE NATURAL WORLD

It was a surprise to us all, was it not, Dear Reader, to suddenly be told to isolate ourselves. We had never considered the possibility that the freedoms we took so much for granted would be suddenly taken away. Some of us were to be confined indoors. Others were to be allowed to exercise. Some were only allowed up to a distance of five miles from our homes. We were not only unable to seek a rural respite from our urban existence, but we could not even walk safely in our local parks. We were all isolated, and some of us had to quarantine for a fortnight. Naturally, we began to dream of the simple pleasures that had been ours yesterday. They were no longer ours today and were unlikely to be ours in the near future. Along with simple dreams of communing with nature came nostalgic memories of trips and journeys we had made in the past. Dotted about in my 100 days of blogs, nature came to play a huge part.

The Owl, the Beaver
and the Heron

My friend, Nigel, and I walked past Mackay Creek on an evening several weeks ago as we frequently do. We are happily amazed at the work that has gone into making the creek a more natural and beautiful place than it once was. One Monday we stood on the sidewalk with the busy road behind us and the creek passing beneath us. We watched a heron wading carefully through the gentle eddies of the water after its prey. Every movement was patient and slow and steady. In his excellent novel *Cold Mountain*, Charles Frazier describes the heron as "everywhere they were seemed far from home." So, it seems, a heron in its natural habitat seems unnaturally placed, even more so in an urban environment. Yet there he stood with his streamlined beak designed perfectly for the job of catching and holding his prey; there were his spindle shanks, his twig-like legs designed to create minimum disturbance as he crept towards his prey in the water. So, even in the short time we watched, he moved from slow and steady to rapid and deadly. A split second saw him fed.

Meanwhile on the other side of the road, Nigel's excellent eyesight spotted our friend from the previous night, the beaver. So, we made our way to the other bank, stood with heron-like stillness and watched as he plashed his flat tail in the water. If ever it is possible for an animal to strut arrogantly in water, then the beaver does it. He owns this particular part of the river. It is his dam that dictates, his felled trees that block and divert, his teeth that gnaw and shape. He is the finest of rodents, the most successful of animals that gnaw.

When I was alone at home that night and reflecting on our early evening dander, I flashed back to an incident that occurred about a decade previous. It was a late winter's evening, that time between day and night that Scots call "the gloaming." The light was not yet night and the day was nudging towards darkness. I had been dropped off at Marine Drive after coaching some rugby at school. I was track-suited and had my Collingwood baseball cap on. I was tired and hungry. I was drawing opposite Norgate Park as I walked down our street. The air was still, not a breath of wind. The trees were silhouetted eerily against the shadows of the fading light, their leafless bows witch-gnarled fingers, ominous spectres lurking with numinous intent. Suddenly, my baseball cap was gone. No problem, must have caught it on a branch, so I looked up. Nope, no tree nearby. Hmm. Looked down at the grassy verge, not a sign. Now phlegmatic insouciance became febrile activity. It was nothing to do with the limited value of the hat, everything to do with the Bermuda Triangle that had taken it from the face of the Earth some years before the end of its natural life. Now I was on my hands and knees, now desperately combing hopelessly through the short grass beside the sidewalk. So focused was I that I failed to notice a guy walking down the street until he was almost upon me. He paused, unsure what to do. I was embarrassed.

"Honestly, I am not drunk or crazy," I said. "I've lost my hat."

Words spilled from me, an elided rapid-fire justification. I stood up sheepishly. At that moment there was a flash of white from the trees on the other side of the road and a flopping sound as something landed on the tarmac in the car park. It was my hat. I dashed over, picked it up and returned to the other side of the street where the guy was now chuckling and shaking his head. The owl that had chosen this tasty morsel had suddenly realized his folly and rejected it in disgust.

"Now I have something to tell the wife," was the man's farewell to me as he laughed his merry way down the street to pick up his car.

So perfect were the adaptations of that beautiful nocturne that I heard nothing, saw nothing and felt nothing. I now know what "one fell swoop" means. Had that hat been Davidson's pet hamster rummaging through the mop of white hair that so clearly represented Davidson's disheveled existence, then Hammy would have been so very alive one moment and so very dead the next.

Admittedly, this owl incident happened a long time before our world became upturned in the upheaval of a pandemic. But it could so easily have happened in our current crisis. The point is that humankind has become so involved in the COVID-19 threat that even when it is not up front and personal there is never a day goes by wherein we do not think of it in some shape or form. It may be at the back of our minds, but it does so easily encroach its way to the front. However, for the beaver, the heron and the owl that live in our urban environment, there is no pandemic. Their crises are the ones they face every day—the continual search for food. Our troubles hold no interest for them, and their lives are proceeding as normal.

I am pretty happy to be a human being but, in our time of trouble, I do cast an envious glance at our local wildlife and wish I was one of them with their simple problems and simple answers. But, then Dear Reader, I turn away to who I am, to where I live, to my family and friends, to the food I can put in my belly and the many pleasures of life that are still available to me here in North Vancouver. The envy passes in the lightning flash of a heron's spear and the speedy dispatch of an owl's swoop.

Springtime in Vancouver

ere in North Vancouver, we occupy land between the mountains to the north and Burrard Inlet to the south. The downtown area is but a bridge away. And yet, the upward lift of the mountains gives us, on average, three times as much precipitation as the city below us. Not being a meteorologist, I know little of weather patterns. I do, however, suspect that this has been a very fine spring for gardens and wilderness. Most of the rain seems to have fallen at night, added to which we have had some cloudless, sunny and warm days.

We have still been allowed to exercise in our isolated state, so my wife and I have walked. There is always a different path not far from us, and we could walk many and various trails every day of the week. We know how spoiled we are.

Just the other day, I decided to wander up the street in the early morning. The sidewalks were still damp from the heavy rainfall during the night. The sun was struggling to lift the moisture from the leaves and trees. Of course, any wet-nosed dog will tell us how water enhances smells. All of us who are blessed with a sense of smell know how evocative it can be. So, as I walked, I was suddenly aware of a smell so familiar, yet so distant in time. A few years ago, I had paused in much the same place to take in a childhood memory. Now I stopped and lingered a mite longer.

My grandparents had a large garden in the small town of Nairn on the Moray Firth in Scotland. Every summer we would decamp there from the south. My dad always booked a rowing boat for our fishing trips. We would either find ourselves on Lochindorb near to the town of Grantown-on-Spey or at Loch Ruthven not far south of Inverness. My two brothers and I would spend the day casting our flies on the water. We would either catch fish or not. Our dad would cast his line with infinite patience. The boat was a source of peace and tranquility, a calm haven of gentle views, lines landing on ripples, flies being pulled temptingly across the loch's surface. Occasionally there was excitement at catching a fish. I can still hear the oars being pulled into the boat, the unbalanced clambering as somebody reached for the fishing net and the proud feeling when we estimated the size of the brown trout. Sometimes a rainy squall, however, changed the idyll, and often the wind blew up. We were then faced with an elemental effort to get the boat back to the boathouse by the end of the day. So, if we came off the loch early because the waters and the winds kept the fish away, we would make the hour journey back to the town with time still to play outside. Northern evenings in the summer are long and light.

Therefore, when we returned to Nairn, we could not wait to get back outside to play football (soccer) on the lawn. One goalie, one defender and one attacker; three goals for the change around. A large beech tree served as one goalpost and a small bush as another. Hours of seamless pleasure before supper. On one occasion, I remember having to retrieve the ball after a wayward shot had skyed it over the wall and into the street. I dashed out of the gate, and in the process caught the fragrance of my grandfather's juniper hedge. Wet from a shower, green with its summer growth, it was only about half of my height and temptingly low to leap over. So, rather than the gate on the way back, I jumped the hedge. More specifically, I caught my foot on a branch and fell. The hedge was now above me, and my teenage senses took in the aroma. My teenage energy did not allow anything but a passing moment of appreciation as I dashed back to the game, but the smell registered, competing with all of the other fluids flowing through my teenage body. So, here am I over fifty years later, with all the life that has gone in between, walking up my street and suddenly, ineluctably back in my grandfather's front garden at Hazelbrae, Viewfield Street, Nairn.

All of our senses are evocations, are they not? They are antipathetic or therapeutic. They take us to different places and different times. They trigger what once was and enhance our realization of what is.

When I walked past this juniper hedge last week, I stopped. I looked about to see if anybody was watching or whether anybody else was on the street. Nobody was. I squatted down, drank in the aroma, stood up and ran my hand through the length of the hedge as I strolled. I milked the moment, savoured the memory, took in its simplicity. Dear Reader, in these times of no touch and social distancing, it is such a pleasure for one living thing to commune closely with another without fear of contaminating or being contaminated. It was an uplifting moment, a deep intake of breath, a closing of eyes, a smile on one's face and a joyous memory of a boy's past and an adult's present.

Be safe, Dear Reader, be safe.

Salad Days and Snowy Ways

Back in the year 1970, I had left school and was about to embark on what nowadays would be called a *"gap year."* I can't remember whether terms like "finding oneself" or the "real world" were prevalent then. At any rate, it was not a gap year in the end but more like a gulf two years—deep holes of experience into which I chaotically tumbled. Various jobs came and went, mostly lurching into view like a drunken man trying to find his way home. One of those jobs found me at the Strathspey Hotel as a porter. This purpose-built monstrosity spoilt the Highland quaintness of the old village community of Aviemore in the north of Scotland. Aviemore was becoming a ski resort for the mountain of Cairngorm in the national park of the same name.

A beautiful, crisp winter day arrived, blue skies contrasting the glittering white that beckoned from the mountain a few miles down the road. I had two days off and was keen to get up and ski, the conditions were perfect. But, dear friends, there is a fickleness about skiing in Scotland not always present in many other resorts. The ski hill was closed. Most of the 3,500- to 4,000-foot peaks of the Cairngorms are treeless, windswept, heather-clad barriers to cold north winds with not much other than a Faeroe, a Shetland or an Orkney island lying between them and the Arctic. So, it is a frustrating experience to see perfect snow, in itself rare, and find that the lifts are closed because of the wind. Or, as was the case on this glorious, windless day, all shut because the access road was blocked. A blizzard had come through, and the road from Loch Morlich at the bottom of the car park at the foot of the chairlift up to the White Lady Sheiling was under at least ten feet of snow. Casual labour was being offered, £3.40 to get up there and help clear the road. I reported for duty.

The bus dropped us at the foot of the hill with spades, pick axes, shovels, barrows and basically any sharpish implement that could be wielded. I was young. I had strength. I enjoyed physical work. So, I attacked the snow and ice with vigour but with little science and no system. Monty, a full-time employee of "The Hill," was working alongside of me. He saw my sweated efforts and was not impressed. With others, he quietly organized barrowing and dumping so that a regular rhythm and method would see systematic progress. It was slow and steady, and the impatience of youth reached lunchtime with seemingly no significant progress. Meanwhile, the loch below us was freezing into a more solid ice, the temperature was dropping, and the snow was getting harder.

As the afternoon rolled forwards, my youthful enthusiasm began to wane. I sweated in the cold, Monty did not. He plodded methodically. He was a silent companion, a man of few words, a toiler for the week, not my pathetic two days. There were other casual workers there with us, mostly students, mostly possessed with the same wish to see the road clear and the ski hill open. Monty dug and shovelled, picked and cleared and uttered never a word. Eventually, one of the younger members of the crew flung down his spade and sat on a lump of ice in frustration, wiping the sweat from his forehead.

"Monty," he said, trying to attract his attention.

Monty paused and leaned on his shovel. "Aye."

"Don't we have a snow-blower?"

"Aye."

"Well, where is it?"

"We're digging for it."

Dear friends, in these days of isolation and a search for a way out of this pandemic, don't we hope for better preparation in the future? Drawing from the experience of my salad years, may I suggest—nay, humbly plead—that even though there may be no blizzard in the immediate forecast, and even though we know the road will be blocked if bad weather comes, that the snow-blower is moved from the high, exposed mountain road to a shed in a sheltered area low down with a weather-protected access road?

Please, please, WHO and governments of the world: be prepared, be ready, forward plan, be innovative, research, and *don't*—please, please don't—lose the bloody snow-blower!

Have a good day.

Wet Noses and "Loud" Smells!

It was a seminal moment, a few years ago now, when somebody explained to me that a dog with a dry nose was an unhealthy dog. A wet nose is exceedingly important to a dog's sense of smell. All of us know that, sure, a dog wants to go for a walk, fetch and carry, herd, meet and greet and all of those social things that make it such a great pet. But the *real* truth is that a dog *really* only wants to sniff, to smell, to sample every aroma on every step of its walk. To a dog, a smell is like mum's apple pie, like unwrapping a Christmas gift—every flower, every bush, every heap of mud is a holy grail found, until around the next bend there is another holy grail.

It rained in North Vancouver yesterday morning. I waited until it stopped and took my walk up through Ashdown Park. Bluebells, daisies and salal bushes luxuriating in the warmth after the showers were encroaching on the path. In the spring, there is always those beautiful aromas of a natural mixed wood springing up through the undergrowth; smells we would bottle if we could but realize it would be sacrilege so to do. Every smell in its place and every place in its smell! As I sweated my way up the hill, breathing more heavily with each ascending step, I realized early on that the rainwater had enhanced the smells, had brought them so much closer to me. On some days they were always present but never there. Yesterday morning they were very much present and very much there. I felt very privileged. As Keats would have it:

"The poetry of earth is ceasing never."

Since I was a child, I have always looked on nature with many questions but very few answers. Many of us feel the same, I'm sure. So many people of the world have based their belief systems on the seasonal rhythm of the natural world. I have always looked up at a craggy rock face, the size and stature of a monolith like the Chief, Uluru, the old Ayers Rock in Australia's red centre, with awe. I cannot look at a peak without thinking that it knows something I don't. There is always an air of brooding mystery about the hills and glens, the coires and hanging valleys, the glaciers and the jagged teeth, the gloomy whale backs. Looking across a moor or a plateau as a storm approaches often leads us towards it as much as we want to retreat. The power of bleakness and distance often feeds our curiosity, and we always want to know what lies beyond the horizon.

So, today on my walk I needed a botanist at hand, somebody to identify what I was smelling, somebody to separate the flower from the bush, the cherry blossom from the cedar tree. Smells evoke, do they not? Easing off from my vigour, warming down from the rigour, I ambled down Tatlow Avenue towards home, and I smelled the juniper hedge three houses to the north of us, an aroma I will always recognize from my youth. Some smells shout louder than others, do they not?

Hope that you can forgive my daily ramblings (no pun intended) and don't spend too much of your valuable time on them. My excuse is, like Charles Lamb,

"I am retired—I walk about; not to and from."

Going Out, Going In

I think that it was John Muir, the famous naturalist and founder of the Sierra Club, who said that when he was going out he was really going in. In other words, his adventures in the outdoors were as much about looking at his inner being as exploring the world. Talking to my brother, George, the other day, we got to chatting about his long-distance walking, in particular his walk on the Coast to Coast Trail, which I mentioned the other day.* One of his goals is to walk the West Highland Way (WHW), which I know that at least two of you who are reading this have done. I did it with some boys and colleagues from my last school and once with a friend. Sadly, my buddy accumulated awful blisters on the first day, took the bus up to Fort William and left me to saunter up on my own.

In the days when we walked the WHW, the beginning was in a car park in Milngavie (pronounced "Mill Guy") in Bearsden in Glasgow. The beauty of going from south to north is that you are walking away from the sun, and you begin walking on fairly flat ground towards Drymen and Loch Lomond. It is a pretty step with a steady transition from Lowland to Highland. So, I cannot remember where I camped on my first few days but, of course, I remember Crianlarich, Tyndrum and the steady ascent up to Rannoch Moor and Glencoe. What I particularly remember is the stage from Tyndrum to Bridge of Orchy. Somehow, I started to run a temperature; a summer cold seemed to have grabbed me, and it looked like the beginnings of a flu. So, I resolved to cut my walking day short and pitch my tent when I arrived at the "Bridge." I arrived at about lunchtime and discovered there were cheap bunkhouses to rent, so I forgot the tent thing and booked my sorry body in for the rest of the day and the night. There followed a luxurious and memorable day. I downed a bar meal in the pub and curled up into bed at about 1:00 p.m. I brought out my novel and did nothing all afternoon but dozed and read. At about 7:00 p.m., I got myself up, went to the pub, had a large whisky and pie and chips and went back to the room. I continued to read and sleep. Morning came. I awoke feeling so much better and ready to walk on. Why do I remember this day with such pleasure? I was just sick enough to be relaxed, just sick enough to realize that what would have been a guilty, unplanned pleasure was a wise necessity, just sick enough not to need to sleep the whole day but had enough in me to read.

Do you remember, Audrey, Rose and John, that as you enter Rannoch Moor there is a cairn by the side of the trail? It is a memorial to Peter Fleming. There is no marker on this, but it is at Black Mount. Peter Fleming was an author. He was the older brother of Ian Fleming, the James Bond creator, and married to the actress Celia Johnson. He was a travel writer as well as a novelist. He died suddenly of a heart attack in 1971 while going out shooting. Why do I mention this? Partly because I have a strange memory for such useless pieces of information, but also because there is a scene in the James Bond movie *Skyfall* that is so obviously filmed just up the road in Glencoe, and I was wondering if anybody involved in the film made the connection 'twixt recent film,

Ian Fleming, and his brother Peter who died just down the road. If you have the inclination, Google Peter Fleming's memorial cairn; it has lovely views.

Now then, where was I? Ah, yes, I was going out and going in at the same time. The head of Glencoe is guarded by Buachaille Etive Mor, the big shepherd, a peak that appears on many a calendar. When I was walking there with Broughton House School and ten or so students, the deputy head, Brian, was with us. He drove down the glen while we hiked over it. He had a cold feeling about the place that he could not put a finger on. He was really quite ill at ease, then somebody took it upon themselves to explain its history, the massacre of the MacDonalds by the Campbells in 1692 after a night of Highland hospitality. A great sacrilege as well as abuse of a Highland custom. There is a memorial cairn to the MacDonalds at the westward end of the glen. Just beneath the Pap of Glencoe, the distinctive peak that overlooks the sea, and up the hill from the memorial is the Glencoe House Hotel. Donald Smith, Lord Strathcona and his wife, Isabella, built it and lived in it. If you have seen the picture of the last spike being driven to complete the CPR railway at Craigellachie just this side of the Rockies, it is he who is posing top-hatted in the picture. So, 1692, 1885 and 1971 are representatives of very diverse events and people. There is the local and worldwide, the narrow and the broad, tragedy and success represented in a few short miles. Going out is indeed going in when one pauses before these worthy monuments. I hope these are three symbols of our past that will not be torn down for some perceived political incorrectness and signaling of virtue. But I am sidetracked here. The WHW is over ninety miles long and ends at the

Glen Nevis Caravan and Camping Park just beneath Ben Nevis, Britain's highest peak. The glen itself is worthy of a visit. Down the glen is the town of Fort William. The short drive up to the east is a dead end for motor traffic but has some lovely little trails girded by the peaks of the Mamores. One could rest up in the Glen Nevis campsite for a couple of days and then could continue one's hike from Fort William north through the Great Glen to Inverness. I have driven this route many times, but I have never hiked it. There is another remarkable statue in this glen. At Spean Bridge, three commandos look out over what was their training ground during the Second World War. There is also a memorial garden close by in memory of those who never returned home. I visited there as the son of one of these was laying a memorial wreath to the father he had never met. He had driven up from the Ayrshire coast to do so. His going out really was a going in.

Sun shining. Off for a bowl of porridge and a crack at the crossword over a cuppa.

Trusting Instincts

nstincts and intuition are difficult to understand. Indeed, some people would say that they are one and the same. A great deal has been written and researched about whether they are the result of nature or nurture. To me, it always comes back to direction finding. I always set off on a journey believing I can get to my destination without too much reference to a map, without too much guidance from somebody who knows the area. Well, Dear Reader, it is **not** true. I am an absolutely ***useless*** direction finder. On drives in the past, I would start well and then lose focus on what I knew and suddenly discover I knew better than the map, at which point failure was inevitable. On a hike in the countryside, I would follow the map religiously until after a few miles, I would see a peak, a river, a landmark and be convinced that it was this on the map and not that very real and obvious other landform. I would inevitably be wrong and need to retrace my steps and think again. Thank goodness when I was with students it was different. Being responsible for others suddenly made the event important, and I would maintain focus and obey the rules. So, I never understood why there was no transference, and I was wholly useless at it when on my own. My instincts are flawed yet I still reinforce the failure.

A couple of years ago, I was staying with friends in Richmond in Yorkshire. Elaine and Charlie are wonderful hosts and made me feel very welcome. By coincidence, my brother, George, and his friend, Nabil, were walking the Coast to Coast Trail at the same time. This is a grueling 182-mile hike beginning at St. Bee's Head on the west coast of Cumbria and coming out, after going through three national parks, at Robin Hood's Bay on the North Yorkshire North Sea coast. Further contact revealed that the two of them would be spending the night in Richmond when I was there. So, we arranged to meet. The plan was for me to walk from Richmond to the village of Marske, meet them there, turn and accompany them back to Richmond. It would be a walk of about ten miles. It was late morning before I started. I had spent some time at Elaine and Charlie's award-winning allotment, revelling in the sun and the greenery. I walked up the hill from their wonderful garden, joined the road and strutted off west. Soon the tree-patterned avenue morphed into a path. I was in Swaledale with views of the River Swale a few hundred feet below. There was a section through some woodland, but the real beauties were the escarpments above that were carved by glaciers some 15,000 years previous. The dry trail, stone dykes and walker's gates were a gentle walking pleasure. Eventually, I came to a "B" road downhill to the left and slightly uphill to the right. I took the right because there looked to be another entry to the path a smidge above me. The sun shone, the day was warm, the world was a wonderful place. The new stretch of path headed downwards through some shrubbery to a stream. As I reached the bottom, the path seemed to disappear into some overgrown ferns, so I prepared to walk along the trail less travelled. It had not occurred to me, even after seeing so many long-distance walkers coming towards me all day, that the new path was sufficiently unbeaten to suggest that this was the wrong way. Much sweating and a bit of uphill later revealed warning flags and a stone dyke with signs that this was a Ministry of Defence firing range. Deciding that this was not a day that I wanted to get shot and killed, particularly by soldiers who were supposed to be on my side, I climbed higher up the hill until, eventually, I was back on the B road. After a long trek, I was back to where I had crossed over, and I finally figured that the village of Marske was just a continuation thereof. A farther walk down the hill brought the realization that it was now late in the day, and I had missed my brother and his friend. Not having a cell phone, I was not able to contact them so there was nothing left for it but for me to retrace my steps. By this time, I was giving myself a mental kicking, muttering things like, "You never bloody learn," "You stupid, stupid old bastard," and "You've done it again, haven't you?"

The view was no longer a consideration but now was the time to hasten my return, to try to catch up and get back so my hosts would not be worried. After a long, sweaty, sore-kneed slog, I found myself back in Richmond Market Square at the hotel where I knew George and Nabil were staying. They weren't there. I limped back to Elaine and Charlie's house to find that Elaine had been out driving the road searching for me. That they had been worried they left me in no doubt, and I was shamed by their justifiable concern. They let me phone George. I discovered that the two of them had switched hotels, and I told them I was going to walk down and meet them after we had eaten. Charlie is a wonderful cook. I was hungry. I ate my fill and, a little apologetically, I took my leave and found my way to the new hotel. I entered and found George and Nabil lingering over the last of their dinner with glasses of red wine half full. I shook George's hand and he introduced me to Nabil. I nodded at him, and he reached forward and said by way of introduction,

"Get a fucking cell phone."

I smiled ruefully and took an instant liking to my new acquaintance and George's long-time buddy.

Of course, Dear Reader, I am sorry I caused worry and concern to four people. Of course, dear friends, I am disappointed that I was unable to spend that extra time with George. Of course, I am ashamed that I have had so much incompetence and failure from which I have not learned. I have tried to find appropriate quotations to justify my actions. Ralph Waldo Emerson:

> ### *"Do not follow where the path may lead.*
> ### *Go instead where there is no path and leave*
> ### *a trail."*

Well, the trail I left would have been overgrown again in very short order!

> ### *"A good traveler has no fixed plans and is*
> ### *not intent on arriving." Lao Tzu*

Hmm. I **did** have fixed plans, plus if I had quoted this to Nabil and George when we first met, they would have told me in no uncertain terms where I could shove my Lao Tzu.

"Like all great travelers, I have seen more than I remember, and remember more than I have seen." Benjamin Disraeli

This would seem to be getting closer to the truth except that "great" does not apply, my memory does play tricks, and many of my stories become the victims of hyperbole. I would not have dared to spout this to Elaine and Charlie after they had been so concerned for my welfare as that would have risked my delicious dinner, and they would have rightfully gifted me with a flea in my ear.

Looking through these excellent quotes, I have come to the conclusion that Nabil's introduction is by far and away the best and most appropriate given the circumstances.

Safe travels, my friends.

"A talent is formed in stillness; a character in the world's torrent."
Goethe

CHAPTER 3

EDUCATION
AND SCHOOL

I suppose it would have been easy to say that education and school were one and the same thing. It seems, at my time of life, that they are not; that if we have done our job properly as teachers, we have created learners who learn way beyond the school environment. Indeed, we hope they have acquired education as a lifelong habit. The following are memories of my time in school and education.

The Hawthorne Effect

"The idea that emotional reward is more important than material compensation."

I t is nice to be paid well as recognition for what one does at work, but we all know that it isn't enough. That's not being greedy, that, apparently, is just how we are. We all know how impressive and goose-bumpy Martin Luther King's "I Have a Dream" speech was. In his recent book, Martin Gladwell pointed out that MLK's speech was not "I have a plan." If we say that to ourselves over and over again, we hear how uninspiring that is. I am sorry to say, "I have a plan" would likely glaze over the Davidson eyes, whereas "I have a cunning plan," a la Baldrick, would perk up the little grey cells. Language, and how we use it to praise or crucify, matters.

When I taught in the Collingwood KEY programme, I somehow managed to get involved in provincial exams. (Requiring a KEY student to read *Cat's Eye* by Margaret Atwood was a big ask, particularly as I didn't understand it either. The event became worse because, somehow, we ended up with *Wuthering Heights*. Requiring a young fellow born and raised in West Vancouver to suddenly find himself on the Yorkshire moors was another reason why I did not age well. I guess I could just have played him hours and hours of Kate Bush, and he might have got something out of it.) Any rate, cometh the hour and cometh the exam, and Dan was due to sit his provincial examination. At least I thought so, but then Dan explained to me, as if to a child, that he did not have to do the formal examination.

> *"No, no Mr. Davidson, I am exhumed from*
> *the exam."*

I had this sudden image of a couple of gravediggers, spades to the ready, trekking off to the local cemetery to dig up Dan so he could sit his provincial examination. I put the image out of my head and wiped the smirk off my face. It would indeed be serious if Dan was not to write the exam, but maybe more so if he did with a creative vocabulary like that!!

Studies of medieval history when I was at school were pretty interesting to me. Like all perspectives, the teacher was unable to hide his true feelings despite it being his duty to remain apolitical so as not to indoctrinate. Mr. King was not a huge fan of the feudal system, feeling that many lords of the manor were corrupted by absolute power. He did somehow get into the farming of the time, and along the way he explained that many of the animals roamed free. The pigs, for instance, found their main sustenance in the woods. We were all asked to write an essay based on what we had been taught. One of my fellow students amused Mr. King with the following wise statement:

> *"The lord of the manor was a tyrant. The*
> *swine lived in the woods."*

Mr. King really did hope that the second sentence referred back to the first one!

My mother asked my brother, Bill, what he had learnt at school that day. He had discovered that the ducking stool was used in the villages to determine whether or not a woman was a witch.

"Just as well you weren't alive then, Mum."

Loud guffaw from Dad, and a smile from Mum.

Words *do* matter. So, receiving a letter of praise from a parent or manager produced a huge boost to my self-esteem, just as the opposite was discouraging and causing of a loss of sleep.

The problem with teachers and the giving of praise is that one always wants to give a boost. Giving a boost through praise of something that is not very good cheapens the outstanding piece of work that the other child completed. Also, words for words' sake will lack sincerity. If there is one thing that children do well it is see through flattering bafflegab. And it is not only children. Diplomats are trained to use words carefully, to sugar-coat bad news, to veil their threats. Until, of course, diplomacy fails and that is called by another name, which is "war."

"A diplomat is somebody who tells you to go to hell in such a way that has you looking forward to the trip." Cassie Stinnett

Many people in their professional lives trade in words. The back and forth over the phone or in person is how business is conducted. It stands to reason that although the best is always attempted, there will inevitably be failures.

A nuance here, an intonation there and the deal is lost or won. Miscommunication and lack of the correct word can cause failure or hurt. One of the classic examples of this occurred when a much-respected member of a community in England went into work one day and found windows broken and red graffiti-daubed obscenities all over his place of work. The locals had heard that a convicted pedophile had recently moved into the area and had fuelled their hatred of an evening and found where he worked. Trouble is that they were not able to distinguish between a "pedophile" and a "pediatrician"!! Words and knowledge matter, do they not? But we have to be cautious when we listen to she who praises or he who compliments, for in the words of Mark Twain:

> **"He who knows how to flatter, knows how to slander."**

Have a good day, dear friends.

Wisdom and Knowledge

I s it possible to have one without the other? I was thinking about this today in the context of leadership and learning. Admiral Horatio Nelson, after whom "The Nelson Touch" was named, was a true leader. Who knows how much of his skill with people was nature and how much was nurtured? It is certain that he had a much harder apprenticeship than many of his contemporaries. He began his career at sea in the merchant marine as opposed to its military equivalent, the Royal Navy. There, he was exposed to a far more forthright and democratic experience than the military would have allowed. He came to learn what made the ordinary seaman tick. He came up from below rather than down from above. He learned about the "soft" skills of managing human beings but also the "hard" skills of practical seamanship. I like the following:

> *"Knowledge is knowing that a tomato is a fruit. Wisdom is not putting it in a fruit salad."*

My best friend at teacher's college was a mature student, having served as a fighter pilot in the RAF. He was twenty-seven years old, and most of us were south of 20. He seemed to breeze through life with never-ending success. It all came so easily for him. He could talk himself into and out of any situation. He saw things ahead of time and had the skills to head them off at the pass or to milk them for all they were worth. When it came to finding a teaching job, I knew that Keith van Bergen would get the job if he got the interview, and he *would* get the interview. Conscious of my blundering, bull-in-the-china-shop crashing failures, I asked for his help. Being a kindly man, as well as owing me a beer, he allowed me to follow him through on his interview preparation. We started with his CV with a view to me completing mine. Well, friends, every word, every nuance, every piece of punctuation, grammar and spelling was analysed, torn to shreds, vamped and revamped. It seemed to take hours. Then there were the questions that were likely to be asked at interview within the context of the job specifications and some that were outside the job specifications. We formulated answers and discussed and questioned ad infinitum and, from my point of view, ad nauseam. Finally, there was the neatly-pressed suit, the white shirt, the polished black shoes, the RAF tie, the neatly-styled haircut. There was nothing left to chance. Hours of hard work had gone into making Keith van Bergen come across as casually relaxed at interview. He became head of a prestigious PE department at Lincoln College of Technology, much lauded for his teaching style, much praised for his "busses and buns" organizational skill. It was a very fine example of the combination of wisdom and knowledge. And it all came so easily to him??!!

I am a huge fan of Malcolm Gladwell as a writer. He writes about things that are tied up with human psychology. He is an easy read. In his book *Blink*, there are two memorable instances. One is the story of the 2,000-year-old Greek vase that The Met Museum in New York was eager to buy at an outlay of millions of dollars. Of course, the museum had to establish its authenticity, so it employed experts to confirm that this piece of exquisite craftsmanship met the claims. All said "Yes, sign the cheque, get it on display." But the high heidyin, he of the final say, wanted to test it through one more expert. So, he assessed the vase yet again and informed the museum it was a fake. Why and how was it a fake? Well, the final expert, sorry I do not have his name to hand, did *not* know how he knew, but he knew that he knew.

In another scenario in the Persian Gulf War in 1990, an American operative was watching his radar screen noting the many dots proceeding from A to B—planes and missiles and so forth. Suddenly, his attention is drawn to one particular blip that is moving towards an American target. He does not know whether it is friendly or not. He has seconds to decide whether to order its destruction or not. Wrong decision will kill his own pilot. He presses the button to blow it out of the sky. He then has a nerve-wracking hour or so not knowing whether his decision was the right one or not. He had taken the right action but, like the art expert, had no idea why.

The point that Gladwell is trying to make, I think, is that instinct and intuition, if they exist at all, are based on experience and knowledge. Both of these men had lifetimes of experience and hours of training for just such occasions. That knowledge had given them the wisdom to not put the tomato in the fruit salad.

It is always the job of a teacher to know her students. At Collingwood and as a homeroom teacher of Grade IV nine- and ten-year-old students, it was my job in the morning to call attendance, which I routinely did:

"Johnny Appleblossom?"
"Yes."
"Erica Brathlethwaite?"
"Yes."
"Natasha Phagash?"
"Yes."

Children would arrive, note the instructions on the whiteboard, go to their lockers and prepare for the day. I would be about the classroom, meeting and greeting and insisting on a "Good morning" before hearing about last night's hockey game. I knew who was there and who was not way before I sat down at my desk to call the roll. In fact, there was rarely a need for that "name and answer" formality. I could have submitted the electronic data without it. "Why bother then?" you might ask. Well, partly I bothered because I wanted settlement and calm before the day began, and I also wanted ears instead of voices for any important announcement. But those were not the real reasons. I wanted to hear the "Yes" from the wee takkers. Why? Well, because that little three-letter word gave forth so much meaning. It told me if Johnny had eaten his breakfast, had a good night's sleep, was excited by the day. It told me if Erica had had an argument with her dad in the car, if breakfast was a rushed Pop Tart or the dog really had eaten her homework. OK, it was an old teacher's puerile game, a piece of trivia designed to flatter a paucity of omniscience, but it was also a pride in my own years of experience getting up on my hind legs and pontificating to nests of many wee sparrows eager to be fed!! (Sorry about the outburst of wordiness here, but you get my drift!) Incidentally, I think I was always guarded in any pretence of expertise in anything other than my profession.

It may have been tempting on occasions to play amateur psychologist or to counsel students, but I believe I was always aware enough to know when I was out of my depth and hand things over to the experts.

I have mentioned before the plethora of pundits we now see on the TV. I am always impressed when they appear from their homes in isolation and do so with shelves of books behind them. Irene is a bit more cynical than me, seeing that as a pretentious affectation. I may be old-fashioned, but I believe that well-read people should be our leaders. What is more, they should read material that puts forth views opposite to their own. They should know more about the opposition than they do about their supporters. They should be well-informed before they make their decisions. They should cultivate wisdom based on knowledge.

Bo

eather, Anne and I were sitting outside Bean Around
the World the other day when Bo arrived on his bicycle.
He leaned against the wooden planters near where we
were seated, so we greeted him with a smile and a wave. Bo
did not react, no hint of interest crossed his face, he did
not blink, he did not smile. We tried to get him to take an
interest in the plants, but he looked away with disinterested
disdain. We persisted with our smiles and our waves. The
lady he was with also encouraged him but to no avail. He
sat, he pondered, his bike helmet was tilted jauntily to one
side, we felt somewhat flirtatious in intent. We sensed that
underneath that unforthcoming exterior there was charm
and charisma. We were slightly chagrined that despite much
effort on our part we were not to be granted a mere glimmer,
a slight glitter of a smile. Then it happened. Bo raised his
right hand and waved. We waved back and—and?—could
it be? Yes, it was. We were sure. Bo smiled. It was beatific, it
was open-hearted, it lit up his whole face. We felt honoured.

Bo is a bonny wee laddie who is one year old. He was sitting
on the front seat of his mother's bike while his dad was in
getting coffee. He started to look at the plants, to touch the
plants, to hear about the plants from his mother. It was not
yet the season to smell the plants, and it was unlikely he
would ever taste the plants, but three out of the five senses
is not bad for the first hours of the day, is it, Dear Reader?

I was thinking on the way home how great it was to be one year old at this time of pandemic. For one quarter of his life, Bo has had so much time with his mum and dad. He has not been rushed off to a daycare when he should still be tucked up in bed. He has been able to sit and have a leisurely, unhurried breakfast, not a hasty Pop Tart in the back of the car. If there had been puddles on that day, I am sure Bo would have had time to jump in them. If he had wanted to stop and examine rocks on the way home, there would have been time. If Mum had online work to do at home, then Dad was on hand to play, to read, to make lunch, to change his diaper.

So, Dear Reader, we have had the "baby boomers," the silent generation, the Millennials, Generation X. So now do we have the COVID generation, those children who were born in our current time of trouble? To Bo and any other young children living in and around Norgate in detached houses with gardens during this pandemic, what a fortuitous blessing this disease has been. Of course, there is the other tragic side of this pandemic for young children. There are apartments in tower blocks where the stress of being stuck at home produces unbearable pressure on the adults that is transferred to the children. Those children need daycare or school or summer camp to get relief and release from friction from fractious parents or an exhausted single parent. COVID infants are becoming, maybe, a different type of "haves" or "have nots" in our society, do you think? There will be studies produced on the "COVID generation" in years to come, don't you think? I believe that this disease will be an exceptionally good start for many young lives, an exceptionally bad one for others. I like what Confucius says about education:

> *"If your plan is for one year, plant rice.*
> *If your plan is for ten years, plant a tree.*
> *If your plan is for 100 years, educate*
> *children."*

So the Bos and Bo Peeps we are seeing out and about, walking and talking with their parents in the parks and trails of the North Shore, stopping to throw a stone in running water, stroking friendly dogs, learning to ride their bikes and, Dear Friends, are having the most wonderful of beginnings. If they are a few years older, sure, they are missing out a bit. But that is a different piece of research, is it not? There are some subjects too big, too overwhelming, too mountainous to cover in a short scribble!!

> *"It's not the mountains ahead that wear*
> *you out, it's the pebble in your shoe."*
> *Muhammed Ali*

Happy Sunday, friends.

Concrete and Abstract

Nobody's schooling is the same, is it? Teaching and education are very human activities, are they not? When I was a child, and even when I was an adolescent, I thought that education was all about learning facts and not much about what to do with those facts. Later—probably too late—it came to me that there is a difference between facts and what we should do with those facts. Training somebody in first aid or how to pass a rugby ball is coaching, is it not? There is nothing abstract in how to give somebody CPR or when to turn right at a red light. Neither occasion provides an opportunity for a philosophical debate. Whispering "Come away from the light" to somebody who is having a jammer on the street ain't gonna save her life. The great philosophical plea "Why are we here?" ain't gonna tackle that bull of a rugby player charging towards one with intent on progress.

"Education" has its Latin root in "leading out." Therefore, "education" is more a matter of coaxing and nurturing what is already inside us than drumming facts into a child's mind. It is designed, at least in the primary and secondary years, to give pupils experience in a variety of options so that when a career decision is made, it is decided upon through interest, passion and love. OK that may be a First World wish. I ***do*** understand that in the Third World the business of survival does not give the young that option.

There is going to be a new, miniature wooden deck built in the back garden of Chez Davidson. I would love to say that this is something I could throw together with ease. People who are more practical than I am will try to convince me that, because I can read, then I can do anything. I can wire a house, I can lay a concrete slab, I can fix the plumbing. I did, it is true, used to work as a concreter when I lived in Australia. The concrete used to arrive on the site, seemingly always at the hottest part of the day, and we spent a sweaty hour barrowing it to where it needed to go. When we dumped it, it was the boss and his son's job to level it so that a perfectly flat floor was the result. Occasionally, I helped with this, but the surface I created was indeed flat but never level. My eye tells me that the pictures I put on the wall are level, but the bubble level disagrees. Thus, it was on the concrete slabs. I realized this weakness early on, so my sole purpose on the site was to barrow from A to B. I was exclusively a piano mover not a piano player, but I became very fit and strong very quickly. I suppose that with persistence and practice I could have adapted and become adept. But thereby hangs another side of character: one needs one's work to be a passion, to be a challenge and a source of enjoyment. Getting fit was my passion, getting level was not. So, when it comes to building this new wee deck, I will be a presence, but our son, Grant, will be a ***presence***. He will turn the abstract into the concrete with ease. He will see the steps on the way to the completion, and I will only see the completion.

When I last taught in England, I arrived at the old manor house that was Broughton House School (you well remember it, Audrey) at the beginning of term to be greeted by a very proud looking headmaster.

"What do you think, Pete?"

Nice haircut, nice tan, nice jacket and so on flit through my mind. What was I supposed to say?

"Er, did you have a good holiday, Mike?"

No, that was not it. Did I not notice the new colour of the paintwork and redesign of the front hall? No, I didn't. What was the colour before? I had no clue. Even though I walked through that front entrance every working morning, my abstract brain was on a different planet, spaced out in a different world. Thus, do I remember that Dr. Gorgas was responsible for clearing the Panama region of malaria to allow the canal to be built but forget to buy milk when grocery shopping! Thus, am I terrified when my son throws away the instructions for building the shed before it is built. Thus, do I not notice the difference between a vacuumed carpet and a non-vacuumed carpet. Irene made the conscious decision to marry an abstract in hopes of nudging him towards concrete over the years. Ho hum, she still holds out hope!

Off to make lunch, an abstract idea with a concrete conclusion. Have a good day.

Moments and Momentum

We have all had seminal moments in our lives that have sent us in a different direction for better or worse. I recall the story of the two twenty-two-year-old friends who ran into each other at the supermarket four years after they had graduated from high school together. They had not seen each other since they had left. Maggie was stacking shelves in the store, a job she had been doing ever since she was a teenager. Penny had been travelling the world, gap-yearing, "finding herself," but now she was heading to Capilano College to pursue tertiary education. She was enthused about the new student career upon which she was going to embark, which twigged Maggie's interest.

"It was easy to get in. Why don't you come along? It'll be fun. You'll enjoy it."

So, Maggie enrolled, gave up her work and went on to bigger and greater things. Maggie is now a hugely successful lawyer in New York City. A chance meeting in a grocery store aisle, the changing of a life. A moment to provide momentum.

I am no expert, so I do not know whether this is an example of Carl Jung's theory of synchronicity, which is described as:

> *"The acausal connection of two or more psychic and physical phenomena."*

The way I understand it is being in the right place at the right time or, presumably, the opposite. It could be how we met our wives or partners, how we discovered a particular passion or any seminal event that persuaded us to change direction.

When I lived in London, I was driving through Isleworth one night when a car came around the corner on the wrong side of the road. I swerved too late, mounted the kerb and hit a lamp-post. I must have hit my head on the steering wheel (no air bags in those days), and I am sure I was unconscious for about ten seconds or so. I stumbled out of the car in a daze, and saw the other driver was also out of his car and standing. I did not approach him. Instead, I sat down on the sidewalk. I was pretty much out of it until I felt a tap on my shoulder and found something thrust into my hands. It was some moments before I realized what it was. I can't remember anybody asking me if I was OK or, indeed, anybody saying anything to me, but I finally remembered I was holding something in my hands. Eventually I looked down and discovered I was holding a steaming cup of tea!!

I guess that that gesture was a very British thing to do. I have used it on occasions when there has been a bit of a crisis and I have not known what to do or how to act. When confronted by a tale of woe or a piece of bad news, I have used "putting the kettle on" as a form of running away, a chance to think or an act of kindness. It seems to be a very male thing to do. It's a cry for help. It's "I have no idea what to do but I know that I have to move, I have to do something, I cannot sit still and listen to this problem without adopting some action." I do not understand whether this behaviour has stemmed from that moment of crisis or not. Oh yes, I do also remember that the police woman who drove me home that fateful night was stunningly beautiful, but in my state of heightened awareness, Godzilla would have been Helen of Troy!

I guess we know where we were when men landed on the moon, when John Lennon was shot, when Princess Diana was in a car accident, and when toilet rolls became important. If there are moments that were not seminal to us or did not change our lives at least they are still with us. There are moments on large and small living canvasses that can lead to momentum in many different directions. We can use them or not, but it seems to me that every moment is a time for forward or backward momentum however big or small.

Think that I will pop downstairs and make a cuppa tea.

Have a good day, my friends.

Control

"I claim not to have controlled events but confess plainly that events have controlled me." Abraham Lincoln

It is very hard not to like and admire Abraham Lincoln. Years ago, I promised myself I would read at least one biography of an American president per year. I saw it as a way to plug the gaps in my knowledge of American history because the medium of biography is an excellent means of understanding history. I became hooked on Lincoln and read more than one. A group of us even went to see the excellent Daniel Day-Lewis movie about the man. This is beside the point except that if a person of the stature of Abraham Lincoln cannot control events then who can?! Of course, sadly, his story benefitted by being assassinated in office. As we know through the assassination of Kennedy, the myth of a Camelot arises and there are so many questions of what might have been. Chances are there wouldn't have been the sunny uplands that people would have predicted. Camelot is Arthurian. Camelot comes about when there is a desperation for somebody else to take control, a panicked seeking of a solution to a war, a revolution or a pandemic. I will always believe that President Johnson's "Great Society" was a product of the death of JFK, and it is, indeed, unfortunate that his reputation cannot rise above Vietnam. LBJ could not manage the war but he sure did a great deal for civil rights. Some things he could control, other things he could not.

> **"There is no such uncertainty as a sure thing." Robbie Burns**

As a young teacher, loss of control of a situation was hard for me to take. When things got out of hand then I used to try—ineffectively—to bring them back into acceptability. It seemed that the harder I tried the worse they became. What was I doing wrong? In hindsight, I was failing to sit back. Sitting back and watching and learning was something that did not come naturally to me. I believe that whatever job one is in, there is huge merit in "sitting back." If that means a loss of control at that moment then so be it, because often there are long-term benefits.

I remember a nine-year-old boy called Eric. He was a criminal of the first order. His "crime" was that he simply could not sit still. How could that be? How could a child not sit still when so many pearls of wisdom were being laid before him? How dare he. It was my unforgivable naïvety that did not inform me that it was not the natural way of being for all young children to sit still and listen. Having forgotten my own youth and denied the fact that a child's natural state is one of movement, I was on a hiding to nothing. Eric had had a morning of annoying movement. He had dropped things noisily. He had fallen off his chair. He had knocked over Penelope's open water bottle on his way to the washroom. He had tripped over something on his return to class. I calmed myself but resolved that Eric would spend some time at recess having a forthright chat with me on how to keep still. So, he was surprised not to be heading out for a run about with his buddies when the time came. I called him up to my desk and sat him in a chair in front of me. I was sat opposite him on my office chair. I am tall, so my chair was set at a height that towered above the wee laddie in front of me.

"So, Eric, you know why you are here, don't you?" I smiled patronizingly.

Eric looked at me quizzically. He had no idea why he was there. Why would he? That was up there with the dumbest opening statements in teaching history.

"No, Mr. Davidson."

"Well, you are here because you don't sit still," I said, looking down from my superior perch, facial expression conveying my annoyance, superiority and adult righteousness. "I am going to help you to learn to sit still in my class."

I smiled benignly. Here was the solution to Eric's movement woes—woes which he didn't know he had. At that moment, Eric's right foot shot out, hit the pedal on my chair, and I slowly sank until I was looking up at him. He peered down at me as if nothing had happened.

"Thank you, Mr. Davidson, I appreciate that."

I failed to get my message across except that I didn't! You see, Dear Reader, Eric's irritating clumsiness had absolutely *no* negative impact on his ability to learn. It was just the opposite. It helped him. It was my equanimity that was the problem, my belief that he was ill-disciplined and, importantly for my ego, that I had lost control. I hadn't. I had physically and metaphorically descended from hubris to humility through the short movement of a child's foot. It was a loss of control that did not matter.

Eric has now completed his university degree. He is working. He stopped me and a friend on our walk while he was out for a run with his girlfriend the other week. He is still moving and so, my friends, he should be.

I do not want politicians to control my destiny. At the moment, I want medical experts to decide what we can and cannot do. I do still have the freedom and power to make decisions. I have lost some control, but then none of us has ever been in complete control of our destinies. If we had been, then life would have plodded along without the excitement and mystery that makes living much, much more than existing. Control is a double-edged sword because along with it comes responsibility, and very few of us want that as well.

It's Friday night, the end of a long, easy week. A glass of wine, one of Irene's famed chicken curries, and maybe if I am very good and do the washing up, Irene will allow me the remote and thus I can gain some control.

*"The fatal metaphor
of progress, which means
leaving things behind us, has
utterly obscured the real idea
of growth, which means leaving
things inside us."*
GK Chesterton

CHAPTER 4

WORDS, BOOKS AND PHRASES

Chesterton sums up what I feel about the written word. I believe the written word leaves far more inside us than radio, TV, cinema or the spoken word. I am not alone in believing that in order to be a most effective member of society, one needs to be an active reader. One who reads with a critical eye, a loving heart, a wise head and who embraces the written word with passion. I read a great deal but find analytical, reasoned reading difficult. I wish I read with more perception.

Language

As some of you may be aware, I spent forty-three years of my professional life boring children to death. Sleep-deprived children whose parents have let them stay up too late and woken them far too early have flourished in the deep recesses at the back of my classroom. Meanwhile at the front, their teacher has put paid to the laudable philosophy that "children learn by doing not by watching and queuing." I am thankful to have realized late in my career that I talked too much, so I employed a child at the front of the class whose job was to give a "talk alert" when I was rabbiting on ad nauseam and, sometimes, ad finitum. The child was normally a keener who was eager to tackle the task, and so he or she took delight in bringing my bloviations to a close, albeit not abruptly; the train often slowly edged its way to its terminus. Any rate, now you understand why this is a long-winded interruption with seemingly absence of point. Ahhhh, my friends, but there is a point.

My good friend, Jamie, locked down in the ancient pile of St. Leonard's School in the university town on the Fifeshire coast of Scotland's east, has been seeking reparation for flights lost on British Airways. His wife, Jenn, is busy with her house-mothering duties. Young Harry, their boy, is back at school online. The esteemed British Airways that flies the flag around the world has diverted Jamie towards words that are from other languages and have strange meanings. I hope he doesn't mind me stealing some of his polyglot thunder here by quoting from his list:

> ***Petrichor = the scent that emanates from dry soil after it has rained. It is an English word but comes from the Greek "petra" meaning "stone" and "ichor" the liquid that flows through the veins of the gods.***

Of course, I would inevitably choose this one because it involves my name. Far from being Peter, the rock upon which Christ built his church, it was bequeathed to me for different reasons. I was so named because it was hoped I would have the emotional range of a rock, that very little would grow from within me, and that when everything else jumped for joy in rain and snow and sun and shine, I didn't! I jest, of course—at least I hope I do!

Medusa of the snake-filled hair turned all who looked upon her face to stone. Certain things **petrify** us to this day, not least good-looking partners who have just been to the hairdressers, and we haven't noticed. Maybe that is where the Medusa myth came from!

So, Davidson once taught mathematics and, inevitably, polygons, the many-sided figures of geometrical fame. After the children had recovered from the explanation that a polygon was a parrot that had escaped, then discovered that the Greek word "gonum" meant "knee," so "many kneed" was a more literal explanation, we did progress to learning about the different types without too many more red herrings. Science brought forth the explanation for the word "muscle," which is the diminutive Latin word for "little mouse" because when we flex our biceps it is as a little mouse scampering up and down under our skin. History gave us "curfew," which is from the French "couvre feu": to cover the flame; in other words, to put the lights out. Speaking of French, we occasionally found that the children were involved in a "querelle de clocher," a "clock tower quarrel," therefore something of nothing. My warped sense of humour had French campanologists turning up at the village church of a Sunday to herald the call to worship, Jean grabbing the wrong rope, Gerard taking exception, a donnybrook ensuing and the villagers being treated to a cacophony rather than a harmony! We have a term in English for the German "Einen vogel haben," to "have a bird in the head," to be crazy, cuckoo; much the same is it not.

Enough of this drivel. Just remember, John Angus, when you are considering planting an Eriogonum in your magnificent front yard that it is a plant with many "knees" on its stem, and that they are "woolly"!

Have a good day, my friends.

Downtown Dopiness

I had to travel downtown for the first time since early March today for a medical appointment at VGH. So, I guess, I had the debate that we all have these days: What is the most responsible way to travel? I am an early riser, so I thought about walking, but then I am not a very good judge of timing. Rarely late for anything but often ridiculously early. So, partly through laziness but more from a timing perspective, I decided to discard that option. I thought about biking, but all of my bike trips in the past have had me remaining with the bike at all times so I have no lock. I don't think the doctor would have welcomed a sweat-drenched piece of equipment taking up space in her office. My normal method of getting downtown since I retired has been to take the bus. Hmmm! That was my favoured option. Sitting and looking out of the window or doing my crossword are lovely ways to spend a journey rather than focusing totally on the road in front. Then I thought of the people on the bus and how an old fogey like me has become a threat. So, I settled on driving and came to terms with the fact that I would have to pay an exorbitant parking fee. I would have NO contact with people on the way across and would not have to wear my face mask in transit (a hazard in itself because it causes my spectacles to mist up). So, I allowed plenty of time— time I did not need. Little traffic and free parking at the hospital for patients and staff was a surprise that delighted my Scottish wallet. There was a problem, however.

Throughout my non-productive but very pleasant life, there have been occasions where I have ended up working in rural areas of the world for months at a time. So, trips back to the city after these boondock sojourns—hiccups in Hicksville—have resulted in me returning to the metropolis "struck with wonder all too dread for words." I have wanted to greet every bustle and hustle, every Stanley Park, each store face, every pedestrian on the sidewalk, all old sights and sites, like long lost friends. So, I have had to pull up my distracted driver socks and remind myself that that traffic light is red, that the bus pulling out has the right of way, and that the bike lane is not for me but for cyclists. I have become a naïf gullible travelling through a strange "new" world.

There is a wonderful Australian poem called *The Man from Ironbark*. It is a story of a bushman from the settlement of Ironbark in New South Wales visiting the city of Sydney for the first time. He wonders and wanders and eventually his senses are so overwhelmed that he seeks some place to take a rest. He settles on a barber's shop and sits down for a haircut and a shave. The barber recognizes his customer as a country cousin and decides to have some fun at his expense, a bit of a lark to entertain his regular customers. He winks mischievously at them after he has trimmed the hair and sharpened his cutthroat razor. Flamboyantly, he is ready to shave. He heats the razor up in his sterilizer. He lines up the chin and with a swift, vigorous movement, runs the back of the blade over the man's throat. The sense is that he has cut it. Yer man thinks he is dying and resolves to not go out without a fight. So, there are fisticuffs in which the barber and his regulars are no match for the strength and energy of a man who earns his living shearing sheep and other physical pursuits. Banjo Paterson weaves his rhyming magic and concludes his poem so wonderfully with the shearer back home, telling the story of his visit to the big city, holding his fellow sheep shearers aghast and spellbound in the process. Rural heads shake at the appalling behaviour of their urban compatriots and draw the conclusion that this very scenario is why there are no clean-shaven men in the settlement of Ironbark and that their throats are too tough and gnarled to sever!

Have a look at the poem at: http://www.australianculture. org/the-man-from-ironbark-paterson/

I was very focused on my driving on the way home, partly because the novelty had worn off but mostly because my eyes were dilated, and I shouldn't have been driving!

Sun continues to shine, at least my blurred vision suggests that it does!

Pan - & Omni -

Parents know best, do they not? Mine certainly did. Thus, did I complete my French exam a year early, at the age of fifteen, so I could take up Ancient Greek. Being a passionless child who followed where he was led and did as he was told, I never questioned the decision. So, it was in my final exams at the age of eighteen, I found myself doing Ancient history, Greek and Latin. Through many spectacular failures throughout my life, this one was low on the totem pole but a failure none the less. I had never been told what I was going to do with these subjects had I been successful at them. Thus, it was that I failed entry into university but matriculated into life. The two years prior to teacher's training college, the "wilderness" years, were a gentle saunter through a variety of jobs varying from van boy to hotel porter to washing machine repair "person" to building sites to barman and so forth. It was not a gap year, nothing to do with finding myself, nor a hiatus until I had settled on a career. All of these jobs were of the moment, and they became who and what I was at the time, and I became who and what they were. But all of that is another story. Back to my classical education.

Greek and Latin are with me still. I have tried to shake them off but failed. My first teaching job was as a Latin teacher in a large secondary school in West London. The old headmaster at Collingwood School had me teaching basic Latin. Indeed, I taught the last student in the province ever to sit the Latin provincial examination! Maybe there is a plaque somewhere honouring this; after all, every pigeon needs a place to poop.

Here we are in a *pan*-demic. *"Pan" is literally an "all-"* encompassing prefix 'cos that is what it means. Greek mythology had Pandora's box. *"Pan-dora"* means "all the gifts," although there is some confusion over this because when they were let out of the box by Pandora herself, all of the bad things—disease, famine, pestilence, envy, jealousy, hatred and so on—escaped. They were gifts??!! All that was left when the lid was finally banged shut was hope. As an aside, if you know somebody called "Dorothy" then that means "gift of the gods." There was a "Dorothy" in the Davidson family back in the day; she was, I suspect, a gift, but thereafter may have been a bit suspect. So, there is no escape in the Davidson mind from "panorama," "panacea," "panoply." A personal favourite has always been "Pangaea," when billions of years ago there was a supercontinent of "all" the lands around the world. We can see how neatly South America is part of the jigsaw that was married to Africa.

Of course, typical of the Davidson upbringing things were done out of order. I had Latin before Greek, and it should have been the other way around. So, I knew about "omnis" for "all" before "pan" and, in particular, the dative case plural "omnibus," meaning "for all" from which we get the abbreviation "bus." Then I discovered I was an "omnivore" in that I ate everything. If it moved, I ate it until it didn't, and if it didn't move, I ate it until it did. Apparently, we are in the presence of an omniscient, omnipotent God. All knowing, all powerful She may be but all benevolent, hardly. The philosopher Bertrand Russell suggested that all churches have posted outside their doors *"Important if true."* It seems strange that if She does exist, She is still letting thousands of African children go blind through a disease called African River Blindness. She also seems to be shrugging her shoulders and looking the other way when the current pandemic arrives and kills thousands. She may be omniscient but not omnipotent, otherwise She, with assumed kindness, would do something about it. But what do I know? I am not President Trump who is omnicritical, omninasty, omnidumb and omnitweeting. Nor I am Justin Trudeau who is omnivirtuous, nor Boris the omniscruffy, nor Angela Merkel the omniteutonic (and I mean that as a compliment). Nor am I a student of theology, so there is much in religion that remains a mystery to me. So, apologies to you who believe; your belief is your own, and if I tread on your toes I hope you recognize that I do so lightly.

Probably, however, as an offshoot of my classical education I am, I think, a theist, albeit a polytheist. It seems to me that the Greeks and the Romans had it right. They had so many gods and all of them had human failings and human frailty in abundance. I can relate to a Bacchus who likes his wine, a Cyclops who tries so hard to have an acceptance of differing ideas and thoughts but, in the end, is one-eyed with little interest in a periphery. Maybe that is simply age setting me in my ways. I love the myths of our indigenous peoples who look upon our magnificent natural world and respect it and understand it through story. And I suppose that in the current world crisis I am able to have a positive take on things because whatever we as humans do to spoil our planet, nature is in control and never so much as She is at the moment.

Hats off to you, Mother Nature. You are reasserting your omnipresence, pan-globally!!

Have a wonderful day, my friends.

Pachyderm-atology?

As I was washing my hands for the umpteenth time just now, I noticed how reptilian in texture my skin was becoming. I have always admired the pachyderms of this world. You know, the thick-skinned elephants and rhinoceros, the individuals for whom criticism is water off a duck's back, who do not respond with heart-on-one's-sleeve sensitivity. And yet—and yet—I *don't* really admire them. I suspect that during all of our lives we have had the occasional sleepless night, that time in the wee small hours when all of our chickens seem to have come home to roost. With the dawn comes reason and a resolve to either fix it or put it behind us. During the first Gulf War, the American general, Colin Powell, was asked how he slept at night knowing he was responsible for so many lives:

> *"I sleep like a baby—I wake up screaming every two hours."*

To me, Mandy and friends, that qualifies as a paraprosdokian, does it not? I think so.

I think that I do not admire the thick skinned because they have no self-doubt. Of course, one can become so thin skinned, suffering paralysis through analysis, that a decision becomes impossible. And we all need to make a decision at sometime in our lives, do we not?

A decision was made for me this morning. Of course, I did not have to follow through, but I thought I had better, otherwise there would have been no lunch at the bottom of the stairs. There is a window up here which is rarely opened. My beloved asked me to force it open, which, with my manly strength, I surely did. Underneath, its tracks were shrouded with the effects of damp, a miasmic mildew announced its presence. So thus, I was given a mixture of bleach and water, and I rubbed and scrubbed, then applied WD-40 so now we have a smooth-running window again. One which we will rarely open but *that*, my friends, is not the point. Thus, did this peacock puff up his plumage, preen himself at a task tackled, fluff up his rainbowed feathers at a job begun and completed. The pride at his prowess far exceeds this minor achievement, which, after all, was such a mundane, banausic task. So now, I am "puffed up wi' windy pride" even more because my computer has red-lined "banausic." Suggesting what? It is misspelled? It is not a real word? But aaah, my omniscient, omnipotent, robotic, doctrinaire, technological tool of mine, *this* human being knows you are wrong. There *is* such a word. Admittedly, nobody would ever use it. Only we quest-seeking, quarantined, stimulation-deprived individuals would seek out something so obscure and make it our raison d'être for the day! And that, my friends, is the quintessential question, is it not? When we eventually emerge from our cocooned existence and become butterflies yet again, what will be really important to us?

We will all have a different perspective, will we not? There should be a scale designed with "thick skinned" at one extreme and "thin skinned" at the other. What should be the levels on the way?

Let's start at the pachydermic end. Edging its way from west to east, we very soon reach *"Trump,"* which I suppose means that he sleeps like a baby because he whines like a baby, he has tantrums on the playground like a baby, he bullies in the park like a baby, he speaks English like a baby, and he has never done anything wrong like a baby, so he sleeps like a baby.

Edging farther towards the centre, the *"sales representative"* for whom his or her product is the best thing since sliced bread. It has matchless body work, sleek lines, acceleration nonpareil (and that's just the bread). She sleeps well at night except when she wakes once because she has dreamed up a new sales pitch. She is the *"con artist"* whose house is built on straw, who has spent her life convincing others so that finally she has convinced herself. Although she can no longer lie straight in her bed, she can sleep the night through at an angle.

Then there is the *"virtue signaller."* There are a lot of these about these days. So convinced are they at the ethical rightness of their cause that they come across as gung-holier-than-thou to the extent that they are not open to civilized debate. They are still to the west of the line but are getting close to the middle.

Up next come the *"talkers,"* those who love the sound of their own voice, those who do not understand that they were given two ears and only one mouth. They are still pachyderms but more gentle elephants than aggressive rhinos.

Aaaah, now we hit the middle, the **"talkers and listeners,"** those who often say, "On the one hand—this" and "on the other hand—that." These are great people, but they can be fence sitters, which can be a problem in a crisis. Such people are often the squirrels who are found flat on the highway because they could not make a decision. Now we are moving into healthier territory.

Now we come to the **"listeners,"** those who rarely speak. They have, in the words of Khalid Gibran, "learned silence from the talkative, toleration from the intolerant and kindness from the unkind." All too often, however, they believe that last argument they heard, the last opinion they read.

The **"thoughtful listeners,"** however, hear and think and plan and act invariably with common sense and with the greater good to the fore.

Finally, we come to the eastern most point of the line. There we team-up with Nelson Mandela, Gandhi, Pericles and Confucius, thin-skinned philosophers who spent a lifetime in thought with interludes of effective action. They may be thin skinned, but their actions prove the opposite. Maybe it is not a line but a circle of life. I do NOT rest my case!

Pachyderms---------------Trump------------Sales Rep----- -----------------Con Artist-------------Virtue Signaller----- -----------Talkers-------------------Talkers & Listeners----- ---------------Listeners------------- Thoughtful Listeners--- ---------Gandhi, etc.

Sorry guys, my techie skills don't run to a circle.

Reading this through, I have been unfair to the "sales rep," and I do, sometimes these days, have more sympathy for the "con artist" than the "virtue signaller," but that is the point, is it not? One person's opinion is another's fake news. Ho hum!

Off to create a password book so that all of my passwords are safe in one place and not dotted about various notebooks I can never find.

Paraprosdokian Ponderings?

"**A**aaargh!" I hear the cry. "Where on Earth are we going with this? Plot lost finally. Barking mad. Quarantine finally cracked him up."

Not so, my fellow splendid isolates, not so indeed. But before we head off into paraprosdokian, let me doff an imaginary hat to Anne who came up with the wonderful "seeking quest" as a tautology. Good one, Anne. More, please, from others of you. Kathi has asked for a solution to her chimney-tapping woodpecker. I suggested a bird of the female persuasion working on the Martin Amis theory that the "male libido is like being chained to an idiot for fifty years." I don't think he was talking about birds, however. If that doesn't work, I also suggested a fire. Nothing like a fire to disguise a fire, eh! Any rate, any further word or phrase suggestions or solutions to tapping birds then please send them in on a post card to—. Sorry, you are isolated so maybe just an email to all of us.

Now then, about those paraprosdokians about which I had no knowledge until my good friend, Mandy Richmond, directed me towards them yesterday. So now I have stolen her thunder and usurped her knowledge. She kindly explained a paraprosdokian as follows:

> *"A paraprosdokian is a sentence with an ending that is completely unexpected."*

Like all of these things, they are best explained with examples.

"If I agreed with you, we'd both be wrong."

"War does not determine who is right, only who is left."

"I didn't say it was your fault, I said I was blaming you."

"A clear conscience is usually the sign of a bad memory."

Be great if any of you could submit more of these. I find them sources of endless fun. Thanks so much for this, Mandy.

Well Day 8 is over. I was handed the garden shears to sharpen today. Having done as bid, I went downstairs and into the kitchen and out the back door for the first time. I noticed the new, handmade kitchen curtains. I was informed they were more old hat than curtains, given they had been up for a month or so. Och well, I have been in turbulent waters and not been able to pause in an eddy for a wee while. The back garden is prepared now for planting. Rich, black soil ready to nurture and nestle new beginnings. I do so hate the term "dirt" for "soil," by the way. "Dirt" is "filth," is polluting; soil is a new beginning, a giver of life. Any rate, that is just me being pedantic and pretentious to boot. I noted the short sprigs of our yearly yield of hostas making an appearance. No wonder, by the way, the shears needed sharpening. The princess of pollarding, Irene Davidson, has wrought havoc on innocent laurels and ebullient bamboo with all the vigour of an explorer thrashing her way eagerly through virgin bush in search of the source of a hitherto undiscovered Canadian river. Why, oh why, did the shears need sharpening? There was surely nothing left to trim, but just in case another use was to be found for them, I decided to be far more polite when requesting the odd cuppa tea here or more lunch there. The cold, brisk air was a welcome change from my stale inner confinement. I walked, and worked my dumbbells for forty minutes. There is always so much pleasure in the joy of movement. Wanderings promote wonderings, do they not?

Congratulations to Paul and Melanie Klintworth, whose premature trip to the UK came to an end and who have now served their fortnight behind closed doors. Like the rest of you, Paul and Melanie can now join you on parole.

In the light of Kathi's woodpecker issue, I thought it would be a good idea to set up a section a la the "Dear Mary" in that famed British magazine *The Spectator*. Something along the lines of:

> Dear Mary,
>
> Although I brush my teeth in the morning fresh out of the shower, I get dressed and always seem to find a smear of toothpaste has somehow found its way onto my clothes! How can this be?
>
> Yours frustratedly, Pete

> Dear Pete,
>
> I suspect you have been secretly hoarding toothpaste a la the toilet paper scandal. (We all

have our pet hordes. Mine is Cabernet.) One errant tube may have escaped from the horde store. I suspect you are not the most tidy person, that your bookshelves are a mess, that there are piles of "useful" stuff that has waited to be sorted since the millennium. Let me ask you this, Peter: are you the type of man, I suspect that you are a *man*, who dresses to go out and thinks he is the smartest, most together man in the restaurant/wedding party/job interview and has a lovely white shirt on inside out, buttons in the wrong holes, a tie that is tucked into one's pant fronts, odd socks and a pizza stain in an awkward place? If you are, then you need to tidy your room, store your toothpaste all together on a shelf marked "Toothpaste Only" and then await success. I suspect you are married and have been for a long time. I believe that you have gone from being a "project" to a "problem." Take my advice and your problems will disappear into a sunny upland of calm and order. Hope this helps.

Yours condescendingly, Mary.

Dear Mary,

It was only one minuscule, almost invisible blob of white toothpaste!

Yours devastated, Pete

Would someone like to volunteer to be "Mary"?

Hot of the press: Young Harry Turner, resident with Mum and Dad at St. Leonard's School in the Kingdom of Fife on the east coast of Scotland, noticed the garbage pick up truck in his area doing its weekly round. The garbage contraption did not fully embrace the detritus leaving a trail of debris behind it. He observed that they were *"rubbish rubbishmen."* Aaaah, my tautological young friend, indeed they were, indeed they were.

Any rate, I dug out some other wee expressions I thought might qualify as paraprosdokian statements. What do you think?

"If at first you don't succeed, try two more times so that your failure is statistically significant."

"Women can remember stuff that hasn't happened yet."

"No matter where you are, there you are." M. Manson

"Whatever you say, say nothing." Seumas Heaney

"Old is not an age, it's a demeanour." Grant Davidson (Yes, I was surprised too!)

"Voters prefer 'I like' over 'IQ.'" Mark Shields

I hope, friends, that your day's isolation is idyllic. Pete

"Sitzfleisch" and Why German Is Such a Great Language

I grew up (yes, I know not all of you will agree with that rash statement!) with a wonderful father who flitted in and out of fads and fancies. One of those that stuck with him for some time was his desire to learn the German language. Thus, was it mandated that we should all speak it at mealtimes. Thus, is my brother, George, now fluent in French and German with smatterings of other languages. I, however, have accomplished a fluency in laziness and clowning about. But German is such a great language because of its ability to create longer and longer compound words. Mark Twain once complained that some of its words were *"so long that they had a perspective."*

So, for example, after war was declared in 1939, there was a period where nothing warlike actually happened. The Brits called it the "phony war," the Germans called it the "sitzkrieg," the "sitting war." Such words as "schadenfreude," "angst" and "bergschrund" are now so much a part of English that they are almost English themselves. There is no one word in English to express "joy at the misfortune of others" or "a moderate fleeting anxiety" or "the gap between the top of the glacier and the rock face." So, Davidson thought it was time that we English speakers usurped the German language and explored our skills to create compound words of our own. Here are some examples:

Winsumsprifallclimdumm = The tendency to have all four seasons appear in the weather pattern in one day as so frequently happens at this time of year.

Geheimstukken= Quarantine.

Kanatabessereh = Jingoism and patriotism rolled into one meaning "Canada is the best country in the world."

Rotnekzeit = A tendency that only simple opinions and solutions are correct, best expressed by American border guards.

Kaltweissweinlieber = Someone who likes to participate in a glass of white wine of an evening.

Blitzdieheimenextedummkopfhaben = Going to war with noisy neighbours.

Ausfahrengutesarbeitsich = "Go away, my job is important."

Pufofahren = Pack up and go away.

Zweibiersehen = An optimistic outlook, literally "two beers seeing" meaning if I can drink one beer I will likely survive so that I can have a second.

Nichtmannsweltschaften = The belief that women rule the world. Found on Angela Merkel's desk.

Hamburgerbekommenzeit = the end of the world as we know it, a sort of German Armageddon.

Your turn, my friends. Oh yes, back to "sitzfleisch." Apparently, it means "sit meat," which means the ability and the stamina to sit at one's desk and focus until the task is done. It can go as far as to mean "endurance." Apparently, it is a skill that the aforementioned Angela Merkel has in spades, and those people diagnosed with "Attention Deficit Disorder" need to work on.

Quarantine Quizzicallities: Day 8

Actually, spellcheck says there is no such word as "quizzicality." Given that "quizzes" may have been enough then it should have been left hanging. A short telephone chat with Anne and Laura today brought up "tautology" and "oxymoron." Even though I had discussed these with Marie Scott at Bean Around the World a few weeks ago, I inevitably forgot the difference so after I put the phone down I resolved to seek their definitions out once and for all and see if I could finally have a good handle on them. Thus we have:

> *"Tautology is a phrase or expression in which the same thing is said twice using different words, such as 'new innovation,' 'male widower' and 'added bonus.'*
>
> *"Oxymoron is a figure of speech in which apparently contradictory terms appear in conjunction (e.g., Faith unfaithful kept him falsely true)."*

So how do these definitions fit into our lives? "A moment in time" has always been an irritation. Surely, it is impossible to have a moment that is not in time.

A "Trump truth": Is this a contradiction, a tautology or an oxymoron? Far from me to point a finger at a U.S. president, but I have heard it said that he "views the truth as a second home and visits it occasionally." So, maybe his statements are "fake news," which raises the question of how real news can be fake! So what is that? Oh dear, oh dear!

2nd April and it snowed out there. We all knew the pandemic would have a great effect on the climate, did we not? Increased glaciation, no more calving off the Antarctic ice shelf, fish in Venice, no more plastic dropped into the ocean 'cos we dare not sail, paddle, swim, sit by it any more. Adopting the North American attitude of putting an optimistic picture on everything is the only way to go.

"Go, COVID, go. Right the world."

We have a long, tall hedge outside our house. It runs the length of the garden. Nobody can see over it. Yesterday from my window upstairs, I watched a father walking up the street, laughing and giggling with his little girl. As they were about to disappear behind the hedge, he grabbed her, turned her upside down and began to tickle her. I watched for a further ten seconds until they reappeared. There they were again, totally immersed in each other, bantering and smiling, oblivious to the rest of the world. It was a simple moment but a joyous one. It had me thinking back to summer noises in our back garden. We have sat down to supper on our patio as the heathens next door have spent endless hours in their pool with their floating board game, their beer and their dope. The raucous laugh every ten seconds, their innate inanity increasing with every passing beer, every languid intake of influential smoke. (So easy to be holier than thou when one is in enforced sequestration, is it not? Preaching and sermonizing one should leave to those with white tieless collars, should one not?)

One summer I was raking leaves round about the patch of grass, Jamie, Jenn and Harry, where the tent is pitched for your pleasant sunny sojourns in our backyard. Things were heating up next door. A discussion had morphed to a debate, to laughter and onwards to a heated argument.

"Bucharest is the !@#%$# capital of Albania, you're talking out of !@$^^^% @#$%."

"No, it's not, it's Sofia, I #^%@&& know it."

One closed one's eyes, one rested on one's rake, one rubbed one's forehead. The temptation was to shout out the answer, to at least create an awareness that there were in fact others in the neighbourhood. To intrude on their privacy as they had intruded on ours for years not without, I hasten to add, 1:00 a.m. incursions into their public, private (tautology, oxymoron, etc.!) world. I am not a complete wimp.

"It's Tirana, you @#%$ wits," I muttered, dropping the rake and going back to the patio table to open a bottle of red wine. Well, one does, doesn't one? Beating them or joining them? Well, what would you do?

Anyhow, those were truly awful human noises that grated on one's nerves for hours on end, as my English/Canadian friends from Scotland will attest to. (Tautology, oxymoron or identity issue?)

In contrast, there is a young family southeast of our house. We have never seen the children but we have heard them. They bounce on the trampoline, they laugh, the to-ing and fro-ing of childish interaction. They, too, are out there for many hours while we are enjoying our back garden. You know, my friends, where I am going with this, do you not!? Their noises are a continuous pleasure. They are the same noises we would have heard from children a thousand years ago. Just as when we walk along the margin of a deserted beach with nothing but the sounds of the crashing turbulence, or maybe through the woods accompanied by a gentle stream with the trickle and tinkle of eddies and flowings, the splashing and quacking of a duck. Or, as again for me this morning, the announcement of the day with the twitterings and songs of birds that know the season better than we, the sounds of nature, atavistic and ingrained, subliminally sublime, are wonderful reminders of all that is great, removing us from all that is grate.

Can there be a "great grate"? (A tautology and so on??). OK, I'll call it a day in a moment. You will have noticed an outbreak of "One's" in this piece: "One is very happy, angry, sad." According to John Cleese's excellent autobiography *So Anyway*, which I completed last night., this is a Britishism exclusive to a certain class. It is a way of avoiding committing oneself. It's not what "I" think, it's what "one" thinks. One should never offer an opinion or a feeling using "I" because it suggests what "you" really believe and thus leaves "I" open to criticism or possibly recrimination and one can't have that, can one??

Is "I, one thinks —" a tautology and so on? So, I will stop now afore I become even sillier. Hope that you are having an inspirational isolation, as you can see I am having a questioning quarantine. Sun is out. Have a good day, my friends.

Verse and Worse!

There is much that is so good in poetry and much that is not so good. I love the way rhyme can give reason in a few short words. Pithy sayings often explain people without the bombast and bloviations of prose. Short, sharp and succinct shrewd observations abound in poetry. Indeed, if one wants to find a good description of a character trait, one can almost certainly find it well expressed by William Shakespeare. Robert Burns would not be far behind him, I suggest. There is a certain rhythm to limericks that seems to appeal to many, many minds. Nonsense verse also tickles, whether a limerick or not. Here are some examples:

> *"A strange bird the cuckoo,*
> *It sits upon the grass,*
> *Its wings neatly folded,*
> *Its beak up its arse.*
> *In this strange position it murmurs 'Twit,*
> *twit'*
> *'Cos it's hard to sing cuckoo with a beak*
> *full of s@#$"*
> *Anon*

And a limerick:

> *"A fat wifie's knickers in Crail,*
> *Blew clean off the rope in a gale,*

Her husband said, "Hen
Ye'll nae see them again"
But she did—on a yacht, as a sail."
Ali Christie

And the lazy poet's limerick!

"There was a young man from Peru,
Whose limericks end at line two."

Back to Ali Christie:

"A bletherin barber frae Ayr,
Said tae the man in the chair,
"It's snawin, I fear"
But the man couldnae hear
Cause his lugs were lyin on the flair."

Or the political statement in verse. This from an Ireland that was fed up of being under the English yoke and English laws:

"So Paddy dear and did ye hear,
The word that's going around,
The shamrock is, by law, forbid,
To grow on Irish ground."
Anon

That would seem to have summed up the situation in Ireland back in the day in a nutshell.

Or the perennial problem of teachers:

"Billy McBone had a mind of his own,
Which his teachers had searched for, for
years."

On alcohol:

"Ho! Ho! Ho! To the bottle I'll go
To heal my heart and drown my woe."
J.R.R. Tolkien

Or with the current pandemic:

"I called my chiefs to council
In the din of a troubled year;
For the sake of a sign ye would not see,
And a word ye would not hear."
Rudyard Kipling

Or a feminist plea:

"So it cames that Man, the coward, when
he gathers to confer
With his fellow-braves in council, dare not
leave a place for her."
Rudyard Kipling

On what not to believe:

"Beware of fair and painted talk,
beware of flattering tongues:
The Mermaids do pretend no good
for all their pleasant songs."
Isabella Whitney

How many of us, men, have been lured onto the rocks by a beautiful siren call over the years? Sounds like a problem that "Dear Mary" should offer a solution to!

Sun is shining. I am off to VGH for a medical appointment. It could be an adventure! Have a good day, my friends.

I Wish I —

— had said that! Apparently Oscar Wilde, the Irish playwright, was well known for stealing other people's "bon mots." At a dinner party in Paris, the artist James McNeill Whistler made a particularly witty remark. He overheard Wilde saying,

"I wish I'd said that!"

"You will, Oscar, you will."

How often have we come away from a meeting or a confrontation and suddenly found the words we needed at the time. A bit cruel perhaps, but how many bosses have been able to say the following to uppity employees or indeed vice versa:

> *"Put your hand in a glass of water, now take it out. That is how hard it is to replace you." Steve Hansen, New Zealand rugby coach*

Then there is the wisdom of the ancients in shape of the Athenian, Pericles:

"What you leave behind is not what is engraved in stone monuments but what is woven into the lives of others."

Good advice but a great shame for pooping pigeons! Then, of course, so many of us are involved in children's education as parents, grandparents or teachers. This from Sir Walter Scott, the novelist, writing in the nineteenth century:

"The ability to succeed without an education is there but it's like climbing over a wall rather than handing in your ticket at the door."

Most of us use technology, but we realize it can take away from our humanity and too much screen time impacts the development of children. This one struck a chord:

"Technology is the knack of so arranging the world that we do not experience it."
Max Frisch

Yann Martel in *Life of Pi* struck a nerve in the current crisis with this statement:

"You might think I lost all hope and, at that point, I did. And, as a result I perked up and felt much better."

I had a wonderful student in my class a few years back, a serious, quiet, unforthcoming boy. Wyatt Anderson is one of nature's gentlemen. Indeed, I ran into his mother downtown pre-lockdown; she is probably the real reason Wyatt is who he is. I came across this quotation of his as I was browsing my notebooks today, and it reminded me of the occasion. Every Wednesday in our mathematics class at Collingwood, we used to "teach" problem-solving. The quotation marks are there because I didn't teach it. I preferred that the children find their way, in groups or as individuals. I was a mute adult, a background silence, albeit prepared to step in for the really desperate. Wyatt arrived at my desk, relaxed but puzzled.

"I have a problem, Mr. Davidson."

"So does everybody else, that's the point of the experience," said I with an unnecessary superiority and a grin of arrant superciliousness.

If Wyatt had been an adult I would not have blamed him if he had given me a quick slap on my ear. Wyatt searched for the words. He was determined to get his message across.

> **"Mr. Davidson, the mystery thickens, my patience thinnens."**

Ahhh, well done, Wyatt. I deserved that.

Speaking of which, here is the report card I never wrote:

> **"He is a youth by no means above mediocrity in his abilities." Robbie Burns**

Those of you who are gardeners:

"A weed is a plant whose virtues have not been discovered yet." RW Emerson

That is the lazy husband's plea, which does not wash at Chez Davidson.

Then there is the person for whom life is a continuous battle to overcome hardships:

"I'll bet his toast always lands on the carpet butter-side down," says Jeremy Clarkson.

There is a wonderful quotation from sportswriter Simon Barnes, the best in his genre for the last thirty years, in my opinion. He said of Ricky Ponting, one of the most successful Australian cricket captains in the history of the game:

"Ricky Ponting has always given the impression of a man who has escaped the tyranny of abstract thought."

Hmmm, it says something about the absence of that tyranny when one looks up Ponting's bio and finds his fortune to be something above $95,000,000!

More from Simon Barnes, this time on the golfer Colin Montgomerie:

"[His] response to every setback is to behave like a spinster finding a man beneath her bed."

Dear Reader, it is now time for breakfast. As you sit down before your bacon and eggs and mull over your plans for the day, please reflect on those plans that are a "may do" and that are a "shall do"; the difference between involvement and commitment. It is right there on your plate in the shape of where your breakfast came from:

> *"Bacon and eggs show commitment and involvement. Take your breakfast egg: the chicken was involved. Now look at your bacon. Well now, the poor old pig, HE was committed."*

Decisions about Decadence

I rene pointed me in the direction of an article in yesterday's *National Post* called **The West Needs to Shake Off Its Decadence** by Sean Speer. He uses as his basis a new book called **The Decadent Society: How we became the victims of our own success** by Ross Douthat. Significant is the fact that the book was written before the current crisis.

I think we all make decisions about decadence every day. They could be as big as a New Year's Resolution or giving up something for Lent. I know one person who never drinks alcohol in January. Many people have purges. We hear about the modern day "cleanse," which seems to mean people sort of chloroxing their insides by drinking nothing but green sludge for weeks on end thus risking another worldwide shortage of toilet paper.

One of the features of this article that hit home loud and clear was the tendency for people who work to have never-ending meetings that are inevitably inconclusive. They only ever result in the decision to meet at another meeting being scheduled for a month's time! Also, the liberality and slack tendencies of people who are unwilling to confront a situation struck a chord with me. I wondered about whether there would have been those tragic crashes of the Boeing 737 MAX aircraft if there had been less liberality and more rigour in the testing process from the beginning. Maybe the pandemic has finally focused the decision-making part of our minds so that we are no longer of the opinion that "tomorrow comes a day too soon." I have a friend who used to work in the bureaucracy of the NHS back in the UK. She relates a tale of taking the train to London and back, a distance of 120 miles, for a meeting that lasted thirty minutes and was a waste of time. Money that could have been spent on somebody's health, presumably, was wasted on that. Maybe we are finally able to do away with such events. To me, in my ignorance, travelling exclusively for a meeting is a form of decadence.

The Latin root of decadence suggests a "falling off," a dropping away from a standard of excellence. We have all heard of the "fall of the Roman Empire." We all realize what energy must have been expended to advance one's frontiers, what bravery it must have taken to expand into hostile territory and, once there, to maintain order and impose a different culture on an indigenous people. Once we have reached the top of the mountain, we pose for the picture, we raise our hands in triumph, we eat a snack, and then we breathe a sigh of relief and relax our guard. Many people, sadly, die on the way down. Growing up in the 1960s in the UK, we probably heard from our elders that carefree youth needed "another war" to make us appreciate things a bit more.

Chocolate is often described as "decadent" as a selling point in a commercial. It is, I suppose, a whole philosophical discussion to debate whether acts of altruism and self-sacrifice are really about helping others or really a kind of chocolate for the soul, acts that make one feel good. Certainlym when I have bought a coffee and a muffin for homeless, jobless Patrick outside Tim Hortons, it has been more about making me feel good than it has about the recipient. Mother Theresa I ain't. Indeed, I do hope you are not reading these scribbles of mine out of a mistaken loyalty; they are a luxurious catharsis for me. I do like you guys so much and am lucky to have you as friends, but I really write as a release from the uncertainty of the times. They are written for *my* mental health.

At my boarding school in Somerset in the west of England, we had a dining room that seated the eighty boys for three meals per day. Grace before every meal, an impatient wait while the prefect at the head of the table served it out, a speedy scoffing in hopes of seconds and so forth. Behind the head table, where sat the housemaster and his wife, was a picture. It was modern art. I guess it was impressionism. It depicted shapes of a group of wraith-like creatures, which, presumably, were human beings. I remember it to this day. I did not really understand it at the time, but this article and the prospect of this book sparked the memory and brought it vividly back to me. I remember the quotation under the picture, it is etched on my befuddled brain. It read:

> *"The cessation of strife will wither and wear the aspirations of a vigorous race."*

Maybe that is what the message is in this article and this book.

Have a good day, my friends.

Make-Up

Camp Sasamat is a wonderfully relaxing children's camp out near Port Moody on Sasamat Lake. It is not a long journey by mini-bus from the "wilderness" in which the camp is set to the dormitory community of Port Moody. The four Grade IV teachers and their classes used to spend two and a half days there at the beginning of the school year in late September. Occasionally, I used to spend the full week there. As I had a Class 4 driving licence, I was able to drive the emergency vehicle, which was also the school mini-bus. It was a busy week. Occasionally, I liked to escape on my own. I always used the pretext of a Starbucks run with an offer to buy my colleagues coffee. Totally unnecessary as we had an abundance of caffeine, but an excuse for a brief piece of solitary that I selfishly valued.

Wednesday evening arrived. The new batch of Grade IV students had settled in. My class was no longer there. The new teachers were with their own classes, so I offered the coffee run and it was gratefully accepted. Oh yes, and could I drop in to the local pharmacist and pick up some rouge, a reddish make-up? Not a problem!

Dear Reader, I have heard of mascara, but I don't know what it is. I recognise lipstick but have never understood its point. I remember musty old ladies applying some white clouds of dust to their cheeks. I do, however, remember that the Picts, early inhabitants of what became Scotland, used to daub woad on their faces, giving themselves blue cheeks to make themselves look fierce in battle. ("Pict" comes from the Latin word for "painted ones," which the Romans noted as they looked north from Hadrian's Wall, now the boundary of empire between England and Scotland.) So, the Davidson experience of make-up is that clowns wear it to make themselves look sad or funny, and Donald Trump wears orange to make himself look, ummm, to make himself look, well, something. So, off I trekked to Port Moody.

I found myself in the local pharmacy opposite the Starbuck's. I looked at my list of coffees and noted I had failed to write down the make-up order for my respected colleague. No worries, I was confident I knew what I am buying. In I go. There is no pharmacist on duty. They have finished for the day. So, I peruse the shelves, searching for the word that will trigger the memory of what I am supposed to buy. I cannot for the life of me find it. So I have to ask. There are a couple of teenage girls who are minding the store, so I ask them.

"Hi, I wonder if you can help me. I am looking for some douche."

Quizzical looks come from the shop assistants! They look at each other, confused. I elaborate.

"It's that stuff that women put on their faces?"

Further confusion. Then a slow dawning from me, a memory of the conversation back at the camp.

"I think it makes women's faces red? Yes, that's it, a jar of douche please," I say triumphantly and confidently at last.

Knowing look of relief from the assistants.

"Do you mean 'rouge'?"

"Yes, yes, that's it. Silly me, 'douche' is wrong, I don't mean 'douche' at all, I mean 'rouge.' Yes, yes, where's the rouge?"

So, they helped me. I am ecstatic. I am over the moon. I am bantering. The shop assistants look totally nonplussed, a bit timid. But I have a big smile, a skip in my step. All I need now are the various coffees and I can return, having had a successful trip. Indeed, such is my joy that I buy some cookie treats to go with the caffeine. I expect to return to camp as the conquering hero. I dish out coffees and give Lise her rouge, happy that it is the right shade.

Later that evening, the children are abed and settled. We are sat around the dying embers of the campfire, and I tell the tale of my trip to the pharmacy. Laughter breaks out, and it is my turn to be nonplussed. I turn to my male colleague for an explanation. He, too, is holding his sides. I become frustrated, eyes to the heavens, hands in the air.

"What?"

He has to explain. As he gives the definition of a douche, my gab doth start to gape, the colour in my cheeks becomes red in the dark, I begin to cringe at the memory, I fidget, my head goes down. Finally, I muster a sheepish grin. I hope that this further tale of Davidson forgetfulness is forgotten, and yet it surfaces again as I am given the speech that accompanies my retirement gifts on my last day at Collingwood School!!

The Living Mountain
by Nan Shepherd

Dear Reader, I am a bit of a reading slut. I will curl up with any book of an evening. I will pick it up, read it, digest it, discard it, throw it to one side. Sometimes, however, my lust gives way to love. Then every sentence flows and trickles and eddies into my consciousness so it becomes not an act of reading but a balm for the soul. *The Living Mountain* by Nan Shepherd is such a book. Every time I pick it up, I become very quickly serene, very gently calm and very subtly transported. Miss Shepherd grew up on the periphery of the Cairngorm National Park in Aberdeenshire. There it was that she explored and embraced the local mountains as a child and an adult until, during the Second World War, she wrote this little gem of a book, which remained unseen by the public until 1977 when it was published some four years before her death.

So, I had leant it to a friend. Then today I was walking with another friend when it was kindly returned to me. I sat in the back garden, poured myself a glass of red wine, picked it out of its socially-distanced plastic bag and browsed through the introduction, which Robert Macfarlane wrote. It, in itself, is about a third of the size of the book and supports the book so much better in that it was written in 2011. It is a contemporary picture of an old classic. So, I was reminded again that here was a man, an outstanding author is his own right, who was writing a paean for an author whom he so much admired. He obviously was passionate about her writing and no praise was too high; she had written a classic, the only real book worth reading about the Cairngorms. What was so interesting to me about this introduction was that the skills in the language of the eulogist were so much better than those of the author herself. Quite simply, Robert Macfarlane is a better writer than Nan Shepherd.

My brother, George, put me onto Robert Macfarlane a few years ago. I have read and re-read *The Old Ways* and *Mountains of the Mind*. If ever I want to move away from the stress and anxiety of life, then I only need to reach and read a chapter of his trickling flow to be in an English meadow, gallivanting a Scottish glen or nursing a Norwegian memory. To me this is a greater transport than a TV travelogue, more inducing of a sunny somnolence than any photograph or picture of a natural scene. Like every act of reading we are not influenced by anybody's commentary or any film crew's preference. All is in our mind's eye, all is ours and ours alone. Very rarely is the film better than the book.

I have walked Lairig Ghru, the "gloomy path," several times in my life. It is a long day hike. Walking from west to east, from Aviemore to Linn of Dee, it splits the Cairngorm massif. One starts at Rothiemurchus along a cushioned, peaty path by a tinkling burn accompanied by heather and Scots pine. One occasionally sees deer and grouse. Soon one leaves the vegetation behind and moves into sparse rockiness, a barren bleakness where weather can change in the blink of an eye. Cold winds whistle down the gap, which soon becomes shadowed by the peaks of Ben Macdhui on one side and Braeriach on the other. The ascent becomes rocky until one reaches the source of the River Dee, that which gives its name to Royal Deeside and eventually Aberdeen where it enters the sea. The descent to Aberdeenshire and Mar Lodge eventually becomes a repetition, a bookend of where one started the day amongst the heather, the trees and the wildlife. My father once dropped my two brothers and me at the western end, drove around the northern periphery and walked up to meet us from the other side. We sensed him around the bend before we saw because he used to smoke Henri Wintermann cigarillos, so there was a puff of smoke ahead of him and he was suddenly there. I do not know what Macfarlane and Shepherd would have made of the smoking hiker, but then we used to identify him on the ski slopes of Austria and Switzerland by the puff of smoke and rather incongruous smell of tobacco, not unpleasant, which was so much a part of his athleticism! The smell of tobacco will always be a most abiding and pleasant memory of who and what my father was. What he smoked was not the offence of a cigarette but an attractive aroma of comfortable happiness and well-being. Dear Reader, you really had to be there. I have heard it said that nobody sees a piece of art in the same way.

So, I cannot possibly imagine what a living mountain is for anybody else. Even without the skills of a Macfarlane or a Shepherd, I cannot convey what memories of these places mean to me. They cannot convey to anybody else, really and truly, what they were to them. But they sure do a convincing job.

Have a great day.

Juniper Hedges

*T*he *Old Ways* by Robert Macfarlane was a revelation of a read to me. It was not that because he wrote and writes about nature and his experiences in it. It was not because he is a philosopher and a historian, both subjects that are dear to my heart. Nor was it that he is an adventurer and an explorer. None of that. No, quite simply, it is because he writes from the heart. His words have soul and passion. They flow easily. They soothe the troubled mind. I have read this book twice. His *Mountains of the Mind* is, arguably, a better book. I challenge any one of us to read his works and not be lulled and calmed, minds massaged by the gentle eddying of his trickling rills.

> *"Different paths have different characteristics, geology and purpose. Certain coffin paths in Cumbria have flat 'resting stones' on the uphill side, on which the bearers could place their load, shake out tired arms and roll stiff shoulders; certain coffin paths in the west of Ireland have recessed resting stones, in the alcoves of which each mourner would place a pebble. The prehistoric trackways of the English Downs can still be traced because on their close, chalky soil, hard packed by centuries of trampling, daisies flourish."*

There was a damp morning a few years back when, walking up Tatlow Avenue, I caught an aroma I recognized and was immediately transported to a different time and place. It was the fragrance of a juniper hedge so familiar to me growing up. The sense of smell is so evocative of times and places, people and past, is it not?

There is a quietness over our cities at this time. Mountain goats have made their way into the Welsh town of Llandudno. For some reason, that took me back to a day when I walked along Marine Drive to Capilano Mall. The traffic was cheek by jowl, the sidewalks were busy. I reached Mackay Creek and, looking upstream a short distance from the turmoil on the roads, I saw a heron poised to spear a passing fish. Immediately, I was with the heron in Charles Frazier's American Civil War novel where the war-ravaged hero has deserted and is walking home. He, too, sees a heron and finds the bird's presence equally incongruous.

"Wherever he was, seemed far from home."

Frazier's description was so perfect. He could have been standing on a dirt road in 1863 or on Marine Drive in 2014. It could have been the same bird.

Sun shining bright out there today, my friends. Tomorrow, I graduate from quarantine to isolation. It will be a new world, stepping away from the Davidson domain, the queendom of Irene. I shall probably go for an early morning dander along the Spirit Trail and, maybe, up the stairs to Pemberton Heights. I am unsure as yet whether to don the face mask that Irene made for me or the much more enveloping underpants. The latter appeals more because the rest of the population are more protected, I feel. Nobody in their right mind would want to break down the barriers of social distancing to talk to a nutter with underpants on his head, I believe. In the UK, hoods and helmets have to be removed before one enters a store. Shall I be asked to remove my underpants, eh? Ha. I guess, in Quebec, my heady underpants may be associated with religious headgear. I certainly do feel like I am having an epiphany when I put them on! Tomorrow, I can escape and maybe get a chance to smell the juniper hedge up the street.

Ah, yes, found this wonderful chapter on puns in my book *Stuff Brits Like* by Fraser McAlpine. I love them. Here are a few from British newspaper headlines:

Kim Jong launches nuclear tests: "How do you solve a problem like Korea?"

Bank bosses apologise for global financial crisis: "Scumbag Millionaires."

George Michael falls from his car: "Scrape me up before you go slow."

Inverness football team Caledonian Thistle (nicknamed Caley Thistle) beat Glasgow Celtic:

"Super Caley go ballistic. Celtic are atrocious."

Journalist deserves the freedom of Inverness for that one! Also loved some of the creative names for businesses. Here are some hairdressers: "British Hairways," "Choppy Toffs" and "Jack the Clipper."

There's the tanning business "U-Rang-A-Tan."

Second-hand shop: "Junk and Disorderly."

Cleaning service: "Spruce Springclean."

The plumbers: "Suck-Cess."

Hours of endless fun, eh!

Enjoy the sun, my friends.

Lost in Translation

Boris Pasternak's *Dr. Zhivago* is a classic novel. Set at the time of the Russian Revolution in 1917, it traces the turmoil at that time through Yuri, his marriage, and his lover, Lara. The David Lean movie of the 1960s had a long-lasting effect on me, not least because of Julie Christie and my teenage "brain." I always promised myself I would read the book at some point, and so, in 2014, I did. It is a magnificent panorama, wonderful description, but, of course, it is translated from the Russian. The book carried me along, but I occasionally had to stop and retrace my steps because something just did not ring true to me—it was lost in translation. Looking back, most of my difficulties were with the Russian winter. Most of us have experienced winter in some form or other, but the firm affinity between the Russian people and their climate lost me. It was as if their winter and their culture were interchangeable.

> *"The wind swept the snow aside, ever faster and thicker, as if it were trying to catch up with something, and, Yurie Andreievich, stared ahead of him, out of the window, as if he were not looking at the snow but were still reading Tonia's letter and, as if what flickered past him were not small dry snow crystals but the spaces between the small blank letters, white, white, endless, endless." Boris Pasternak*

See what I mean? I guess you not only had to be there, you also had to be Russian.

I often look a similar way at British humour, be it Spike Milligan, Billy Connolly, *Monty Python* or Fawlty Towers. How does *Blackadder* translate to a foreign audience? To me, there is something very funny about the chronically absurd. Situation comedy complemented with the absence of a smile and the dryness of a desert appeals to me. There is so much humour conveyed when the expression of the comic is a furrowed brow, a quizzical expression, an appearance of turbulent confusion. So, I am Canadian. It was not that difficult a transition when I arrived here in my late thirties. When I became familiar with my place of work, my colleagues and my friends, I am afraid that my cultural heritage occasionally took over. I was appalled when I said something with my tongue in my cheek and my new friends took it seriously. I had to learn to suffix outrageous statements with, "I'm only joking," and eventually adapt to my new status as a Canadian so that I was not losing friends and becoming labelled as another British eccentric unfresh off the boat. Much of what I was saying demonstrated that Canadians and Brits were two peoples separated, rather than joined, by a common language. I was in danger of becoming lost in translation.

One day there was a problem with the ATM at the TD Bank, my bank card, my secret code. There was the distinct possibility that the hole in the wall would eat my card if I wronged it further. So, a queue (British for "line up") began to form behind me. Immediately next to me was a gentleman who, by his accent, was from London or its environs. We started a merry banter about the machine and its temperament. It was only a short encounter but was quite funny to both of us. Eventually, we gave up and went our separate ways but not before the lady who had waited patiently behind both of us had passed comment about our "friendship." I was confused, and as I left mentioned that I had never met the fellow in my life. As I walked away, I realized that this nice woman did not believe me. Any further explanation would have been a bridge too far given the circumstances and, I sensed, would have required a long-winded, carefully-worded denouement of something which was a common thread for us but uncommon for her. There is something, Dear Reader, very weird and very strange about the British sense of humour. It can be offensive, it makes fun of idiosyncrasies, it can be cruel, it can be bizarre. I know it is out of step with much of the rest of the world—perhaps not the Antipodes. It may be a weakness, and it may be a strength. I do like its healthy disrespect. British humour just is!

Irene and I have taken to watching foreign TV shows. English subtitles are our preference rather than dubbed translations. Danish, Icelandic and Swedish murder mysteries seem to be our preference at the moment. The English script beneath is usually pretty clear and accurate, but just occasionally one realizes that whatever was said in "Scandinavian" comes into the English as a bit strange. The gist is clear, but the nuance has been lost in the translation. Sadly, I have come to terms with the fact that even if I were to muster the determination to understand a foreign language—in itself a forlorn hope—I am now too old to understand the subtleties and nuances that are a part of the differences. I would become, indeed I already am, the woman lined up behind the two Brits in the money queue; I, too, am lost in translation.

WMD

To so many, "WMD" means "Weapons of Mass Destruction," but to some, I have read, it means "Words of Mass Deception." In this era of "fake news," as many would have it, it raises the question about whether there was ever a time when aspects of the news were not untrue. We all know that orators and demagogues can put a "spin" on events, can make them sound so wonderful that you want nothing more than to be a part of them. Indeed, I love the following definition of a diplomat:

> *"Someone who tells you to go to hell in a way that leads you to ask for directions and has you looking forward to the trip."*

It is often said that the victors of war write history. Growing up learning British history, I don't remember ever being taught that there was actually a Republic of Ireland, but I did learn about Northern Ireland. It was a sin of omission and indeed it can be true that the greatest lies are often told in silence. It leads into the Jared Diamond statement that:

> *"Those who study just one country end up understanding no country."*

There is always another point of view, another side of the story. Opinion, we teach our children, should be based on facts, but we know, to our cost, that the facts can also be manipulated to suit an agenda or even ignored to marry with our opinion. There were no "Weapons of Mass Destruction" to justify the invasion of Iraq. Sure, there was oil and a thoroughly nasty dictator, but if the west were to invade every country lead by a thoroughly "bad egg" we would be in a perpetual state of war. There is an excellent senior history teacher at Collingwood School who has just retired. Robert Sword always taught his students to doubt what they hear, to question what they see. Because not only can we be left pretending to understand bafflegab but, contrary to popular opinion, photographs do lie, and video is not the whole truth. The *Mona Lisa* is an iconic picture worthy of reckless praise and priceless to buy. To me it is another Old Master. If somebody had not told me of its greatness, I would have never have picked it as the outstanding example it is. I don't understand it, I need an expert, I need a history lesson. There is something about the "smile" and the fact that it is "enigmatic," but other than that I am a bestial Neanderthal regarding my understanding of this iconic masterpiece. Arthur Koestler once said that:

> *"No death is so sad and so final as the death of an illusion."*

How often have we seen the media hype up the next great politician or sportsman or pop group only to suddenly rip the pedestal from underneath them? English football managers are classic examples. The greatest thing since sliced bread soon morphs into a useless has-been who needs to find a new home on the scrap heap. I have suffered disillusionment over my heroes over the years. I was a fan of Charlie Rose until his fall. I am still a fan of Christopher Hitchens although I wish he hadn't looked down so much on those of us with lesser intelligence, and I regret the fact that he used to refer to women as "Darling." But he is dead now, his writings and interviews and debates are for the history books, and it is, happily, too late for me to fall off that bandwagon. I would be disillusioned and saddened if Bruce Springsteen fell from grace. Jordan Peterson has edged his way into my pantheon. I am happy that John McCain remains a war hero and a "good" man. I hope that an historical revisionist does not shatter that illusion. WH Auden said:

> *"It is very unfair to judge anybody's conduct without an intimate knowledge of their situation."*

We have to make unfair judgments of people all of the time. We are out in public, and we see the behaviour of others, and we give our approval, tacit or otherwise, or disapproval. But we really have no idea of their lives and what has caused them to act the way they did at that particular moment, for good or bad. President Warren Harding had apparently perfected "the art of speaking for as long as the occasion warranted and saying nothing." He bloviated. I doubt he was the first politician to do this, and we know he certainly wasn't the last.

I guess one can always return to nature for honesty. Take mountains, for example. If one climbs a mountain ill-prepared, it will injure or kill you. We can climb mountains and fall off mountains. They are not empathetic, sympathetic, carefree, courageous or any other human quality. Hmmm! Maybe they have one human quality: they are honest. There is no fake news about them. They don't put a spin on things. I loved the slogan I read early this morning, and I think it is an appropriate statement to end this pathetic piece of scribble I have carelessly flung together today. It reads:

> *Message from the mountain: "It's my birthright to take up space and look fucking fantastic."*

Tenuous Tenets!!?

T hose of you who have wasted time reading my meanderings over the last few days will have noticed a certain clutching at straws, a drowning man reaching for a lifeline. It is difficult within the limitations of our isolation to find something interesting to talk about, so I have inevitably fallen back on myself as the self-centred subject of my machinations. I could have moved the subject towards Irene, but then I thought I had better not as I have a real interest in remaining married to her. So, I probably come across as a narcissist of the worst kind. But my resolve has been to write something every day even if those "some things" have little interest. I hope you are not too irritated, but if you are, then reach for the "delete" button.

I am a huge fan of talented people who create funny or relevant T-shirt slogans. I came across one many years ago when Quebec was holding its referendum regarding separation. It read:

> *"My Canada includes Blind River, Ontario."*

It still produces a smile as I write. There is an advertisement for swimming lessons for children that often appears on Capilano Road at certain times of year. It reads:

"Learn to swim at a higher level."

Presumably that "higher level" means "on the surface"?? It would not be great to have children swimming "at a lower level" without a snorkel or aqualung, would it?

"He said he was approaching forty and everybody wondered from which direction."

A bit unkind but clever. The world of literature is full of aphorisms and wisdom put in clear language that makes it axiomatic. It also makes us wish we had said it first! Here are some:

"It's very unfair to judge anybody's conduct without an intimate knowledge of their situation." W.H.Auden

"For success, attitude is equally as important as ability." Sir Walter Scott

"What comes from the heart goes to the heart." Samuel Taylor Coleridge

"Prejudice, not being founded on reason, cannot be removed by argument." Samuel Johnson

"The future is purchased by the present." Samuel Johnson

"When you choose the behaviour, you choose the consequences." Phillip McGraw

*If you are walking on thin ice, you may as well dance." **Men with Brooms***

"Minds are like parachutes—they only function when they are open." James Dewar

Some of these seem so appropriate to our current situation. Indeed, given the title of today's piece, they do not seem at all *tenuous*. It always brings me up short on the occasions when I dip into the classical literature of a Dickens or one of the Romantic poets or back to the ancients of Greece and Rome, that really nothing is new in humankind. Certainly, we have technology our ancestors did not have, but our own characters are always atavistic in their content. We cannot escape that nature of our birth or the nurture of our forebears, can we? How many parents have vowed never to sound like their fathers or mothers and then, in the act of rearing their children, are suddenly brought up short when they realize they have just said what their own parent would have said!

"It's not the mountains ahead that wear you out, it's the pebble in your shoe." Muhammed Ali

"A little water seeping through a small hole can swamp a canoe." Maori proverb

"The first stage of learning is silence; the second stage is listening." Maori proverb

OK, I'll stop in a minute. I'll end with a couple of T-shirt slogans:

> ***"7 days without a pun makes one weak."***

> ***"Never trust an atom, they make up everything."***

Beautiful day out there. Go forth and enjoy, mes amis.

Cromwells

The surname "Cromwell" is not one to bring joy and laughter into an English household, still less an Irish one where up until very recently "The curse of Oliver Cromwell" was called forth. The English Civil War fought back in the 1600s between the roundheads and cavaliers, the parliamentarians and the royalists, Cromwell against King Charles I, was fought for extremely laudable reasons. The divine right of kings—the silly belief that one man had the right to make decisions because he was blessed with the wisdom of God—had surely been debunked in the year 1215 at Magna Carta. Charles I surely deserved his decapitation for his refusal to surrender it, indeed he would have been a better king without his head than with it! The trouble with Oliver Cromwell's rule was not that it gave more rights to the parliament but that they were puritans. I imagine that even back then, as now, your average Englishman liked his government to be based on the rule of law, and to at least go through the motions of equality, to be fair. He or she wanted all of those things. But he couldn't stand them if they did not come along with a sense of humour, the quirkier the better. The "warts and all" painting of the Lord Protector projects many things, but it also suggests that yer man there did not have a funny bone in his body. That would not have washed well in England, and done so even less in Ireland, where the "craic" is so much a part of life. This was the Oliver variety of the name. His predecessor back in the time of Henry VIII and his six wives was Thomas Cromwell. To this day one cannot rule Britain or Ireland if you have no sense of fun.

I am reading *The Mirror and the Light*, the third in the trilogy of the life and times of Thomas Cromwell, who rose from humble roots to become the most powerful man at the Tudor court. *Wolf Hall*, the first of the books, won the Man Booker Prize and, in the process, takes us on Cromwell's journey to power and ends with the execution of Henry's second wife, Anne Boleyn. The second book, *Bring up the Bodies*, takes us through the marriage to Jane Seymour. It also won the Man Booker Prize. Religion is the huge backdrop to all of this. The king's quarrels with the Catholic Church, which led to the "Reformation" and he electing himself as head of the Church in England, form the meat and drink of the novels. To this day, there are ruined monasteries dotted throughout the land that are marvelous places to visit and study. Henry's legacy is still around nearly 500 years after his time.

Thomas Cromwell is ruthless in his climbing of the slippery pole. The jury is out on whether he deserves our sympathy or should be damned as a ruthless, power-hungry manipulator. Queen Victoria once came out in support of one of her rival prime ministers, Benjamin Disraeli. He had had a hard life, not least because he was Jewish at a time of anti-Semitism. Considering her very privileged background, she showed perspicacious understanding of the man's character, but then she wasn't a great fan of his rival, William Ewart Gladstone, who wanted to solve the "Irish Question" by granting Home Rule. This is a long-winded way of saying that Lord Cromwell came by his ruthlessness honestly because he was the blacksmith's son. So, these novels are inspiring in so many ways, not least of which is a renewed interest in the history of the Tudors. We know so little, but we know so much more with hindsight. Lurking in the background of the problem of who is going to succeed Henry as king, is Anne Boleyn's daughter, Little Eliza. She is a footnote to the novels, barely a mention, but we know she was to become Elizabeth I, the Virgin Queen, and one of the greatest monarchs England ever had.

So where am I going with this? Probably nowhere. Except that there is nothing more nepotistic than a monarchy, is there? Inheriting power because of one's name and heritage goes against the ideas of meritocracy and democracy, does it not? Yet it happens. To some extent we have all experienced the employee who receives a promotion so that he or she does less harm! We have also seen the poor little rich child who is forever going to live in the shadow of a parent. It is a fine line that we have as parents when we want what is best for our children and use our financial resources to give our children a start in life, a step up. At this time, we do need experts and we do **not** need glib phrases, throwaway remarks, seat-of-the-pants solutions. Justin Trudeau's twenty-one seconds of silence before answering a question speaks far louder than any political noise to me. The jury is out whether the "Trudeau" name will match that of "Cromwell" as one that itches our emotions when we are able to find hindsight in the future. Cromwell = Nepotism, Trudeau = Nepotism?!

Have a great day. No need to water the garden.

Quick Wittedness

How many times have we been in situations when we have regretted not having said something and thought with marvelous hindsight what we could have said if only we could go back and impress the situation with our quick-witted verbiage. We all know the one:

"Waiter, there's a fly in my soup."

"Don't shout it out loud or everybody will want one."

Dr. Henry Kissinger was once described as "paying more attention to his principals than his principles." That sums up Nixon's henchman and the man Christopher Hitchens wanted tried as a war criminal pretty succinctly. Who was the man who described Napoleon's character as "being shit next to gold"? Back to Kissinger again, this time with his offsider, Nixon: "Neither had the ability to rejoice in someone else's success."

A message for us oldies whose bodies are "hurting in the places we used to play":

"My joints are stiff."

"You're rolling them too tight."

Or truly awful verse:

> *"I was standin' in ma kitchen,*
> *A combing of ma hair,*
> *When I saw a wee bit robin*
> *And he gied me a stare."*

Is there any worse verse? No Robbie Burns he!

Then there was the mother and father of three horrendously-behaved children whom Stuart MacBride suggested that "They went through babysitters like vomit through a sock." Or even better, the clumsy klutz at the cocktail party was "like a hand grenade in a septic tank." Rose, Di, Anne, Paul, Muir, Mandy and I were probably not permitted to use similes like these when we were teaching our language arts lessons but now, ex-colleagues, if we are called back in to teach that wonderful simile lesson we have up our sleeves, we can advance the cause with wonderful, colourful impunity. Sadly, Jamie Turner, your pees and queues still have to be watched! There is Rod Liddle in *The Spectator* talking about somebody having "the intellect of pre-set concrete." Or Rex Murphy on the current Liberal government's efforts to get re-elected back in October: "The days of whine and poses are nearly over." Talking of politics, there was Dalrymple writing way before Trump was nothing more than an ordinary run-of-the-mill billionaire:

> *"The cult of celebrity is the marriage of*
> *glamour and banality."*

How true is that?! And the same brilliant Theodore Dalrymple:

"It's not the personal that is political but the political that is personal."

We who are men and driving to an unknown destination will never, ever stop and ask directions. It's simply not in our DNA. All of us have a feminine side, of course, but it never, ever results in us pulling over and asking a bystander the way to Ashby-de-la-Zouch.

"Of course we weren't lost. We were merely where we shouldn't have been without knowing where that was." Longstaff

Ah, Mr. Longstaff. I would like to meet and, on behalf of men everywhere (wherever everywhere is), I would like to shake you by the hand.

I love this from Victor Hugo:

"Stronger than all the armies is an idea whose time is come."

Pretty relevant at the moment, I think. Hefferman takes it a step further:

"While doubt isn't a very pleasant condition, certainty is absurd."

George Bernard Shaw rather pithily said:

"There are two tragedies in life. One is not getting what you want and the other is getting what you want."

Which Dorothy Rowe would seem to understand as:

> *"Without dark we would not know the light,*
>
> *Without imperfection we would not know perfection."*

Talking of the arts and in this case movies, William Holden, the actor, said:

> *"There are only six basic plots.* **Frankenstein** *and* **My Fair Lady** *are mostly the same story."*

And another famous actor, Marilyn Monroe:

> *"Ever noticed that 'What the hell' is always the right decision?"*

Back to authors. Here is Martin Amis with a racist comment:

> *"The French they say, live to eat. The English, on the other hand, eat to die."*

Don't worry, Martin, the English and the French won't be knocking down the doors at the Court of Human Rights; they know when a tongue has been put in a cheek.

Wise man is Mr. Amis. He also said:

> *"The male libido is like being chained to an idiot for fifty years."*

Jeffrey Arnold summed up the five stages of drunkenness with brevity aforethought:

"Verbose, jocose, lachrymose, bellicose, comatose."

Talking of sins and sinning, that old philosopher and atheist Bertrand Russell summed up the Ten Commandments:

"The Ten Commandments should be treated as an examination. Only six need to be attempted."

He also wanted all churches to put up signs saying:

"Important if true."

And here we are in a pandemic and in a world where Britain has left the EU. It seems Britain always felt a wee bit superior to its continental cousins. Witness a weather report from about fifty years ago:

"Fog in the Channel. Continent cut off."

Not a hint of irony there, but even more parochial was this headline from 1912 in *The Press and Journal*, the local Aberdeen newspaper.

"Titanic sunk. Aberdeen man feared drowned."

Frederick Langbridge summed up optimism and pessimism as follows:

"Two men look out through the same bars,
One sees the mud and one the stars."

Talking of optimism, Christopher Hitchens does not share the view that the reign of JFK was "Camelot":

"It is pardonable for children to yell that they believe in fairies, but it is somewhat sinister when the piping note shifts from the puerile to the senile."

In the immortal words of Marilyn Monroe:

"Happy Birthday, Mr. President."

On a serious note:

"Kindness in words creates confidence.
Kindness in thinking creates profoundness.
Kindness in giving creates love."
Lao Tze

Who would have thought that Rudyard Kipling wanted to empower women? He wrote:

"So it comes that Man, the coward, when he gathers to confer

With his fellow-braves in council, dare not leave a place for her."

Just in case we forget that the world has gone through many crises in the past and has come through them, there is the following Mongolian proverb:

> *"Not forever can one enjoy stillness and peace. But misfortune and destruction are not final. When the grass has been burnt by the fire of the Steppe, it will grow again in summer."*

Avez-vous un grand jour, mes amis? Et ne pas permittez les buggers to get vous la bas!!??

Flowers v. Weeds

H ave you who live in the Norgate area noticed the prevalence of foxgloves both in the natural areas and in people's gardens? For me, the foxglove is another flashback to my youth. Old bomb sites from WWII and areas that had been logged always seemed to produce foxgloves. Up until the present I had thought of them as weeds. But there is a wonderful garden near Norgate School that is all foxgloves. So, I have Googled to find out what they really are. Is a foxglove a weed or a flower? I discover that it is **_digitalis purpurea_**, the original source of the heart medication digitalis. So if it is a weed then it is an useful weed. I had never really thought of weeds as being useful before, but then second thoughts came to that other weed, the dandelion. Wine can be made from this weed, something else that is useful. Our back grass produces buttercups, which are weeds. So, these are ruminations and thoughts and we all have the evidence at our fingertips to discover what is the difference, the one from the other. You are now saying, Dear Reader, Google it, Davidson, get to the point. We know the difference, get it over with. Ha, well I'm sorry but I'm not going to do so quite yet.

My brother, Bill, is a gardener in the west of England. He lives just outside a village. He has a property that is far too large for him to fully work, so there is an area behind his house that he has no time to cultivate. There the grass is tall;

the land is given over to its natural state. He tells me there are adders there, the UK's only poisonous snake. There is a path through the shrubbery where he goes to walk his dog towards the old disused railway line at the back. But to all intents and purposes this is an area that has returned to what it would have been before human beings came along and cultivated it. To me, a non-gardener, a naïf in the world of plants and growth, it is a beautiful thing. There are flowering shrubs and bushes that have encroached their way into his "wilderness," brambles and nettles that will scratch or sting, a wealth of nature in a countryside that is fast losing its green belt. Indeed, when one walks through it one can hear the constant sound of the motor traffic heading south or north along the M5 motorway. So, I have talked before in these blogs about "Sweet William" or "Stinking Billy," a plant so named because of a religious divide.

I have no time for the snobbery that tells me something is a "nose-in-the-air" much-despised weed and something is a floral aristocrat, a rose of exquisite design. It is time for us to be allowed to judge on what we like or dislike based on our five senses. Generally, for example, I like bus drivers, dog owners, the staff of Tim Hortons, the Yukon breakfast at The Tomahawk, and the Meridian grocery store. I like the beaver, the ducks and the heron in Mackay Creek. I like the new pedestrian crossing on Tatlow Avenue. I love the fact that Sowden is the bumpiest street in North Vancouver on which to drive. I love the speciality cheese shop. I do not like drivers who drive too fast down Pemberton in the early morning, and I hate cars and trucks that are far too noisy. I am fast developing an antipathy towards cyclists on the Spirit Trail. I try not to like Walmart, but its prices are hard to beat. I worship at the shrine of Everything Wine and love the fact that I can now have a glass legally in a public park. I hate the fact that Bard on the Beach is not happening this summer but, in mitigation, Irene and I have a new deck that we love. I love our neighbours to the north, and I like our neighbours to the south, but there are exceptions! I love the fact I can walk to most places of interest. I hate isolation and love gatherings of people. I love adventurous people, artistic people, kind people, people with a smile on their faces and energy in their attitude. I don't like strangers who won't say "Good morning/afternoon/evening." I cannot understand people who walk, run or cycle wired for sound where there are so many wonderful natural and live sounds to be heard. I like genuine people. Shallow as a bird bath characters don't cut it for me. I like people who don't tell me they love me but obviously do, and I despise people who tell me they love me and obviously don't. I like people who tell me how it is. I like the homeless man with the pet skunk, the body odour and the shopping cart. I don't like the Mercedes suit with his dealership cars parked on the street. I love the guy who stopped his car and apologised to me after he failed to stop at the pedestrian crossing I was about to step out on. I don't like the lady who butted in and interrupted me as I was ordering coffee because she did not have butter for her muffin.

So, Dear Reader, I promised to Google the difference between a weed and a flower. But I have decided not to. I think I will leave it up to you to tell me. Why? Because there is no accounting for taste. If I love a weed that happens to be a flower, then it is not a weed to me. And vice versa. Have a wonderful weekend.

"With well doing ye may put to silence the ignorance of foolish men."
Peter II (XV), the Bible.

CHAPTER 5

PHILOSOPHY

It should come as no surprise to any of us, as we are all affected by a world crisis, that we hang on every word of our newscasts at night. We are looking for strength in our leaders, but all too often seeing fallibility and frailty. So, we huddle amongst ourselves, pore over the media and pour our ideas and concerns forth to others.

A Rocket Launcher??!!

Yesterday's *BBC News* had much about the anniversary of the end of the Second World War. Yesterday it was the end of the war in the Channel Islands, occupied by the Nazis for five years. Then it switched to Russia, fly pasts but an empty Red Square for the "Great Patriotic War." My interest perked as I witnessed a fireman's cradle rising up to a balcony to give a socially-distanced vet a medal, and it perked up even further when a ninety-four-year-old veteran was presented with a WWII...rocket launcher!? Try pinning that on your chest, Sergei! It wasn't one of those off the shoulder numbers either, no. It was towed by a truck and stuck next to other artillery pieces. It even fired salvos of large, eerie-sounding rockets. Can you imagine living in our lovely Norgate homes and having a knock on the door on Remembrance Day and being gifted one of those? The Davidsons would not be able to get it in the front driveway. We could get it into the back garden out of the way if we had a crane to help. In reality, it would have to sit on the front lawn. On occasions when the neighbours have been in their pool, arguing drunkenly over what the capital of Albania is or debating a fictional, albeit hopeful, sex life, then we could have used a rocket launcher. (Be not concerned, Mosers. I am talking about the southern bunch). It would seem that enshrined in Russian law there is an equivalent to the 2nd Amendment. Although for all his health and fitness, this ninety-four-year-old did not look likely to be able to bear his new arms into his local A&W. Maybe he could tow it behind his car through the drive through. It would certainly prevent him from being out-merged on the Lions Gate.

Useless gifts are out there and, I feel, are often victims of re-gifting. I do not know in which dusty attic lurks my friend's hairbrush container in the shape of a boomerang, which, when opened, plays "Waltzing Matilda." Nor do I know what happened to the giant lime-green bathmat in the shape of a human foot. It would have been OK for an evening shower but a bit of a shock to the eyes of an early morning. We have a Queen Elizabeth II bobblehead in our kitchen, complete with waving hand and customary handbag. We knew a couple who were about to get married and were given his and hers movie passes as a wedding gift. My mum and dad were given a bread board, which did the job in our house for at least twenty-five years. Indeed, my dad was upset when it fell to the floor and broke one day. He would have superglued it had my mother not persuaded him to buy a new one. Our son once made a rectangular plant holder for his mother on Mother's Day. It is made from concrete. It has had many blooms in it. It is difficult to move. We still have it after many years.

Talking of Mother's Day, 32 Books & Gallery at Edgemont Village sent out a couple of nice quotes:

> *"Nothing is lost until your mother can't find it."* Anon

> *"To describe my mother would be to write about a hurricane in its perfect power."* Maya Angelou

A wonderful mother lights a fire under her children after she has given the security and building blocks on the ground. She ensures they are ready to be launched. In the UK, the event is called "Mothering Sunday" and takes place in March. That title always sounded a bit crass to me. It suggested that on that particular day, husband and children took over the job of "mothering" in its old-fashioned, traditional sense. They made massive fry-ups for her breakfast, none of which she had ever been known to eat. They then washed all the dishes, putting them in the wrong cupboards afterwards. They vacuumed the house, which was only ever done on a Sunday on Mother's Day. They bought her flowers excessively and abundantly so that there were not enough vases to accommodate them. They insisted on taking Mum out for lunch even though she was still full from the 9:00 a.m. bacon and eggs. They then took her for a long walk on a beach or up a hill. At about 5:00 p.m. as husband was clattering around in the kitchen searching for the pots and pans his children had put away earlier in order to make that special dinner, Mum was installed in the front room, slumped in front of the TV, watching the 60s equivalent of a Hallmark movie and desperately worried about what was happening in the kitchen. Occasionally, Husband would stick his head around the door and ask if she wanted yet another cup of tea to go with the four or five she had had already. When the day was over, the "perpetrators" would ask if she had enjoyed her day. She would then be expected to lavish praise on them with flourishing hyperbole, while inwardly reflecting that these were the actions she took every day and for which she never achieved recognition. On the following day when Dad was at work and children were at school, Mum spent a steady day searching and finding, cleaning and organizing the chaos from the day before.

> *"Life doesn't come with a manual. It comes with a mother."*

We are the rockets she launches!!

Enjoy the sun, my friends. Allow yourselves to be spoiled, mothers.

Uplifting

Well, Dear Reader, as of last Wednesday I have been thrashing around making a mess of the planet for exactly sixty-eight years. Yes, May 20ᵗʰ saw remarkable tolerance from the powers that be by allowing my family to raise a glass to somebody who has muddled through. So my good friend, David Speirs, invited me to be a part of a "Zoom" experience whereby we chatted with Aussie rugby coaches whom we have met and communed over many, many years. Collingwood School has gone there, and Blue Mountain Grammar School has come here. Despite being a reluctant fan of technology, this chat, which began at 7:30 p.m. on Friday night on our time and ended nearly two and a half hours later, was the most uplifting experience of my week. To chat with people who are half a world away, to hear their stories, to reminisce and to be apart and yet a part was really, truly uplifting.

Australia is a truly wonderful country. Being from the UK, I will never, ever admit to this in front of Australians. Brits and Aussies pretend to have a mutual dislike of each other, a "pommie bastard" is a much-bantered term. I was a "bleeding one tubber" for my time down under due to the British propensity to have a bath only once a week because there wasn't enough hot water. England v. Australia cricket tests were filled with jingoistic subtleties and nuances. (What am I saying? No they weren't. There was never anything subtle or nuanced about the Cyclopean support for either country). So I was wonderfully amused when one or two of my fellow rugby coaches from Collingwood suggested, with the best intentions, that we give our Aussie host, Dave Cobb, an England rugby jersey as a sign of appreciation. That well-intentioned gesture "doth butter no parsnips" as the saying goes! So, my virtue-signaling friends, in this current climate of political correctness, I could have strutted self-righteously along to a court of human rights and complained about discrimination, insults and persecution. I could have been filled with self-righteous indignation. Dear friends, that was never a consideration. Why? Because I loved every minute of the "defamation." Now, in case you think I am some sort of masochist, please be assured I am not. I gave as good as I got. There was mutual understanding. I loved every Australian ocker who had ever sheared a sheep, every Aussie cricketer who had ever bowled a ball and every Aussie drinker who had browbeat me, denigrated me and bought me a cold one. There is no point in explaining this relationship to an outsider, particularly to a North American, because they weren't there physically but, more importantly, they aren't there metaphysically. One needs to know the history, appreciate the culture and understand the shared heritage.

I remember my first game of rugby at Northern Suburbs, Sydney. The guys were going out after the game, and I had no money so could not join them. A guy slips me $20 and asks me to pay him back on my first pay cheque. Two weeks later I give him his money back, but he won't accept it. He simply asks me to "pass it on." I remember the free drink I was offered at the Rose Hotel in Bunbury, Western Australia, as long as I picked up Warren, who was drunkenly asleep on the floor, and returned him to the Youth Hostel. No need for the police, no need for the law, just a couple of mates, a strong pair of shoulders and a free beer.

I have always said that, despite my Scottish heritage and my English boarding school, I never really understood what it was to be a "mate" until I spent eighteen months in Australia. I do not understand the Bermuda Triangle, the theory of relativity, American democracy. I do not understand the relationship between Brits and Aussies, but I know I like it very, very much, and I would not change a thing.

So, I am uplifted by being virtually in the same room as them, relaxed by the common threads of education, rugby, humour and comfortable companionship. That "Zoom" call to Australia was, Dear Reader, the most pleasant and uplifting time of my week.

Enjoy your Saturday.

British Eccentricity

L ike fish, we only recognize water when we come up for air. I think those of us who grew up in the UK only noticed how different our humour was when we left. Am I right, Paul and Mandy?

There is an incident in one of Bill Bryson's books when he was travelling around the UK in the 1970s. He caught a train to a stop in Wales, planning to get a bus from the station to his final destination. Upon arrival he discovered that not only had the last bus left five minutes before but it had been scheduled so to do! When he eventually confronted a bus company employee with this obvious anomaly and a suggestion that the timetable be changed so that the final bus became due to leave five minutes after the arrival of the train, he received the reply:

"Why the hell should we?"

One rests one's case, doesn't one? Barrelling northwards up the motorway in the UK a few years back, I had a sudden need for sweet coffee to keep me focused and awake. (Nigel, who kindly drove around Iceland with me in 2016, will tell you that it is best to get the Davidson driving out of the way in the morning as he has a tendency towards a post-prandial nap in the afternoons!) So, I lined up for my coffee and was confronted with sullen teenage-hood, no doubt on a youth opportunities scheme. As I waited, I saw that one could get a Cadbury's Flake with one's mocha. The temptation was too much. I love the texture of the flakiness; it is indeed a gentle bark peeling of a chocolate. I imagined a luxuriating bite, a short delay and then a sip of coffee. So I ordered, and "Her Sullenship" moved from the till to prepare the treat. It came back with the Flake basking temptingly on the saucer. Before handing it to me, she reached down and immersed the chocolate into the liquid! What and why? My inner apoplexy was about to come to the fore. I looked around to see an amused truck driver who understood the situation perfectly. He grinned knowingly.

"I shouldn't bother, Mate."

So I didn't.

Similarly, returning to Lincoln, where we used to live and work, after a weekend in London with the boys involving a rugby international and the accompanying alcohol, we pulled off the A1 main road for breakfast at a greasy spoon. We all wanted the "Full English." However, we could have "eggs and toast" or "bacon and toast" or "sausage and toast," but we could not have all three on the same plate. We pleaded, we begged, we increduled to no avail. Nothing daunted, the three us ordered three breakfasts each and proceeded to put three into one and ask the waiter to take away the now empty extras. Honour was satisfied. He had done the right thing. We ate, paid and left, vowing never to darken the doors of that establishment again. Bad business practice, eccentric business practice, British eccentric business practice.

After the war, the actor Sir Alec Guinness believed he was destined to play Adolf Hitler in the inevitable movie. In a piquant moment, he rented a "Der Fuhrer" costume, donned it and the moustache, found a friend with an open-top car and the two of them drove the streets of London with the actor standing in the back giving the Nazi salute to a stunned populace. Eventually, they parked and Guinness continued to strut his stuff up and down the sidewalk. Ineluctably, he was tapped on the shoulder by a traffic warden with pencil raised to issue a ticket. No word of humour, a serious demeanour.

> *"Excuse me sir, do you realize you are parked on a double yellow line?"*

British officialdom has its moments. Spike Milligan's publisher, a gentleman called Jack Hobbs, had returned from holiday with a bout of stomach flu. Undaunted, he arrived off the train at his London office in the traditional pinstripes and bowler hat. Very early on he realized he was not fit for work so decided to go home. On his way to the station the poor man failed to make it. Put it this way: the bottom did not fall out of his world, but the world fell out of his bottom. So he dashed into a department store, bought himself new pinstripes and new underwear, grabbed his package quickly and left. On board the train he hastened to the washroom, removed his soiled garments, threw them out of the window and opened his bag to find a pink woman's cardigan therein. Nothing for it but to manipulate his legs and his manhood into the sleeves of the garment and button it up the front. On arrival at his station, he marched up the platform and gave his ticket to the employee, whom he had known for years. As he took the ticket he said to Mr.Hobbs,

"Been away on holiday have we, Sir?"

(Search YouTube for the late lamented Spike telling this story, he does a far better job of it than me.)

My father, Wattie Davidson—yes, he who insisted we speak German at table—had a day off on Wednesdays. In one inspired moment he decided he was going to take his teenage boys the thirteen-mile drive to watch a matinee performance of the new film production of *The Sound of Music* at The Odeon in Bristol. We would rather have been playing football in the garden, but we knew there was no gainsaying the bee in his bonnet once lodged therein.

"You'll love it," he said. "Music and scenery, a true story, a history lesson to boot."

I don't know about my younger brothers, but I did **not** love it. I couldn't have cared less about a lonely goatherd high on a hill, tea, a drink with jam and bread, and it really was **not** one of my favourite things to do of an afternoon. Still and all, we got through it, although not without teenage resentment. Nowadays I thank my lucky stars we avoided *Mary Poppins*, which would not have been a jolly holiday with you, Bert. Don't get me wrong, those movies have grown on me. But back then they were a groan. Inevitably, there was going to be another movie that would come along and we would be shipped out on Wednesday afternoon, sometimes on our school holidays. So along came *Dr. Zhivago*.

"Beautiful views of the Russian wastes in winter, Peter, an incredible musical score," he said.

OK, OK, best bib and tucker (we were never to be allowed out in our usual holiday scruffiness), off we trekked, teenage resentment and sullen cynicism intact. Yeah, yeah, lots of ice, sad funeral at the beginning, pretty impressive music it has to be said, Rod Steiger, Omar Shariff and then, suddenly, joy of joys, splendour of splendours, I was the happiest of teenage boys. Yes, there was Julie Christie! Yes, the pleasure of kicking a ball in the mud and the rain suddenly gave way to an unusual stirring. Julie Christie! Hmmm! I guess that it was a bit of an eccentricity to cart teenage boys off to the cinema in their best clothes on a Wednesday afternoon, but my dad must have seen how enamoured I was with the *Dr. Zhivago* experience 'cos we never did it again. I guess that that is another eccentricity of the country, the class or the age. If one finds that one's children are enjoying the experience too much, then one has to put a stop to it!

Nowadays, nearly thirty years removed from living in the UK, I still find hours of endless pleasure in the humour and strange world of a society that has always been outré and a little bit removed from the run of the mill.

Have a good day, friends.

The Theory of Relativity

Yes, Albert Einstein's $E = mc^2$. We all have heard of it but, if you are like me, you have no idea what it means. But, my friends, I am prepared to bet we all have our own "theory of relativity" 'cos we all have relatives. Think about them: they are full of quirks and quarks as we all are. A friend of mine had a mother-in-law who put on white gloves to read the newspaper. Then there was the woman who phoned the police because there was a drunken man asleep on her front lawn. Did she recognize him? she was asked.

"Yes, he's my husband."

So, my friends, dig into your distant pasts, cast around into your translucent presents and think about that one relative who doesn't do things like you do, who brings quirkiness to a new level. They are out there, are they not?

I had a chain-smoking granny who drove everywhere dangerously. She liked to sit upon the white lines in the middle of the road, and she never ever did learn to reverse. Occasionally, when she cooked us a meal, we would find a strange ingredient on top of the potatoes. My wise father confirmed it was cigarette ash and instructed us not to mention it. So come along, friends, you must have them too. How about the sink-or-swim uncle who decided that the only way for children to learn to swim was to throw all of the non-swimming children into the deep end of the pool causing a great deal of work for young teenage lifeguards? Uncle Ted, he was called, but he was not a relation. He was always the first person crossed off the wedding invitation sheets.

Still on the subject of relatives, the aforementioned grandma was very kind to me after I had left school. I lived with her for a while in the seaside town of Nairn where I was a van boy for the Nairnshire Laundry. She cooked for me in the evenings. I lived like a king on her meat and vegetables. She roamed the kitchen with the inevitable cigarette and the radio constantly tuned to Radio 4. I was reminded of this yesterday when reading an article about the *Shipping Forecast*. I don't know whether you erstwhile Brits remember this while growing, but I certainly do. It used to come onto the radio four times a day and reel off the weather to all those people at sea or about to go to sea. The seas off the coast were divided into blocks. South Utsire, Dogger, Hebrides, Trafalgar, Viking, Faeroes, German Bight. Totally out of context, if one of the thirty-one regions is now mentioned, I may not know exactly where it is on the map but I know that it is a part of my youth. I know that the wind speeds are mentioned using the Beaufort scale, and there will be barometric pressure. But, to me, hearing the *Shipping Forecast* as I did back in those days is very much like listening to the rain in one's cosy, dry, warm tent. There I was in my late teens in Granny's Hieland Hame, well fed, a roaring fire, comfortable and secure, appreciating that I was not a fisherman in a storm-tossed trawler somewhere off the south coast of Iceland. They were hardy, tough people, tossed about in rough seas, chilled by driving rain and seeking an increasingly elusive cod so that the likes of me could return from my rugby game on a Saturday night and stumble into the local fish 'n chip shop. Any rate, that is a speedy flashback to the early 1970s and to a granny who was far too kind to an immature young man.

This being the 13th day of the Davidson quarantine, you will be grateful that my boring bloviations are petering out. Pun intended. Enjoy the weather, mes amis.

Walking Wonders

O n one of our evening walks the other evening, Nigel and I came up with a solution. Now in case you think this is a rarity, then be assured, Dear Reader, that we frequently do come up with solutions. Indeed, who better to come up with world-shattering ideas than a practical, down to earth, realistic engineer and a teacher of English and history (with a wee bit of Latin flung in when energetic headmasters have rushes of blood!). We had walked through the pan banging, bell ringing, hoots and hollers for the healthcare workers at the end of Redwood. Indeed, our evening timing was such that we were beginning to feel that the noise was in honour of us. I had indeed recommended that Irene have an afternoon nap that particular day, so I guess that that makes me a sort of "health worker." We were walking past the Pemberton Pub, cobwebs over the doorways, canvas overlay flapping sorrowfully in the breeze, beer festering into a stale memory of a happier past in the pumps. We elbow-pressed the pedestrian crossing, no need to wait for the go sign. We strolled past the Vanleena Dance Academy, no SUVeed parents checking their cell phones and awaiting young ballerinas from the deserted building. Bell-ringing bicyclists frequently passed. As we approached Mackay Creek, we noticed a couple leaning over the fence watching something. We asked what they were looking at. There in the drainage ditch was a beaver making its way towards the grid that gave a floating access to the other side of the road. In twenty-nine years living in Canada I had never seen a beaver, so this was a first for me. Nigel had seen many before. All of these fleeting experiences must have influenced us to come up with a solution for one of the world's abiding problems.

Plastic.

Nigel came up with the figure that something like 85% of the world's plastic has not been destroyed and is polluting the planet. In a moment of mutual inspiration, we decided the solution was to get the plastic off the planet by shooting it not only into space but also pointing the detritus towards the sun so that it would burn off! In a single thought we had returned the Earth's surface to a regained virginity (Hmm, this may not be possible!), a pristine presence unseen since our simian simulacrums were scratching their heads over how best to hunt their next prey many millennia ago.

Now then, the ever-practical Nigel pointed out that our municipal taxes would have to go up if we were to export all of our plastic outside the atmosphere. There would also be a crisis of identity amongst so many of us men who like nothing better than to borrow a truck, don our baseball caps, grab a Timmy's coffee and drive to the town dump. Synchronized grunts of disgust when we are cut off at a traffic light, rueful grinning pleasure when we enter the hallowed ground in the covered area having bantered briefly with the weigh-scale safety vester. Oh, the joy—the joy!—Dear Reader. We then feel the familiar slime under our feet, sniff the familiar air of rotting cabbage and unload our household garbage before returning home to a smiling "she who must be obeyed." All that would be lost if it were mandated that it be catapulted into space. Also, there would no longer be the cheery approach of the radio, the squeak of brakes, the cheery greetings of the garbage men (hoping for a better Christmas box than the really awful, stale box of chocolate liqueurs they got last year). No, those poor guys would be giving way to the Chris Hatfields of this world, up in orbit, strumming on his guitar in between hooking up the booster rockets to the numerous garbage trucks clamped to the outside of the international space station, awaiting jettisoning on the next occasion that the sun comes into view.

Now there have been many other wonderful solutions to the problems of the world that we who walk have come up with. Now I shed a tear. It is not for restaurants that used to be open, barbers to cut my barbaric growth, bookshops in which to browse, sporting events to attend, festive gatherings on weekends. No, dear friends, the pining, the longing, the yearning, the memory is *all* for the joy, the exuberance, the camaraderie, the companionable silence that those of us who are unfortunate enough to have "male" on our driving licences, is a plea for the dump run to be as it was. Come to think of it, Nigel, the shooting of plastic into space may demand a rethink on that very basis.

There is a sun out there into which I must go.

Throwing Things Away

Warren was, and hopefully still is, a wonderful fellow. Friendly, open-hearted, everybody's pal, he would inevitably cheer people up. One could be tired and down after a hard day's work and in would walk Warren, a presence that forbade doom and gloom.

In the early 1980s, I was living in a Youth Hostel in Bunbury, South-West Australia. I was a concrete worker, which was physically tiring. I would come home at night, shower and join the travelling public in the communal kitchen.

One night, Warren arrived in the kitchen just ecstatic. He had shopped at Coles and discovered they were selling flagons of white wine for $5. He persuaded me to join him for a drink. It was hard to refuse Warren. So, we sat down in the communal lounge. Warren unscrewed the top and threw it into the garbage.

"We won't be needing that again."

Throwing things away can be dangerous!

So, before I retired, I was right up there with the most poorly-organized teachers in the world. However, I did not throw things away. Occasionally, I came across a lesson that really gelled with the children. They became excited and enthralled, and both teacher and class ended up in a state of flow. So a resolution was set that when the lesson was over, I would file the plan for future use. Thereby was the problem. I would file the thing in my large filing cabinet. It would be nestling in a comfortable filing system, a pearl of wisdom lying in wait for October of the following year. Self-satisfied smiles, smug inner congratulation, deep sigh of relief at something less to think about cometh the hour in the following year. When the following year came, I would remember the brilliance of the lesson and reach in my filing cabinet for the plan. Dear Reader, you've guessed it, it was nowhere to be found. I rummaged and I searched. The furrow on my brow became deeper, the fluster in my desperation became harsher, the irritation in my soul became desperate. Inevitably and eventually, I gave up and flopped down at my desk to spend an unhappy hour reinventing the wheel. I may as well have recycled the thing from the previous year, thrown it away.

I thought it was just me. Then Collingwood went all technological, and I had to embrace or die. So I battled my way through jargon and systems and became a bit computer literate, enough to get by. Then along came the computer department who told us that, because systems become so insecure so quickly, we must change our passwords every six weeks or so. My gab did gape, my head did slump. I had just made ends meet and somebody was moving the ends. I could NOT complain because that would have been simply the old boy who couldn't keep up with the programme, a chuckle of ageism from behind a hand from one young colleague to another. But, Dear Reader, I was pleasantly surprised because I discovered that the young and the savvy were just as up in arms at the change as I was and were confident enough to voice it. I breathed a sigh when it was announced that the password issue was not going to necessitate a frequent change. Something I would not have to discard.

So, I became a computer evangelist with passwords for everything from magazine subscriptions to teacher certification. I would be writing down new passwords willy-nilly. Useful, eh! Not a bit of it. I could never remember where I had written them. Could I not have had a notebook with the title something like:

> **"The Davidson Password Book So the Stupid Bastard Doesn't Forget Where He Has Written Them Down."**

Or is that a bit excessive?

Years ago, Irene's Auntie Joyce came to stay from Warwick in England. While she was here, we decided to hide our four passports in a safe place. Accordingly, we wrapped them up, placed them in a Tupperware jug, and positioned them somewhere between the hammer and the saw on our tool rack in the boiler room. We asked Auntie Joyce to witness this. Why? So that when we could not remember where we had hidden them we could make a phone call to her in England and she could tell us! Oh dear, oh dear! What a rigmarole, what a flaw, what a schmoz! We have fixed that at last. Alison and Grant have their own passports. Irene keeps hers separate from mine. I know where my passports are. We had to fix this system partly because poor old Auntie Joyce, at the remarkable age of ninety-something, having had a good long life, went and died on us. Giving her a phone call now would be a smidge difficult!

If nothing else, the pandemic **has** resulted in the creation and "safe-place" protection of a password notebook. I know where it is. I have not thrown it away.

I love words, and I love experiencing new words. So, dear friends, I am always dipping into dictionaries or Googling. It is so logical and reasonable for a system to be organized alphabetically. So why can I not have organized my worksheets thus, my passwords thus, my life thus?! Trouble is that one has to remember the title, and that is where the difficulty lies. So, I have taken the lazy route and passed the buck. When I was a teacher, I used to share my lessons when I remembered to. I would give them to colleagues in hopes that when I could not find them the following year they could. Irene has a filing system and it works. What used to be exclusively mine is now ours when "ours" is really a euphemism for "hers." It is an abnegation of responsibility. I need the sign on my desk reading:

"The buck stops with Irene."

It is not, Dear Reader, a happy state of mind.

There Will Come a Time!

There will come a time, Dear Reader, when we will look back upon the early months of 2020. We will take a deep breath, slump back in our couches, flop our heads onto the cushion and wonder what happened to us. At that moment, we will probably finally realize that what we experienced was what every last one of us on the planet experienced. Nobody escaped, nobody was unaware, nobody was totally safe. There was no dark and gloomy foreshadowing, no ominous musical score, no building of tension, no explosion of turmoil. All seemed the same but suddenly it wasn't. We were caught between a rock and a hard place.

Habits become important at this time, do they not? I have no need to shave every morning, and yet I do. Does the bed need to be made? It doesn't, but it is. I don't need to write this blog, but I enjoy the challenge. Dear Reader, I hope you are not offended, but you are serving a need. My writing is selfish. I hope that it gives you pleasure, but I understand completely if you reach for the "delete" button as soon as you see it. There will come a time when we are free of this virus, life will take a more normal turn, and I shall disappear from your air waves. We are all different. Writing and reading, a bore and a drudge to many, is a cathartic release to me. So I owe you a debt of thanks for taking the time to read them. I am naturally of a happy and optimistic disposition. It is hard to be otherwise considering the wonderful neighbours, coffee drinkers, colleagues, parents and children I have had dealings with over the years. Generally, people have hearts of gold. They reach out to others. They want to make others feel good and, in doing so, feel good themselves.

The current crisis has done so much to restore my faith in human nature and humble me as to my own inadequacies. So, I have been critical of Millennials just as many of them have been critical of selfish baby boomers. In those generalizations, the individual is forgotten. I don't care when you were born, where you were born, what your belief system is, what the colour of your skin is, what your sexual orientation is. What offends me is that someone would insult my intelligence and accuse me of being anti any of those "groupings." To me, there are no groupings, there are only people. People are frail and fallible. People are not perfect.

When our son, Grant, returned from playing in the Under 19 World Cup Rugby Championship in Dubai in 2006, we were so proud of his athletic achievements. We were, however, more proud when he told us that the older guy who was delivering fresh towels to his hotel room called him "Sir." He told him that nobody of that man's age would ever be allowed to call him, an eighteen-year-old, "Sir."

I hope that this time of crisis, dear friends, will finally allow us to stop looking up to people who do not deserve our respect; that we finally realize there is as much wisdom from below as there is from above. Jeff Beck wrote this song many years ago:

"Dear one the world is waiting for the sunrise.
Every rose is covered with dew.
And while the world is waiting for the sunrise,
And my heart is calling you."

The comedian Billy Connolly added to that by saying:

"The world is waiting for the sunrise. It's
1976, and the world is still waiting."

I hope this pandemic means we wait no longer. If, for example, one doesn't take care of the poorest then their poverty and illness begins to affect us all. If we do not take care of what is happening in the back garden it has a way of encroaching into the front. Therefore, Disunited States of America, spend the money and create an universal health system for all; practice the jingoistic patriotism you preach and laud through military parades and national anthems at football games, so that every African American who has nothing and every Latino who is working three jobs understands that the powers that be are on their sides. There is no individual who is larger than the whole. We may, as individuals, make our own way in the world, but at some time we are going to need the help of other people. Allow us to have that help because "no man is an island." I want my leaders to stand up and say that they are going to try such and such. It may not work, it may be wrong, but we are going to try it. I want them to say that their ego is unimportant, that your loved one is my deepest concern, nothing or nobody matters more. Please don't play or toy with my family and friends.

I hope this is the time when the world finally comes together, the time when we finally recognize the value of honesty, the time when people recognize there is a great deal of wisdom in neighbourhoods that should be carried across into international institutions.

I believe, dear friends, that the time has come now for the sunrise.

Have a great day.

Narrow Paths and Broad Ways

Walking to the cheese shop this morning, I decided on a short cut. Betwixt hedge and fire station there is a tennis court. It is such a narrow path that it is impossible to walk through it without brushing hedge or fence or both. There was nobody to socially distance from, so I risked the three minutes or so to barrel on down it. Such everyday occurrences these days serve as an allegory for how we are living our lives. We have been narrowed into a smaller world through our isolation; over the last few weeks our experiences have been humdrummed into the murally mundane. And yet—and yet—here are the words of Richard Lovelace who wrote them from prison in 1642:

> *"Stone walls do not a prison make,*
> *Nor iron bars a cage."*

Life these days can seem so much "like finding a shadow in a blackout," but I have had so many wonderful exchanges with complete strangers while out walking. I wonder if I would have had similar pleasant encounters if we were ***not*** all in the same boat, facing the same issues. Though much divides us, much also brings us together. This morning, a young mum smiled happily at her wee boy as he had found a hill on which to use his scooter. She and I had a nice exchange. Social distancing, one at a time, at Doug's cheese shop was well planned. I threatened to sue him if the

Davidson waistline budded into expanded growth as a result of his products. Doug did not crack a smile, but his eyes twinkled as he contemplated a retort. I am still awaiting his riposte. I know I will get one next week if I return. Outside the cheese store, an ancient biker was helmeted, beleathered and awaiting his turn. I thanked him for his patience. He smiled back and explained he was renowned for it. On the way there I had phoned my friend, Heather, from the foot of her driveway. She came out. We had a quick crossword exchange. She was awaiting a call from her husband, Nigel, who was at work. Narrow experiences but broad smiles.

I remember the story of a young man who took the wrong path. He was only doing his job and one could not fault his determination. It could all have gone so well. Back in the days when one could order a sort of kissogram, he was the poor student who was earning some money to help supplement something other than Kraft Dinner. You will remember the idea: "Shania Twain" would turn up for your buddy's thirtieth birthday. "Elvis Presley" would come bursting out of a cake when Gina turned sixty years old. That sort of thing.

The church was full for the London wedding of a popular young couple who were very much in love. As befits such an occasion, the pews were crowded, bride's family and friends on one side, groom's people on the other. They had reached the point in the service where hearts miss a beat, that time when the minister asks if anybody knows of any just cause why the couple cannot be joined in holy wedlock. There are always a few moments of nervous silence after the question has been asked, are there not? At that moment, the heavy wooden entrance door to the church opened with accompanying creaking on ancient hinges. There was a sharp collective intake of breath, and the congregation turned its universal head away from the wedding party to the door behind them. There in the doorway, with a ring of bright sunlight behind him—an aura—stood a space-suited man. He was "Neil Armstrong" ready for his one small step and his one giant leap. The audience looked puzzled and confused, but their bated breath brooked no interruption. Laboriously, the spaceman, more equipped for lunar gravity than that of the Earth, clumped his way to the front of the church. When he eventually arrived and effectively became part of the wedding party, the minister exclaimed loudly and with annoyance:

"What are you doing here? What do you want?"

The apparition answered, but because of his helmet and visor, his reply was an incomprehensible muffled mumble. Then the awkward silence returned, only eventually broken as the spaceman ponderously creaked and squeaked an about turn and clumped his way out of the church without so much as a muttered "By your leave…."

It later transpired that the employee had mixed up the event and the venue. He had followed a narrow path believing he was in the right and everybody else was wrong. He should have realized at the church door that something was awry. He should have taken a broader path, a wider way, cut his losses turned on his moon boots and rechecked his destination outside. But he persisted, reinforcing his faux pas with every forward clump of his weighted boot.

What an awkward moment. But what, dear friends, a great story for the newlyweds to tell their children and their grandchildren down the years. If it had been our wedding, Irene and I would have wanted *Lost in Space* man in all of the photographs. The narrow worry of the moment would have given way to the broader tales of the years thereafter. Sometimes the straight and narrow leads us to the broad, sunny uplands, does it not, my friends?

> *"The virtue of the river lies neither in one*
> *pool nor place, but throughout its length."*
> **Kim** *by Rudyard Kipling*

Have a great day. Pete.

Anna Robertson (1860 – 1961)

*"Paintin' is not important. The important
thing is keepin' busy."*

T he above quotation is the only thing I know about
Anna Robertson. I found it in one of my books and
would have thought no more about it except that I was
struck by the length of her life. People over the centuries have
occasionally lived for 100 years or more. If they had been
lucky enough to have done so 500 or 1000 years ago, then I
imagine that, apart from the occasional war, visitation of the
plague, civil unrest or a revolution or two, not much would
have changed in their long lives. But between 1860 and 1961
would have been a period of mind-blowing change.

In 1860, Canada was seven years from being founded, the
Americans had not yet bought Alaska from the Russians.
Italy and Germany had yet to become unified countries. A
civil war was about to be fought to free the African slaves in
the United States. Queen Victoria still had some forty years
to reign in the United Kingdom. Charles Dickens had just
written *Great Expectations*. Two explorers, Speke and Grant,
set off to find the source of the River Nile. The British Open
Golf Championship began, way before any large sporting
championships. In the USA, which wasn't united and did
not have the number of states it now has, the Pony Express
made its first delivery, a Bible. The world's first ocean-going,

iron-hulled battleship was launched. Great Britain found another use for its newspapers when the first Fish 'n Chips shop was opened. Gustav Mahler and Annie Oakley were born.

When Anna Robertson died in 1961, Yuri Gagarin had become the first person to orbit the Earth. I do not know what the Russian for *"Oh look, there's the source of the Nile,"* is, but there was no bush whacking and blundering through miles of rough country for Gagarin; he just pointed as he passed overhead. John Fitzgerald Kennedy, as president of the USA, looked a wee smidge different from Abraham Lincoln, Ms. Robertson's first president. Kruschev was about to position nasty-looking missiles at the Bay of Pigs on the island of Cuba. The only missiles around in 1860 were a rather superior form of cannonball. Nuclear submarines were about to become all of the rage, joining Elvis Presley and a young pop group from Liverpool called The Beatles. Princess Diana, George Clooney, Wayne Gretzky and Barack Obama were all born in 1961.

So, in the hundred years or so that Anna Robertson was kicking around the planet, somebody invented the horseless carriage. The Wright brothers got off the ground in a biplane. People became so confident in their ability to overcome nature that they didn't put enough lifeboats on the *Titanic*. They invented newer and nastier ways of killing people with the result that millions died in war. Antibiotics saved many lives. Infant mortality was not as prevalent, and many more women survived childbirth. Along came Fleming and penicillin and a plethora of antibiotics so that many diseases that had been fatal were survivable. The Suez and Panama Canals made the world a smaller place, and John Logie Baird invented the television. Of course, dear reader, there is much to be added to this list.

What a life of change, eh! And, oh yes, one could throw a pandemic in there for good measure!

Sun is shining. Have a day, my friends.

Glocalization

When I was a lad around about the time when Pontius was a pilate and cholesterol hadn't been invented, I went to school in the little town of Clevedon in Somerset. I had grown away from my Scottish accent and was no longer labelled as "Scotus furiosus" by the history teacher, Mr. King. I was befriended by Paul Toogood whose grandmother was Mrs. Hale whose husband had founded Hales Cakes. There was his factory on the outskirts of the town. Many years later I was driving on the far north coast of Scotland towards the village of Durness. Single-track roads with passing places, meandering around blind corners and vigorous ups and downs. Around one corner on a misty mizzling drizzle of a day, came a large delivery van emblazoned with its company's name. Yes, indeed, friends, there, 700 miles from home, was a Hales Cakes truck. Now the country of my birth has many flaws. Its people have fought amongst themselves far more than against any foreign enemy. They were cleared from the land to be replaced by sheep during the Clearances. The Orcadians were recruited by the Hudson's Bay Company in droves; they welcomed the chance to seek their fortune in northern Canada as an opportunity to keep warm, not to mention that they thought that HBC stood for the "Horny Boys Club." They became explorers, ships' engineers, colonizers—almost anything to get away. And Samuel Johnson famously said that the "greatest prospect that the Scotsman has is the high road that leads to England." But, dear friends, they **can and do** make a tasty homemade jam sponge cake!!? Healthy Highland wifies often appear on the streets in their aprons surrounded by clouds of flour as they dust their hands off. Why would they want a plastic-wrapped and cardboard-boxed equivalent from a long way away? The Scots can and do make magnificent sponge cakes of their own. Who on Earth in their right mind would send a truckload of the things all of the way from England? For me, that was the beginning of the realization that globalization was heavily under way. Then, of course, I saw billions of dollars being made for Scotland through the massive exporting of Scotch whisky all over the world. One can buy a bottle of Dalwhinnie in North Vancouver and, believe me, there is nothing at Dalwhinnie but heather, wind, rain and a distillery. Ask Bruce Angus.

So that was globalization and another kick in the high streets for local businesses. In the current situation globalization is on hold, so we are confined to our local areas, nestled in our neighbourhoods, grooming our gardens and burning out the engines on our vacuum cleaners. No, my friends, "glocalization" is not a spelling error, nor is it a word I have invented. It is also not a recent word but one that sprung up about a decade ago in an attempt to rethink mankind's ridiculous, random assertion that it is good business practice to send a sponge cake several hundred miles across a country. Let's face it, in the old days, corn got to market in two ways either on the back of a horse-pulled wagon or in a pig.

Ahhhh, you say, but what about Marco Polo? Those of you who smoke will talk about tobacco from Virginia? What about Europeans and their love of the imported potato?

Well, you are right, and while I am thinking about that issue, I think I'll take a walk down to the cheese man and see if he has, at last, received his delivery of Gjetost, that wonderful Norwegian cheese that waters old Davidson's taste buds. It is shipped to Oslo by truck or train from rural Norway, from whence it is flown to Montreal before being flown to Vancouver and finally delivered to Doug's local cheese shop. As I said, friends, it is good to buy local produce from local producers.

Sun is shining, heat is generating. Think I'll away and bake a cake, my friends.

A Sunday Drive with Granny

"You will go most safely in the middle." Ovid

My grandmother was a terrible driver. She had never learned to reverse so never did. She drove the roads believing she should straddle the white lines in the middle. It remains one of my most terrifying experiences to be driven out with her to a Sunday lunch. She believed that the middle of the road was her spiritual home, and I was terrified that if we had a head-on collision it was likely to lead to *my* spiritual home as well. However, sitting in the middle can be a good place to be. If one is not, for instance, blinded by a total idealism then it does allow one to analyse ideas and see merits and demerits beyond the limits of a political, religious, jingoistic fanaticism. It is perhaps easier to sit on a fence if one is not expected to lead. Is it OK to be an indecisive leader, to watch and observe, continuously hedging one's bets, and to answer pointed questions by not answering pointed questions?

During my working life, it always used to worry me when the organization, in my case the school, created a new post, a "Minister for Administrative Affairs," to steal something from a British sitcom. Let us say that there had been a "Coordinator for Curriculum Development" suddenly arrive at the beginning of the school year. Suddenly, teachers received a bevy of new emails and were suddenly involved in meetings large and small, soon being asked to create something and report back in a month on that creation. I never had the courage to put my head above the parapet and state categorically that I already had a job and that if I was to do that one properly then I did not need another one on top of it. None of us, certainly, needed to attend yet another decision-less meeting. New leaders always need to make a splash, Dear Reader, I just question whether the rest of us needed to get wet as a result.

I met with friends the other day and the question of leadership came up. Can it be learned or is it natural? It is the old nature versus nurture debate. As a rule, I have always been suspicious of leaders who are desperate to become leaders. I have had more faith in those unwilling participants who suddenly find themselves thrust into leadership positions because of some unfathomable reason. Here in BC, Dr. Bonnie Henry springs to mind. She is there on our TV screens every night because of our pandemic, and she is doing a very good job. I do not think she is seeking the limelight. I expect that when all this is over, she will fade from view, and I would be very surprised if she milked her new-found celebrity. She strikes me as being a "leader" of conviction. In this case, the conviction is based purely and simply on the science of the pandemic.

Conviction politicians can be very dangerous leaders. Tony Benn was a left-wing Labour politician back in the day. He was polls apart from Prime Minister Margaret Thatcher in his beliefs. Yet he had a grudging admiration for the Iron Lady because she was a conviction politician. She rode roughshod over objections to a policy based on what she would have thought was pettiness getting in the way of the bigger picture. The weakness and strength of the bigger picture is that frequently the little people get trampled under foot. The minorities of the world will always suffer more when it comes about that the sunny upland is a peak too far for them.

At times of crisis, suck it and see, havering and hovering, and lurking with no intent becomes a frustrating option and one which can result in lives lost. My granny and I were lucky there was not much traffic on the road in the north of Scotland on a Sunday. Had it been a truck-filled, work-driven, business-busyness midweek dash for a pub lunch, sitting in the middle of the road would have been an option with calamitous consequences. There are peacetime leaders and there are war time leaders. We tend to forget Winston Churchill's Gallipoli blunder in the First World War or his belief that the troops should be sent in during the 1926 General Strike or the diversion of food to the army so that millions starved in WWII. This hero of the 20th century did not lack for decisiveness; he was not a fence sitter. It just so happened that he is remembered for the decisiveness of his victorious leadership in WWII and not his decisive blunders that preceded that war.

True leadership does not expect others to do what the leader would not do herself. True leadership is humble. True leadership is not threatened by the confidence of others, and it allows innovation and initiative to have its head. True leadership recognizes when no decision is the right decision and, equally, when some decision is the right one. True leadership admits when it was wrong and works hard to make amends.

Finally, true leadership orders one's seventy-something grandma to pull over, gets out of the car and explains to his wise old relative that driving in the middle of the road is going to result in devastation. True leadership is being less frightened of one's grandmother than the possibility of death and destruction. True leadership recognizes that a Sunday drive is never a time to be in between, neither one side or the other. The white line in the middle of the road is not the fence to straddle. Have a good day, friends.

Frail Heroes

The beauty of humanity lies in its frailty and fallibility, does it not, Dear Reader? It is always a sad day when somebody for whom we have so much respect falls off the perch of perfection. Labelling somebody a "sporting hero" is a particularly dangerous process because we have appropriated one outstanding characteristic and suddenly given them others. Why would we expect that Wayne Gretzky or Michael Jordan have any more inside information or any more moral standing than the rest of us? One is always suspicious when a celebrity becomes a political pontificator or a climate change campaigner. Sure and all they have that right as the rest of us do, but just because they are a movie star or a famed novelist or a TV reporter does not automatically guarantee them a respected place in a parade of the pantheon of punditry.

Robbie Burns is one of my heroes. I am safe with him because he has been dead for over 200 years. He can now no longer fail. Was he a flawed human being? Absolutely he was. His frailties would have seen him crucified in our current media, would have found roguishness in every perceptive utterance, every naïve nuance. I love Shakespeare's observation in *Hamlet*:

> *"He was a man, take him for all and all, I shall not look upon his like again."*

Of course, he refers to women too. I love the recognition in this that we are all unique. There is nobody in this world, nor has there ever been, anybody quite like us. Our individuality is something nobody can take from us.

Bruce Springsteen is a current hero of mine. I have attended three of his concerts over a span of many years and have never yet been disappointed. I love his gifts with language, his praise and understanding of everyday people in everyday life. Yet here is a man who suffers terribly from depression. He has it all—money, happy marriage, successful children—and yet when he is not performing or writing, he feels himself to be worthless and his life to be meaningless. Perversely, his personal battles and his honesty about them uplift him further in my eyes.

Working with children for a long time, one always accepted that one was the adult and one was partly responsible for helping them to make good decisions. I always told them that whatever they did that was wrong or right, they should **never** lie about it. If John hurls a rock at Penny he should come clean. Homework-eating dogs rarely exist, in my opinion. I used to take cash out of the bank to pay for a Tim Hortons treat without it appearing on my bank statement so Irene would not know how much I had spent. Now we are becoming cashless, and that is no longer possible. I had to brazen out the cheese and salami panini I could not resist at Bean Around the World yesterday. I knew where to stop in my parking space this morning because I felt the faint nudge as I hit the front of the car behind me. I was not going to lie if the car owner had seen me, but I did no damage, so dashed away quickly with sneaky glances here and there. After over thirty years of marriage, I should know that hiding that chocolate bar around the house makes no difference because Irene knows it is there even when she doesn't know it is there. And I shall come clean if I am caught having a surreptitious square of the salted caramel dark chocolate I smuggled into the supermarket trolley as I followed Irene's extremely direct shopping list this morning.

The tragedy of life is that if one errs then not everyone has the opportunity to make up for one's mistakes. John Profumo was a British MP in the 1960s. He became embroiled in a scandal that rocked the British government and establishment. "The Profumo affair" was front page news for a long time thereafter. He disappeared from the public eye. He died in 2006 at the age of ninety-one, having devoted his post-political life to charity and accumulating many awards and much recognition. Lord Longford said, "I felt more admiration for him than for all the men I've known in my lifetime." He had time to make up for his penchant for peccadilloes, and he used his time wisely.

It will always be difficult for me to take off my rose-coloured spectacles to view my heroes in a critical light, but there is enough written out there to reassure me when I have so to do.

Tenses

I am in the last of the trilogy written by Hilary Mantel, *The Mirror and the Light*. They are historical novels tracing the career of Thomas Cromwell, who was an adviser to King Henry VIII in the 1500s. Such events were almost half a millennium ago and have no impact on us now. Ahhh but they do, Dear Reader, they do!! Every year the wealthy citizens of London fled the city to avoid the plague, and they distanced themselves from their wives in childbirth. They socially distanced. Henry VIII flung out the Church of Rome and made himself head of the Church in England, a title the current queen still holds. Some of the many tourist attractions of England are the old monasteries Henry reformed and stole and destroyed. Too many fat friars robbing from the poor to make themselves rich; too much hypocrisy in the rule of celibacy; too much hypocrisy full stop! It would seem likely that the church leaders of the day would have had private jets if they could, a la current TV evangelicals who seem to be storing up riches on Earth pretty well. "The more things change, the more they stay the same." Oh, and is there still hypocrisy surrounding celibate priests?

I don't know whether it is true that those who do not learn from history are condemned to repeat it. It is true, however, that human beings are the same as they always were. The idea that we have a moral superiority over our forebears is, I feel, a wrong one. To me, it is up to Plato and his ilk to help organize laws and government to protect us from ourselves, to suborn our baser instincts to a moral and common good. Peace, order and good government are what most people desire. Thomas Jefferson said:

> *"Every difference of opinion is not a difference of principle."*

The Life and Death of Democracy is an excellent book by John Keane. Like much that one reads, little is remembered, and much is forgotten, particularly if one possesses an undisciplined, disorganized mind like I do. But I do write down salient points, things that strike me at the time, and this book has furnished me with so much that seems relevant today. Two hundred years ago, Monsieur de Jaucourt stated:

> *"It is the fate of the government to become almost infallibly the prey of the ambition of certain citizens or of strangers and so to exchange precious liberty for the greatest servitude."*

Hmmm! Don't know about you but that blast from the distant past is setting some alarm bells ringing in my present mind! No system of government is perfect, and there are many different styles of democracy. Those of you who have watched the Danish political drama *Borgen* will have some insights into the machinations of proportional representation. We have had our own plebiscites here in BC as to whether it is a system we may want to adopt. Critics say PR is a system that becomes too hidebound by compromise and negotiation and therefore nothing gets done and frustration sets in.

Then there are those who say that governments who do nothing are excellent! "Laissez-faire" leads to progress without the interfering hands of government. Some may say minority governments already give us checks and balances and that a hung parliament is excellent because it doesn't allow for sweeping changes.

It would be nice to have speed bumps on Tatlow Avenue, but I don't know whether I want to set up a demonstration at the junction of Marine Drive to get them. Local government is such a good and useful force except when it becomes the "not-in-my-backyard" variety or when the nosy neighbour complains because we put our garbage out the night before pick up. It is far too easy for a "do-gooder" to become a "tin-pot dictator." That is why we need checks and balances, a tradition of law and order, a general consensus that is healthily **never** a unanimous consensus. We should never be afraid of speaking truth to power even though our "truth" is somebody else's "falsehood." Any rate, before I disappear into a deep hole of pretentious claptrap I will end this with some facts I found interesting. According to Keane, the following is true:

> *"In 1900 there were 25 'restricted' democracies accounting for one-eighth of the world's population. In 1950 there were 22 democracies; one-third of the world's population. In the year 2000, there were 119 democratic countries out of 192."*

But, Dear Reader, there are democratic countries that simply are not! It is worth noting that Keane also states that in 1941 during the height of World War II, there were only eleven democracies left in the world. For this very reason, it seems it is important for us to remember our past and take note of our present because we do not want our future to be like building a campfire on ice. The world is a tense place at the moment, so let us consider our tenses.

Have a day, friends.

Engagement and Charisma

How many of us have watched and tried to listen to a speaker either in the company of others or on radio or TV and found our eyes glazing over and our mind drifting away? I am the guy who joined a long line for lunch at Sun Peaks, offering to pay for lunch. What did Jennifer want? Anything but clam chowder. What did Jennifer get? Clam chowder! Shopping list at home: "We have plenty milk. Don't buy milk." I bought milk. What is the message here? I guess it is that Davidson will only act upon the last word spoken, so when ordering lunch or groceries only name things you want. It should be easy for Irene to understand as she has known since the early 1980s, poor woman. She has no excuse. Jennifer has every excuse under the sun. Not her job to understand how the peculiar Davidson mind works.

I am reading *The Songlines* by Bruce Chatwin, and the subject matter is interesting to me. I was in Australia in the 1980s, indeed in Alice Springs where the beginning of his story is written. His writing is brilliant and beautiful and nuanced and calming. If Mr. Chatwin were writing about the inner workings of the vacuum cleaner, then I am convinced I would be equally enthralled by his story. What is the secret of a great writer or a great teacher or a great storyteller? We know they can engage us, but surely the writer's charisma cannot make its way onto the printed page. But, to me, most surely it can and does. Robert Macfarlane, Charles Dickens,

George MacDonald Fraser are but three authors who make Irene think I have left her. And, in a way, she is right! They transport me to another world, another place, another time. They have the gift of taking me away in their virtual time machine, and I am with them on their journey.

Similarly, I can listen to raconteurs for hours. The late Peter Ustinov has me spellbound; I cannot tear myself away from Billy Connolly; I cannot get enough of Gwynne Dyer's political and historical insights. On the other side of the coin, there are people who have talked long and hard about subjects in which I am really interested, but I have been bored to snoredom. The gift of the gab, the ability to stand in front of somebody and convince your audience that your product is matchless and you simply have to buy it, is wonderful. It is also very dangerous. There is much demagoguery present in the world's recent history, rhetoric that has lead people to kill and destroy and be killed and destroyed in their turn. Some believe that with the amount of screen time so many of us devote ourselves to we are in danger of separating ourselves from the natural world, a world which we are part of whether we like it or not. Very few of us bother to read the small print, so that specific neglect often invalidates warranties and insurance policies. On a bigger scale, government employees are at risk of missing things that might be important or, perhaps worse, make a meal of things that aren't. I hope that during the current pandemic our western attention span does not lose focus on other world affairs. Democratic western parliaments *do* need to physically sit sooner rather than later, we should not let the refugee crises fall by the wayside, and we should take further note about what is happening in Hong Kong. It would be sad if we dropped too many other balls because the world was over-focused on one big medicine ball. Linda Stone said:

"We live in a world of continuous partial attention."

I hope governments are employing people who are **over**-focused to the point of fanaticism on their area of expertise whether that be finding a vaccine or the machinations of leadership in mainland China or the Brexit negotiations or solving the homeless situation. We need some Cyclopean individuals with their one eye on one goal with nary time for a glance from side to side.

I am a lucky man. I know a great number of interesting people. Mornings at coffee, evening walks, chats with neighbours over the fence and in driveways, vignettes from Scotland, descriptions from Australia, humorous chats from England. All of these contacts never fail to interest and amuse. There is so much life experience and knowledge, so many new instances and new stories to tell. I always leave these conversations with things to think about and often with a smile on my face. Like most of you, I have video conferenced with friends and family. It is great to have that facility but, truth be known, it ain't one jot like the real thing. We are humans and we need the nuances of the face, the presence of the body language. All of those qualities can only add to engagement and charisma.

Hinterlands

Simon Barnes is, by a long stretch, the finest sports journalist I have ever read. Why? Because he has a perspective on sport that places it in a spot where it is very firmly *not* the most important aspect of life on the planet. Nevertheless, he is not at all without respect for the achievements of athletes. He understands the dedication it takes for them to get to the top of their tree and, more importantly, to stay there. He reports on Djokovic celebrating yet another Grand Slam win by breaking off one square from a bar of dark chocolate and popping it in his mouth; such is his dietary regime. Similarly, he coined the word "Redgrave" to conflate character, grit and determination. Steve Redgrave won five rowing gold medals at five separate Olympics. So, Mr. Barnes admires one-eyed dedication but also admires people and athletes who have a "hinterland." What is a hinterland? Well, Dear Reader, a hinterland is a passion outside of work, and a crutch for busy, stressful lives. So many people don't have one.

Winston Churchill famously used his painting palette as a release from the strains of being a wartime leader. He also re-read the six novels of Jane Austen. Talking of politicians, the leader of the British Labour Party, Hugh Gaitskill, who was gloriously intelligent, a child prodigy, was being walked in his pram one day when a friend of his mother's peered in to admire the youngster and "cooochee-coo" him under his chin. Gaitskill looked up and is reported to have said:

> **"Madam, soon shall you and I be lying each within our narrow tomb."**

History does not relate the reaction of the woman concerned, so it may be an urban legend! But it makes a good story. It also shows that if Gaitskill had not suffered a premature death, he quite possibly would have been a prime minister with a hinterland.

I have always been interested in work colleagues who talk about things other than work. In my first teaching post it was an unwritten rule that discussions about work did not come into the staffroom at recess or lunchtime. I always had more time for the head of the school who would talk to me about his or her hike on the weekend or something they had seen, done or read that had nothing to do with teaching. Such conversations released me from the stresses of the blinkered work issue that was eating me up at the time, they placed things in a better and wiser perspective. Novelist Ian Rankin had this to say about Inspector John Rebus, the hero of his best sellers:

> **"He loathed his free time, dreaded Sundays off. He lived to work, and in a very real sense, he worked to live too, the much-maligned Protestant work ethic. Subtract work from the equation, and the day became flabby, like releasing jelly from its mould." From Let it Bleed.**

We have, no doubt, all come across the workaholic. My cousin, James, an ex-pat engineer, could always be phoned up and found in his office at 10:00 p.m. so I am reliably informed! The trouble with workaholics is that they expect everybody else to be like them. A boss who is a workaholic is the worst. The workforce is suddenly expected to devote hours of their downtime at the drop of a hat based on the mistaken belief that the be-all and end-all is the company or the school. How many unfortunates have tried to impress the boss by being at their desks early and late? There are those who work long hours who are not as effective as those who work shorter. I left Collingwood at the same time as a male colleague who, after he had dismissed his class at the end of the day, spent an hour preparing and marking for the next day. He was pulling out of the school between 4:30 and 5:00 p.m. every day. He was and is very, very good at his job. He has a young family, a mountain bike, a surfboard and a set of skis. He has a healthy hinterland. I like the following quotation:

> *"If you are distressed by anything external, the pain is not due to the thing itself but to your own estimate of it; and this you have the power to revoke at any moment."*

As a wise colleague used to say to me when I was filled with angst over something, "It's only a pay cheque, Pete." He was right, and he is one of the best science teachers I have ever seen enthrall and excite a class of children. You will note I have not attributed the above quotation. I wanted to give you a moment to ponder it. Some modern psychologist, some psychiatric researcher spouting forth her current research, a well-regarded government expert? No, Dear Friend, Marcus Aurelius dropped this pearl 2,000 years ago. There is nothing new under the sun.

So yet again, Dear Reader, if you are taking the time to read the spoutings of Peter Davidson, you are bearing witness to a bit of a hypocrite. When I retired, I went through the emotional turmoil, the grieving of somebody who has suffered a loss. I spent an unhappy summer questioning the decision. Finally, I was able to come to terms with it. Fact really was that I was missing my colleagues who had become my friends. I was not missing the bureaucracy of teaching. I had come to realize that if I did not get out soon then what little credibility I had would be lost. I would cease to be an effective part of the system and would end up being supported by kind colleagues who were going that extra mile to prop up the old guy. I did not want to be a burden. But I was lucky. I have not lost touch with my colleagues. I do have a hinterland and excellent neighbours and friends beyond school. I do have interests and hobbies and a hinterland. The fact is that if you take the time to read this "blog" every day, you have become a victim of one of my "hinterlands"!!

Enjoy the sun, my friends; it is almost summer.

Missing!

Two thousand or so years ago when the Greeks headed east to fight the Persians, the wars were long and drawn out. The Greek soldiers, children of the Mediterranean Sea, had no choice but to be absent from home for months, sometimes years. Then came the day when they finally were on the way back to the islands and "my" lands of their own country. One Greek soldier, no doubt among many, had that magical moment in his life when he came over a rise on a hill and there set before him was what he had grown up with, a vision he never thought to see again:

"Thalassa, Thalassa," he exclaimed, "The sea, the sea!"

So often, as in the words of the song, we don't know what we've got til it's gone. Hunkered down as we all have been, the Davidson thoughts roamed to what he had been missing over the last three months. Some little pleasures we notice more than others. Now that Dr. Henry has eased our restrictions, Irene and I have thought about taking a drive up to Squamish to sit by the river and see if there are any eagles about. Maybe try to get into one of the very eclectic cafés in the downtown area of that wee town and marvel at the people who meet and greet there.

We all miss the ability to move as we wish. I was locked down in Scotland when all of this began and missed four weeks of my journey because I came home early. But all that I have missed is mitigated by a book or a crossword. Lining-up and waiting for something is always an opportunity to get lost in a book. So, I am lucky because I have shelves of books, many of which have been dog-eared through re-reading. But reading is always that much better if one is able to discuss what one has read with another, is it not? So, good company is part of all that we have been missing. That stimulation is an essential part of being a human being as far as I am concerned. But then, I think again. I *have* been mixing with people on a frequent basis. It is an illusion that this has not been the case. All that has been required to meet people has been a bit of planning, a piece of forethought. Meeting friends at the café has required a drive rather than a walk as there is not an open washroom. Dermot's carport, the Wootton's back garden, a backpack with a tub of wipes, a face mask and a bottle of water can carry one a long way.

Do Irene and I miss travelling? Well, I have a sense of incompleteness because of my abbreviated UK visit. Irene and I both miss seeing Alison, our daughter in England. I was lucky enough to see her, Irene could not. I have talked before about the German word *"sehnsucht,"* the "seeking to see" that is a part of every traveller's life. Back in the day when explorers spent years from home, they had *sehnsucht*, which was that yearning to be home. After they had been at home for a short while, the feeling returned to them and they had that yearning again but this time to be away and exploring. It is a part of the human condition to never be satisfied, to always be missing something. Many of us do have the wish to "wake from the sleep of habit" as Montaigne would call it. To have a little adventure, to do something we have not been able to do. A friend of mine celebrated his fortieth anniversary on Monday night with a visit to The Keg. It was not a party with friends and family; it was something simple many of us used to take for granted, but it was enough removed from our new normal to be exciting.

One of the things I am missing is a healthy perspective. It is difficult to find a reasonable balance. That which is now writ large in our minds and our thoughts used to be of minor importance or not something we would think of at all. Of equal concern is that which we do not see as being important and yet actually is. Thinking on our feet, finding speedy solutions, engaging in problem-solving at work and play; all facets of life that were honed to a sharpness by everyday usage are blunted and cobwebbed by lack of practice. Blaire Pascal said:

> *"Human sensitivity to little things and insensitivity to the greatest things are signs of a strange disorder."*

Montaigne said:

> *"We are all huddled and concentrated in ourselves, and our vision is reduced to the length of our nose."*

But on the other hand, Spike Milligan rescues us with:

> *"I haven't organized anything today, so nothing can go wrong."*

Thus spoke the man whose epitaph on his grave reads:

"I told you I was ill."

I suppose there is no benefit in pondering on all of those things we miss. We, as human beings, are capable of reasoning and rising above, and "hope springs eternal." We all have some control of who we are and how we act. As Montaigne would have it:

> *"Yet there is no use our mounting on stilts, for on stilts we must still walk on our own legs. And on the loftiest throne in the world we are still sitting only on our own rump."*

For all of our recent travails we are not languishing in a Chinese prison like the two Canadian Michaels, nor are we walking five miles for fresh water. Those are two things I am very happy to miss.

Thinking and Thought

One of the weaknesses and strengths of our current isolated state is that we have so much time to think. How often have we overthought things at work or play with the result being that we end up taking no action and regretting it afterwards. Indeed, how often has the reverse been the case where we have blundered into a situation with both barrels blazing and found it hard to retreat with our dignity intact? I was never a huge fan of *Star Trek*. Leonard Nimoy and his reliance on reasoned logic and absence of humour, heart and soul seemed to me a wonderful portrayal of what is good and bad about humankind. The head of Collingwood School once admitted frustration with the school's motto, "From vision to reality," saying we seemed to lurch "from vision to vision." So many meetings over the years, and I am sure this is the same in other professions, have concluded with no decision other than to meet again in a month's time. Is no decision better than taking a bad decision? That is arguable. Bad decisions can be tweaked and nudged so they produce some semblance of good.

> *"If you can dream and not make dreams your master." Rudyard Kipling*

Geoff Parks owns and operates Camp Summit, which is in Paradise Valley near Squamish. Parkee is a wonderful man, and Collingwood has been attending this camp in

Grade IV for the past ten years. The high ropes, low ropes, archery, problem-solving, biking and so on are finely tuned to the ages and abilities of the children. As one turns a corner between the cabins and the campfire area, there is a fenced-off area that is out of bounds. As adults, several of us have opened the gate to see and experience what is behind it. There is, Dear Reader, an outdoor swimming pool that is totally natural and was created by Parkee and his dream. It functions cleanly and openly with no chlorine or pumping system. It has been there for a few years now but has never ever been used by children coming to camp. Why? Because the health and safety powers that be will not pass it for general usage. Why will they not do so? It is not because there are people at the camp unqualified to supervise children in the water, it is not because the camp has a bad reputation. (Far from it. Its leaders are hand-picked and very professional and empathetic.) It is, Dear Reader, because the health and safety manual has nothing written about such an innovation. It is so creative and new that it is outside of the box. There is no power that be who has devoted the time or the expertise or the courage to approve Parkee's dream. It is a great shame. It was a thought, a process of thinking, a vision that became a reality, and yet it has fallen short.

It surely should be possible for our leaders to learn from history. And if they can't, there are plenty of historians out there who need a job and who would be very happy to whisper sweet somethings into the ears of prime ministers and presidents. A simple example is this current pandemic. History reveals that such events occur every hundred years or so, thus a word to the wise would have given people a better chance to plan and prepare. Lives might have been saved. It is true that there was a plan in place after the Second World War for the de-Nazification of the German people, but so many Germans had only joined the Nazi Party as a way to get on in that society, rather like joining the Masons. They were not necessarily involved in the genocide and atrocities. The victors succeeded in separating the wheat from the chaff and, by and large, bringing the criminals to justice. But Wernher von Braun went from making flying bombs, doodle bugs, to helping put Americans on the moon. It seems that the Americans and their allies in Iraq singularly failed to do the same with members of the Ba'ath Party, forbidding them from any participation in the post-Saddam regime, thus creating a power vacuum and the inevitable rise of ISIS. Maybe this is an oversimplification and an idea that does not survive greater study, but whatever the truth of the matter, the postbellum Iraq does not seem to have been well thought out and is hardly a wonderful success story, is it, Dear Reader?

As Bakewell would have it, "Aspirations aren't strategies." It is amazing how people spring into action when there is a crisis or a pandemic. Suddenly, we have decisions being made, innovations being tried, initiatives working. I am full of admiration for emergency action. But as a Mulgrave teacher was telling me the other day, teachers have received well-deserved praise for how they have acted over the last three months, but when September comes (or August if one teaches at Mulgrave), there needs to be a concrete and thoughtful plan. It will no longer be acceptable to be just managing and all hands to the pump when there has been time to think. "The paradigm must not overwhelm the reality." It has been said when talking about the problems that existed in Iraq:

> *"Everyone got diverted, trying to solve derivatives of the real problem."* **State of Denial** *by Bob Woodward*

I am grateful I have now retired.

By the way, looking at my notebook, this here daily dose of *The Davidson Diaries* is today making its ninetieth appearance. I suppose that this almost counts for three months of meandering through a maze of myriad musings. Some, of course, are absolute nonsense requiring the author to be straitjacketed and bundled away in a van, some are mediocre, and some of them have given me quiet pride. But they are all serving a purpose for me. They give my day a structure and furnish me with a challenge that I like. So, if you have read them, I am grateful, and I thank you for that, but if you are reaching for the "delete" button on a daily basis then I understand. At some point I will be bringing them to an end, possibly I will try for the century, and then I will seek something different.

Just to finish today, and by dint of nothing in particular except that it seems to be raining a lot at the moment, I found the following bit of verse:

> *"The rain it raineth on the just*
> *And also on the unjust fella;*
> *But chiefly on the just, because*
> *The unjust hath the just's umbrella."*
> *Lord Justice Brown*

Level Playing Fields

From the time of conception to our death, there is no such thing as a level playing field. At least that's what it seems to me. Some of us have been born with a silver spoon in our mouths and some not. Some of us have been given every chance of success and some of us have not. It seems to be axiomatic that this is the case. Abject poverty with no access to fresh water, an economy that allows one to scrape a living and no more are ever-present, harsh realities. So many millions of the world's population face little hope of an education. There are times when, as a teacher, I wish I had bitten my tongue.

> *"That's not fair, Mr. Davidson."*
> *"Life's not fair, young fellow."*

That throwaway statement should be thrown away and never used. Except perhaps in the context of a detailed explanation, a ponderous explanation of human strengths and weaknesses that are unlikely to make much difference because all George is interested in is the fact that his mum forgot to pack his lunch. My offer of a tin of sardines to tie him over is indeed not fair! We all know people who seem to act in ways that are completely opposite to their own best interests. Samuel Johnson, writing in the late 1700s, had this to say about his one-time friend, the poet Richard Savage:

> *"By imputing none of his miseries to himself he continued to act upon the same principles and to follow the same path; was never made wiser by his sufferings, nor preserved by one misfortune from falling into another. He proceeded throughout his life to tread the same steps in the same circle, always applauding his past conduct, or at least forgetting it, to amuse himself with phantoms of happiness which were dancing before him, and willingly turned his eye from the light of reason, when it would have discovered the illusion and shown him, what he never wanted to see, his real state."*

This is brilliant. As I re-read it for the umpteenth time, images of people and friends are flashing past my eyes, many of whom were and remain to this day, their own worst enemies. I remember back in the day having children in my class who were labelled "gifted," a most unfortunate moniker to give to any child, or worse, to the child's parents. It became my job at the beginning of the year to find challenges for these children beyond the ordinary curricula, something to stimulate and excite. I always, always failed. Then would come Parent/Teacher Interviews, and the parents would inform me bluntly and with clarity that "He was bored." So, I resolved to enter the classroom on the following day dressed as a clown and doing cartwheels across the floor. I would do a stand-up comic routine. I would enter with a life-size model of a great white shark and pretend to strangle it while pointing out the complexities of its dorsal fins, its gills, its life cycle, the fact that it will drown if pulled backwards, and so forth. Nothing, Dear Reader, worked. So, head down and tail between my legs, I would trek off to Muir's office knowing that, like all good heads of school, he would do his level best to make me feel better. And he did. He told me that no truly gifted child or adult is never, ever bored because they will find challenges and invent challenges where there seem to be none. They will make their own excitement. I often thought that the educational psychologist who had "gifted" those "gifted" titles on those poor children had done them no favours whatsoever. "Giftedness" is a potential. It tends to allow the child to rest on laurels not yet achieved. It suggests to the child that she doesn't have to work. It gets in the way of reaching a potential. It un-levels the playing field. Johnson again:

"To see men we must see their works."

And so often we didn't, Dear Reader, so often we didn't.

I like the fact that I live in a country with a welfare state. I do understand the need for a safety net for those who need a leg up. A civilized society needs a balance between individualism and community support. I always have a hard time with charity. I contribute but really believe that my tax dollars should be doing the work for me. So when I see Homeless Patrick camped outside Tim Hortons hoping for his double/double and his blueberry muffin, I do occasionally buy him such. But he had a job, he had a place to live, there was help at hand. He made a mess of it. So, I have become hard of heart as far as Patrick is concerned, and I developed the belief of a Theodore Dalrymple, who feels that the welfare state:

"Discourages self-examination by encouraging the imputation of all miseries to others and then has a disastrous effect upon human character."

Sadly, there was an ex-colleague recently who reached out to me for $1800 to pay his rent lest he be evicted. I had not heard from him for a couple of years. I was never going to help him financially, but I felt guilty about this. I tried to walk my guilt away and eventually rationalized it. This gentleman had been born and educated in Vancouver. He was sixty-five years of age. He has a working son locally. He received a good education. He has always worked and managed to hold down a job. He has not come here as a refugee from a poverty-stricken country raked by war and famine. For him, Dear Reader, the playing field was pretty level. Obviously, there are the potholes of a failed marriage, mental illness, poor financial decisions along the way. Who knows what hurdles he has had to jump? It is OK for me to say that I feel sorry for the guy, but "sorry" does not pay the rent or put food on the table. I *am* prepared to walk and talk, to listen and hear, to make all the right noises, but anything else, it seems to me, is not really helping. For him, it is very much what Samuel Johnson said over 300 years ago, and as I quoted earlier.

"You cannot travel on the path before you have become the path itself." Gautama Buddha

For once out there, Dear Friends, we have a sky that is blue and devoid of clouds. I do not believe it will rain today!!

The Individual

Being independent is what we spend our parenting years trying to teach our children, is it not? Of course, we do not allow them to get too close to the fire, but we teach them the reasons why. We want our children to make their own way in the world and we want them to do so independently. At the same time, we want them to operate to some degree for the common good. They should be giving up their seat on busses for the less able; they should have chores around the house; they should know the difference between being a team player and pursuing an individual goal.

Western democracies preach how they enshrine the needs and wants of the individual. We do see the results when innovation and initiative come to the fore. We note how people have become very creative in this lockdown. But then we see a chink of light and an opening in the protocol and we have a beach in the south of England or demonstrations around the world with no social distancing. It becomes difficult in a democracy to ask people to act as an obeisant herd when our system is built on inalienable rights and freedoms. There are societal mores that we need to obey.

I remember back in the day when many of my peers, me included, went for a few pints and then drove home. We knew we were breaking the law, that if we were breath tested we would face legal consequences. Then came a change, and most of us started to take a cab home, walk or get ourselves a ride. It is my belief that this wasn't because we had become older and more responsible, because we saw our younger brethren doing the same. It wasn't because the law and the fines became any stricter. To me, it simply seemed that the moral climate changed, and we stopped doing it because we were putting lives at risk. It went from being a law that we liked to flaunt to being a moral code. To me, there is a similarity with the current attitude to face masks. I don't see the necessity of wearing them when I am out for a walk or taking exercise, but if I am going to the post office or grocery shopping then I will. If the scientists move the goal posts and tell us we should be wearing them more frequently then I will do so. We all know how hot and uncomfortable they can become, but we are members of a society, so what is a bit of individual discomfort if I avoid passing on my bugs and germs to the guy reaching into the freezer for his burgers?

In this technological age, an age of virtual experiences, it should be possible for those who refuse to don a face mask to be rounded up, placed in a room and given the virtual COVID ICU experience for three or so days. Virtual symptoms would be difficult to replicate, I know. It would be hard to manufacture shortness of breath safely, but the drip feeds, the wires and the health workers surrounding the bed should be fine. And, hey, there are some very strong laxatives out there on the market. Point is that if face masks are mandated in certain situations then there can be appropriate consequences so that people buy in and wearing the mask becomes the right and moral thing to do. Not everybody obeyed the seat-belt law when it came into force, but now, for most of us, it is automatic. Helmets for bikers and so forth are the norm. I don't see how such laws are an unreasonable infringement on individual freedoms.

OK, Dear Reader, one might reasonably expect Davidson to dive into the 2nd Amendment here and start talking about the right to bear arms. I recognize there is a major cultural difference between where I grew up, where I now live and the weird and incredible thought processes of some of our neighbours beneath us. We are taught to accept other people with different cultures, to respect them and, often, to embrace them. So, I am asked to accept that it is OK to forbid women in certain countries from driving cars; I am told I cannot speak out against selling arms to dictatorial regimes; So, Dear Reader, am I to accept that it is part of a certain people's culture for a citizen to parade up and down outside a civic building with an automatic weapon draped over their shoulders? That is somebody else's culture that I will be making no attempt to appropriate. However, talking of which, I had thought to spend a day dressed as a Muslim woman covered in a black blanket from head to toe and experience travelling on busses and shopping downtown just to see what that was like. And more to see what the attitudes of others would be towards me. Then, I think, I would experience racism and misogyny in the rough and have some credence when I talked to women and Muslims. I can see but one advantage and one advantage only. I would not, dear friends, need to wear a mask!

To close, Dear Reader, I am reading a book called ***The Inevitability of Tragedy: Henry Kissinger and His World*** **by Barry Gewen.** I don't really know why Kissinger plays such a prominent part in the title because it is more about the

German-Jewish immigrant philosophers who influenced his thinking. Hannah Arendt, Strauss and Morgentau all fled, like Kissinger, the Nazis. What is interesting for these four who fled dictatorial Europe is that democracy is not the be-all and end-all of systems of government they think it should be. They see many flaws in such a system, not the least of which was that Adolf Hitler was democratically elected in 1933. In other words, they are saying it is possible for a population to vote for a racist, a xenophobe, a manipulator of the truth, a "my-country-right-or-wrong" nationalist, a man who has no sympathy or empathy for anything or anybody beyond his narrow vision. Hmmm, food for thought, Dear Reader.

Sun is shining.

Taking as Found

It does seem quite difficult to meet new people and then take them as we find them without fear or prejudice. Sometimes we just click with strangers and pretty soon it seems as though we have known them all of our lives. On other occasions we develop an immediate antipathy and never want to see them again. If we dig deeper, indeed if we can be bothered, we may gain some insight into why they are as they are.

> *"There are no strangers just friends we haven't met yet."*

Irish-British comedian, raconteur and author Spike Milligan served his time in the Second World War. He was in the artillery. On one occasion he fired off his large howitzer and such was the recoil it catapulted over the back of the rampart into a trench, narrowly missing the soldiers who were cowering there. Had it hit them it would have seriously injured or more likely killed them. The white-faced, quaking, shocked troopers who had just seen their lives pass before their eyes were further startled when Milligan appeared over the edge and asked:

> *"Anybody seen a gun?"*

Harry Secombe and Michael Bentine became his friends and fellow comedians on the radio show *The Goons* from that day. It was a chance meeting that led to a most successful and lasting partnership.

On another occasion, Milligan's troop appeared around a corner and saw some American troops coming towards them. When the "Americans" started firing at them, they suddenly realized they were, in fact, German paratroopers. Many years after the war, one of those German soldiers realized he had been firing at Spike and his men, so he contacted him. Mutual correspondence ensued, so Spike invited him out to lunch in London. They enjoyed a hilarious bibulous luncheon and afterwards his new-found friend asked if he could sign the menu for Spike, which he did:

> *"Sorry I missed you on August 5th, 1944. Otto."*

There is an obvious message here, and that is that an enemy in war is only an enemy because somebody else tells you he is. Indeed, war-time experiences are probably so intense it is probably irrelevant which side one was on, and it is entirely possible that enemies and allies have more in common than the people back home who did not experience the terror of the front lines.

I like the statement by Colin Dexter, author of the Morse mysteries, when he has his hero say, "Speech often gets in the way of genuine communication." Having watched and read about various courses on leadership, there are the brash and the brazen types who talk a good line and believe their own propaganda. Then there is the background personality who all too frequently voices the solution to the problem but is equally frequently unheard. We hear much about voices crying in the wilderness, the wise whose faces do not fit, who are condemned to be the silent majority because they are simply not cool. At the other end of a rather tragic scale there are those personalities in prison because they could not articulate their frustrations, lashed out and were caught and now have plenty of time to put their problem into words. That would be when speech should have replaced genuine communication!

I think, Dear Reader, that it is very hard to approach every situation and every new human situation with an open mind when one is in the thick of a busy working day. Being in the swim and battling against the currents of a river in flood does not really give one the time to make balanced, reasoned decisions. In retirement, however, now that it doesn't matter quite so much, it should be easy to run into a stranger at a coffee shop and pass the time of day. It really should be an opportunity to find some common ground, hear a bit about somebody's life and take an interest in what makes them tick. It is easier to take allowances for quirks of character if one walks for a mile in their shoes. Hmmm, I would, however, like to buy a couple of dozen eggs and sit in the front garden and hurl them at motorists who speed along Tatlow Avenue or even Pemberton where I am to be found doing the crossword and becoming caffeinated of a morning. If I am honest, I find that both streets are often treated as race tracks. Taking those drivers as some of us find them is an argument against retirement and having too much time on one's hands!!

Cloisters and Clarity

T here is so much merit in a walk with a friend or alone. I don't know that it works so well with more than one; three can be a crowd. I don't know. What do you think? Opinions, however, are often better when many people are involved; indeed, the more diverse the better. But a back and forth between two people has real merit too. A monastery was a place of cloisters, inner squares around which the monks could walk and talk, assuming that they weren't in a silent order! But even then, silent contemplation while in motion tends to give structure to an idea, give flesh to the skeleton of a plan, does it not? We all know this. When the "world is too much with us late and soon" then a breath of fresh air, a turn around the block, with a dog or without, can ease a crisis of worry, settle an anxiety. I think it was John Muir who said, "When you are going out, you are really going in." In other words, the outward motion in a natural setting is a way of focusing on our innermost thoughts.

If this be true, then it surely must follow that the "BOGSAT Principle" is *not* a great model. A "bunch of guys sat around a table" frequently becomes a battle of egos, long-windedness, boredom and nodding off syndrome. Frequently, a decision is deferred except perhaps the agreement to meet again in a month. How many "meet-again-in-a-month" meetings have we all attended? Often, one understands that acting in haste means repenting at leisure but coming up with nothing is not a model for confidence or moving forward. At a time of crisis such as now, we need people to talk—to walk and talk. To find clarity in a cloister and to make good decisions is a life-saving priority. Trouble is that nobody is really sure what will work. The old military maxim that "no plan survives the first contact" tends to ring true. Thus, do we have governments around the world making decisions based on facts that are not always axiomatic. Best we can say is that they are trying for a balance between safety and the economy and, let's face it, even with bombastic government "puffed up wi' windy pride," the foxes do have a sincere interest in prolonging the lives of the poultry. They want us to be around to spend all our new-found government money, otherwise our billionaires will slump to be mere millionaires and that will never do.

Seeing all of the scientific effort being put forth to find a virus solution, whether that be a vaccine or better ways of curing the sick, one can believe that democracy is the best hope of success. For all its faults, democracy is not threatened by the power of innovation or initiative. Dictatorships are hidebound by the neurosis of paranoia; they see a revolution around every corner. It makes me think of one of the late, great Peter Ustinov's school report cards: "He shows great initiative which should be stifled at all costs." Young Ustinov did **not** go to school in North Korea! CS Lewis said:

> *"I reject slavery because I see no men fit to be masters."*

There are far too many non-democratic countries in the world where the leader acts because he knows best. Democracy is not perfect:

"Two cheers for democracy. One, because it admits variety and two because it permits criticism. Two cheers are quite enough; there is no occasion to give three." E.M. Forster

Boris Johnson may not have had a cloistered walk the other day before laying forth his "word salad," mix-messaged plan. There was a soupcon of clarity somewhere between the lettuce and the tomato. He meant well and, at last, now he seems to have an effective leader of the opposition in Sir Keir Starmer, who is more likely to hold his feet to the fire. And there is a new dawn rising amongst the regional governments, which means they do not have to follow England if indeed it is leading them into the doom and gloom of a second wave. Boris has not failed yet. It would, however, have been a good decision if he had had Donald Trump over for a crisis summit. Great if he could have invited him to Number 10 for canapés and a glass, firm handshake of greeting at the door, warm maskless manly embrace, maybe even continental kisses on both cheeks (sorry about the orange make-up Mr. Johnson!), Boris having to leave the reception early, not feeling great, Boris having to be dashed to hospital, Boris into ICU, Trump panicking, fleet of cars to the airport, Air Force One home, back to the West Wing, Melania wisely deciding she doesn't want to be anywhere near him, goes into self-isolation, heard to mutter "Should have done this ten years ago" as she is whisked away to an undisclosed address. Trump at a press conference, surrounded by his unsocially-distanced, maskless grey men in grey suits. His Orangeship with a dry throat, a slight cough and so on and so forth. Ahhhhh, but one can but hope!

"Gie us anither glass o' that whisky, the clarity is frightening." from Golf in the Kingdom by Michael Murphy.

Rainy day, my friends. May have to visit the Cheeseman. Gjetost beckons.

*"People don't take trips,
trips take people."*
John Steinbeck

CHAPTER 6

TRAVEL

I have never really been on an holiday that is simply a destination. I could go down the pretentious route and talk pedantically about the difference between journeys and trips. I like the George MacDonald quotation, "Out of the everywhere into the here" and think of trips being rather "Out of the here into the everywhere." To so many of us staring at the Taj Mahal, seeing a cougar in the wild is not so much seeing those beautiful things but also who was with us when we saw them. However, I do understand that sometimes the presence only of me, myself and I is all that is needed and all that is required for a moment and a memory.

The following travelogues were some of my most memorable and most meaningful of my COVID writings, possibly because we always want what we can't have more than we have in our present. Also, such nostalgia smacks again of what, hopefully, is part of our future.

It was a bit of an inner debate whether or not to include Bruce Chatwin's *The Song Lines* in this section. This was, after all, someone else's journey, unlike Ålesund and the others. But it is travel, and his story summed up what travelling and journeys should be so perfectly. It was a lesson in how to move across a landscape in our world and, somewhat poignantly, a way of movement that it would have better to have in one's youth rather in later years.

Gullible's Travels

I thought that as a man who is now well into his sixties I would no longer journey as a chronic naïf. I have been lucky enough to travel to many wonderful places around the world in my life. One would think that, by now, I am something of a sophisticate as far as boarding and disembarking from a bus, train or plane is concerned. I have become a worldly member of the jet set, arriving at my destination with blasé aplomb with no sense of an adventure but with every suggestion that I have just bussed from North Vancouver to Park Royal. Sadly, automation came to YVR and destroyed every such self-belief.

I was to submit my landing pass into the slot of a machine. It had become crumbled in my pocket. I submitted it, it ate it and jammed. An official had to come and open up and release the jam. As I waited for my baggage on the carousel, I knew I would not mistake it for somebody else's because it was my Collingwood Aussie rugby touring kit bag. It had the tour date on it, the name of the school and "Davidson" in capitals blazing out from its yellow background. I had thought it would only have been accepted into the oversize baggage at Heathrow, but it wasn't. Then I saw its unmistakable nose appear at the gateway of the tunnel, about to enter the ramp. It appeared briefly and then became a blockage. I knew it would only take a nudge from a human being. I was tempted to skip over the moving ramp and do it for myself but recognized the folly of such a move just in time. People were looking around for an official, but there were none to be seen. Frustration was starting to rise. People were tut-tutting. They were tired, jet-lagged and eager to get away. Eventually, a uniform appeared, pressed a button, stopped the carousel and pulled my bag free. There was no way I was going to claim it immediately. I allowed it to circulate the carousel several times, looked several ways, grabbed it quickly and moved rapidly elsewhere. Did I have anything to declare? Only my innocence and incompetence.

"Honest, Mister Customs Official, the constipated carousel was not my fault. Bag should have been labelled 'oversize.' No, Sir, I am not bringing in ten jars of Marmite for commercial use. Yes, I should have washed my socks before putting them in the bag. Haven't I seen you before on that reality TV series *Border Crossing*? The purpose of my journey? Warm beer, the Sunday newspapers, people telling me they 'mustn't grumble' when asked how they are. Cricket commentary on the radio; the *Shipping Forecast*; understatement on the Tube ("Ladies and Gentlemen, we are sorry for the delay to the train heading from Piccadilly to Hounslow West. This is due to the presence of a suicide bomber in carriage three. We will keep you informed of any progress and let you know as soon as he has been shot. We thank you for travelling by London Transport. Customer Service is our byword.") What did I visit? Crewe Alexandra railway station, the funicular railway at Saltburn, Kerbside Auto Dealership in Clevedon. No, no, no, Sir, I am absolutely respecting you and your uniform. Is somebody meeting me at the airport? I should coco. Is the Pope catholic? Was Pontius a pilot? Let me take a keek and I'll tell you if the trouble and strife is there. Why am I talking like this? Because I have been listening to the prime minister's news conferences every night. I can go? Thank you, thank you, thank you. You have been so kind. Would you like a jar of Marmite for your trouble? No, sir, Marmite is absolutely not a bribe, it's a balm for the soul."

Have a good day, mes amis.

Ålesund

"**W**elcome aboard. For the next twelve days we will be cruising up the coast of Norway from Bergen to Kirkanes on the Russian border and back again. There are a few things you should take note of. Firstly, when the ship is in port, you will be given a set time of departure. Sometimes you will have three hours to explore and sometimes only thirty minutes. This is a working ferry with a tight schedule, so we don't wait. There is the tale of an American couple who missed the boat and had a difficult journey up the coast to rejoin. There is always an expensive helicopter ride if you want not to miss out. Ha! Ha!"

Thus spake the rather unctuous German/Norwegian tour guide as we set sail from Bergen on the Norwegian ferry *MS Lofoten* in May of last year. There were some 130 passengers aboard the ship. The weather and the scenery were already stunningly beautiful, and we had barely left Bergen. I laughed along with our Teutonic tour guide at the poor saps who had missed the ferry last year. *Typical Americans*, I thought to myself, *expecting the world to revolve around them and the God Almighty dollar*. Then I pinched myself at the terrible bias and prejudice of my thoughts and looked around guiltily as though I was surrounded by telepaths who could read my mind. Then I smiled smugly. Pete "The Punctual" Davidson would never, ever do something like that. I had always been super punctual, arriving at events earlier rather than later. I had been known to arrive at parties before they officially began, creating awkward moments where the host and hostess were trying to be polite but were still running around trying to get ready. Pete was never late.

As soon as the ship entered the fjordland that led to the town of Ålesund, I knew I was going to enjoy my visit to this remarkable-looking town. The art nouveau buildings, the surrounding vista of tall snow-clad peaks, the whole feeling of comfortable, relaxed confidence conveyed itself before we docked. The peak that dominated the town, Aksla, was immediately above us. After an ascent of 418 steps, there was a viewing platform and a touristy area at the top. I resolved to make that peak my first port of call. We were to have plenty of time to explore this quaint-looking town, so I felt leisurely relaxed. The weather and the sea were blue and bright. What was not to like?

So, the ship docked. The departure time was chalked on the blackboard by the gangplank, and we were off the boat. I meandered slowly and roughly towards the entrance to the stairway. Soon I was at the foot, and quickly I ascended to the top. The town was spread below us. I was able to see our ship moored at the quayside to the right of the town. Having ooohed and aaaahed at the view and taken numerous pictures, I discovered there was a nice wee hiking trail to the rear of things. I decided that rather than retrace my steps I would take this different route down the hill. Off I set. I soon found myself away from the crowd and, while not quite alone for most of the time, I was significantly removed from the "hoi polloi" to be able to move and stop at my leisure. I came across some interesting wood carvings and some concrete bunkers left over from the German occupation during the war. Slowly, I wended downhill until I found myself back at sea level. There were some very large cruise ships across the road. The statue of Joachim Rønneberg, a World War II hero, stood proudly in a park. At the age of twenty-three, he had led the successful operation to blow up the Nazi heavy water plant thus setting back the German plans to develop an atomic bomb. He died in Ålesund in 2019 at the age of ninety-nine. I paused awhile at the statue before heading back along the quayside in the general direction of the ferry.

The sun continued to shine. The meanderings down the sides of many quays continued to mesmerize, and I was slowly making my way back to the Lofoten mooring. I had not wandered too far when I realized that what had seemed an easy route was fast becoming a maze of differing quaysides with only one way in and much retracing to get back. Time was moving along. I kept losing sight of the Aksla peak I had climbed. I was now trying to turn corners that would bring the mountain back into sight. It was my guiding bearing. Yet more dead ends, more stretches of water the other side of which I needed to be. Now I was upping my pace, was sweating, was becoming nervous. The deadline for the boat's departure was coming up far too fast. Finally, I recognized the quayside and the dock on the other side of which was the boat. It was a mere couple of hundred yards away but still I had to come farther inland to complete the three sides of the square. Now the brisk walk was becoming a near jog. I was drawing closer but then so was the time. Images of the wake of the ferry gently nudging its way out of the fjord with me bereft on the quayside flitted through my mind. Pictures of me finding a bus or train north, desperate phone calls to the company to discover the next port of call, a mad dash northwards. Images of a helicopter ride after the boat, me being dropped into the water, inflatable being dropped to pick me up, my fellow passengers all on deck, shading their faces from the sun, pointing and waving, cameras clicking and the final ignominious arrival at the rope ladder and the even more cringeworthy entry into the dining room for dinner that night. Then a picture in my mind of Irene going through the receipts after my trip and coming across a large bill for a helicopter ride and an explanation and a further few days of anguish. I was shaking my head. If that happened, I would *never* go home again. I would take my tent and sit in it in the Highlands and try desperately to pluck up the courage to face the world.

There were ten minutes to spare as I strolled nonchalantly up the gangplank as though I had timed my arrival to perfection. I sat down to dinner that night with my new acquaintances. We discussed the beauties of the town and its environs. I uttered nary a word of my narrow escape. I crawled out from under my rock of humility and made a special effort to befriend the Americans on board, knowing in my heart of hearts how arrogantly I had silently insulted them earlier in the day.

The Songlines by Bruce Chatwin

The Songlines is one of those books I have often heard praised. It is a book written in the 1980s that I had always intended to read. Yet I would never have done so unless a friend lent it to me. It is about Bruce Chatwin's travels with the Aborigines in the Red Centre of Australia. It is about how those incredible people are so much a part of the wilderness that they are able to find their way from place to place by singing the handed down songs that identify features. It is an incredible tale of mythical direction finding. It is extremely well written. The "tjurna djugurba" are the footprints of the ancestor. To the aboriginal, the song and the land are one.

Chatwin's book, as befits a travel writer, is one of movement. To me, it is one of the finest explanations of why human beings are committed to moving. We all seem to know instinctively that if we have a problem, a worry or an upset in our lives, then a walk alone might help us make a decision. Indeed, meeting with a friend, walking and talking it through sometimes helps us find a way out. Anyhow, this is proving very difficult to write. I have had to read through things several times. I will quote a great deal. I think we all know the benefits of walking for our minds and bodies, but the problem is trying to write about them with clarity. What I need is a walk to get my thoughts in some semblance of order!!

"When I rest my feet, my mind also ceases to function." JG Hamann

It's the monks in the cloister, the dog walkers, the long-distance hikers, the man with a walking stick and a pipe, the woman strolling a beach who are all seeking the balm for the mind that comes from motion of the body. So, what did I discover? I discovered the Greek word for "limb" is "melos" from which we also get "melody." I don't know about you, Dear Reader, but I rather like the idea of a walk being also a melody. I rather like the idea of Irene and me going for a "melody" on the Spirit Trail; it has a certain charm, does it not? Incidentally, if the Ancient Greeks noted that walking was good and equated it to music, when in the Antipodes another people were also singing their movement, then it says something about the human mind, does it not? Two peoples who have had no contact and are physically a world apart having the same philosophy? They have their own creation story and many myths and legends that talk about a devastating flood? How can this be?

Then Chatwin produces "nomos" as the Greek word for "pasture":

> *"Nomos is the Greek word for 'pasture' and the 'Nomad' is a chief who presides over the allocation of pastures. 'Nomos' then came to mean 'law,' 'fair distribution,' 'that which is admitted by custom' and so the basis of all western laws. 'Nemesis' is the distribution of justice."*

So how do we get from people who are nomadic to a word that means making laws? A wanderer as a law giver?? Yet again, dear friends, I am struggling to understand all of this and put it into words except that I have the feeling that all of us, I mean all of us, *do* understand. It is almost an instinct, an intuition. We see babies who crawl, toddlers who toddle and fall over and fail. Yet they get up and they try again. Giving up on the idea of walking doesn't seem to occur to them. Many of the things I have failed in I have *never* returned to. Learning to walk seems to be the most basic of instincts. And here Chatwin uses this to explain all other instincts:

> *"You couldn't pick and choose with instincts, you had to take the lot. You couldn't allow Venus into the pantheon and bolt the door on Mars."*

There seems to lie the strength and weakness of humankind. Love and war are part of our being. If we love, then we will go to war to protect that love. Of course we will. I have heard the story of the Glasgow ratcatcher back in the day. His party piece was to gather with his mates by the River Clyde with a sack of live rats. He would put his hand into the sack, pull out a rat and throw it into the river. Nothing, however, would persuade him to do this when there was only one rat left in the bag. Why? Because the group of rats never believed that that fatal hand was coming for them, it was always going for the other one. But that last rat knew that the hand was coming for him and would fight to the death to prevent it. In our civilized society it takes an awful lot to make us fighting mad, but those dormant instincts are likely still in us. Here is Chatwin again:

> *"As a general rule of biology, migratory species are less aggressive than sedentary ones."*

Taking ourselves off for a walk when we have had a confrontation with somebody can mitigate our anger and help us to put forth a more peaceful perspective.

Any rate, I apologise for imposing these confused ramblings on you today. I have been trying to understand something here and put it into words. I have selfishly used you as a means to an end. It may not have given you clarity, but it has helped me a little. If I am asked to describe my frequent walk along the Spirit Trail, I think I could now explain it. I think if it was a shared walk it would read something like this:

> *"Stroll onto the street, wave across to John's banana tree, walk down past the double storied 'sauna house,' continue to the house that Winston and Beth built, come off the road, turn left on the tarred trail, walk towards the floral bank, past the covered coffee shop that doubles as Dermot's parking space, take careful heed where the path narrows by the tennis courts, acknowledge the children's playground, emerge near the Pemberton Pub, press the button to cross the road, pass the dance academy, cross the junction up which the*

West Van bus park is, approach the creek,
check for wildlife, and so forth."

OK, so I am belabouring the point, but thank your lucky stars I am not singing this to you!! But I think that I can finally see how a people who have inhabited a land for thousands of years before the surprise arrival of Captain Cook were able to navigate and find their way without maps. The oral tradition of handing down their culture would mean they would never be lost in the wilderness because, to them, there was no such thing as wilderness.

"Solvitur ambulando," "It is solved by walking," as the ancients would have it.

"Leaders create the right environment for the right behaviour to occur."
Owen Eastwood

CHAPTER 7

CURRENT AFFAIRS

During the early days of our isolation, I wanted to avoid all the virtue signaling and the political correctness that was rampant. But it proved impossible to ignore. The murder of African Americans in the USA by law enforcement, the sudden realization that certain statues were offensive, and the fashionable current thinking that brooked no opposition are rightly taking a prominent role in our media at the moment. I suppose I was becoming more and more irritated not with the rightness of so many causes but in the fact that there were no shades of grey, that everything was good or it was evil; that everything was black and white, if I can be pardoned for saying so. Woke thoughts, the #MeToo movement and Black Lives Matter are all very necessary movements to correct many wrongs. However, to my simple, white-privileged brain, many of the speeches were too strident, too blinkered, too gung-holier-than-thou. To some people, a man is guilty if we are told he is guilty; to some people, a white-privileged male is guilty because of the colour of his skin and the wealth of his upbringing. To a climatologist, a baby boomer is guilty of climate change because she was born at a certain time. If ever there was an argument for making sure debating societies and philosophy should play a much bigger part in our school curricula, then the current climate of restrictive argument has it.

Sarcasm, Wit and Intelligence

With His Nutship, who runs the country beneath us, telling his citizens that if disinfectant works on the outside then it is bound to work on the inside and to knock back a pint of Lysol, then we are in trouble! Leastways those who believed him are. Forget PPE and ventilators, manufacturing stomach pumps and sending them south would seem to be a great investment opportunity. Who are the fall guys—the clown who made the statement or the clowns who drank the stuff? OK, so in the realm of Trumpton, the Donaldom claimed he was being sarcastic. Last time I read it "sarcasm was the lowest form of wit but the highest form of intelligence." I understand that one can lump these three attributes together in one sentence but don't know how they work the current incumbent of the Orange Office. It could have been sarcasm, but from a man with neither wit nor intelligence? Oh, come on!

It wasn't sarcasm at all. It was a throwaway, top of the head, fly-by-the-seat-of-one's-pants remark. It was one of those many moments when he was not content to be silent or plead ignorance or defer to an expert. It was a silence-filler. If a herd of pigs had flown by when he was speaking, one could not have been less surprised.

"Pour me another drink, Irene, I think I've just seen a pink elephant!"

Charles Dickens called it "streaky bacon," a combination of mixing comedy into tragedy, and tragedy into comedy. Donald Trump treats the presidency like he's running a hobby farm. Disinfectant drunk as Kool Aid is like bringing a knife to a gunfight—those who survive will not be holding the knife. The man needs to make his puerile prognostications and then have a bevy of spokespersons take the mic to replace the balance of power with the power of balance, because the former is unhinged craziness. It does more harm than good. Theodore Dalyrymple talked years ago about "the banality of celebrity." He will take no satisfaction in being proven correct. Yer POTUS there is a "planet without an atmosphere," a desert without an oasis, a storm without a centre. The hope is that he has surrounded himself with people of intelligence who can speak truth to power and put a steady hand on the tiller when the ship is heading to the rocks. Words matter, and the sooner the person in charge of the most powerful nation on Earth realizes it, the better. Ahhhh, but I am ranting. I will seek a lighter note.

As a skill to be admired I do like sarcasm, but I like irony more. Irony pertains to situations whereas sarcasm is a means of expression. It would be ironic if a driving instructor was killed in a road traffic accident or a sleep doctor could not sleep at night. Was John Lennon being ironic when he proclaimed that The Beatles were "more popular than Jesus"? He likely was. His problem was that he was doing it in a nation that in the 1960s didn't do irony very well. There might be irony if the minister of health in a chosen country smoked like a chimney, drank like a fish and ate deep-fried Mars bars. Is it ironic that those who work on the sea, fishermen in deep sea boats for instance, so often cannot swim? It is definitely sarcasm when teacher says "Very good" to Johnny who has just come in from recess soaked to the skin because he forgot his waterproofs on a rainy day. Is it sarcasm to say:

"Oh yeah sure, the American electorate are going to elect a reality TV host over a Hilary Clinton/Joe Biden. Yeah, like that's gonna happen."

I guess it would be ironic if the president was visiting a Lysol factory and a pallet of the stuff slipped off the shelf onto his orange visage! Got to go, Irene is preparing a big feast for tonight. Here is the menu:

Pate de foie Clorox.

T-bone steak with onions, mushrooms and mashed potatoes with Lysol gravy.

Strawberry cheesecake with a Vim drizzle.

A cheese board with crackers with red pepper Tide preserve.

Ha! I jest, but let me ask you this question: Which do you prefer: a witch-hunt or a whitewash?

"May the farce be with you." Pete

Independence and Dependence

I t is an ill wind that blows nobody any good, as they say. I try not to get too involved in the politics of a country in which I do not live. Of course, I have huge respect for Angela Merkel and am pretty impressed with Ardern in New Zealand. Scott Morrison suffers from Pot Noodle Syndrome: speedily prepared, very filling at the time, but thirty minutes later one is hungry for something different. At the moment there is little stability in an Aussie PM's tenure, but then they have had those terrible fires and COVID, so cutting the guy a little slack may be the order of the day. Problem is that they were temporary before those disasters anyway. "Cometh the hour, cometh the errrr woman," a misquote, of course, but at the moment the female leaders of Taiwan, Finland and Germany seem to be doing a far better job of dealing with the crisis than the men folk. Nobody's fault, of course, but men need to move rather than step back and then move. Women consider, ponder, have foresight and are designed to see the details. Massive generalization, of course, but having seen ten-year-old girls sort out their school supplies at the beginning of the school year, I know there is a big difference between them and the boys. The former label their pencils, but with the latter, there is a mess on the floor. Of course, children grow up and there comes a balance between the genders. Yet again, dear friends, guilty of generalization. How would Margaret Thatcher have dealt with the pandemic compared to Boris Johnson? The Iron

Lady, for all her faults, was not afraid of the definite and did not dance around clarity. There was much that was wrong with her as a politician, but lack of conviction was not one of her faults. Now Boris is dealing with an opposition that seems to have a real leader rather than a pie in the sky. Setting loose flying pigs is *not* likely to happen under Sir Keir Starmer as seemed likely when "magic grandpa" was in charge of the British Labour Party.

So, back to the point. I do not really believe sovereign nations can ever be totally independent anymore. Sure and all, borders have been shut where borders had been removed many years before. Certainly, politicians can play the blame game, which is all fine and dandy *after* the crisis is over but smacks of childishness when we are all in the midst of it. Reasoned, logical analysis can come later. There is no point in saying this is China's fault or that the idea of "herd immunity" was not a good one. It seems at the moment that the world is holding its breath. Countries that have delayed opening up are watching with intense interest to what is happening to those that are moving forward.

We are dependent on the scientists and nature at the moment. We know that, despite mankind's habit of despoiling the world we live in, extinguishing flora and fauna with reckless abandon, we know that nature wins in the end. We only have to watch the British TV series on abandoned railways to see how quickly wilderness takes over. Many of them have become lovely little footpaths with a bit of reassuring bushwhacking to avoid a bramble scratch. The world's population is perhaps too many; we may be too cheek by jowl in our ways of living; too crammed aboard life's railway carriages.

Back to dependence and independence. I really am pretty pleased that there is a border between Canada and the USA at the moment. More than that, I am delighted it is difficult to cross. I am not suggesting we build a Trumpian Wall here, but the number of states opening while corona is still wreaking havoc seems callous and irresponsible. It really seemed to be far too soon for the crowds on Kits Beach to be gathering as they did on the weekend. I am glad we are not in Quebec at the moment, and I am pleased with the balance between local initiatives and federal diktats.

There are some differences of opinion between the national government and the "national" governments in the UK. Boris wants the people to be freer, for some businesses to open and for people to "be alert." I have a picture in my mind of the people of England as meerkats, sticking their heads out of their holes, and vigorously scanning the skies and ground for predators before moving from their safe havens. Sadly, people are never going to be as alert as meerkats. I say the people of "England" because the leaders of Scotland, Wales and Northern Ireland seem to be adopting a more cautious approach. There is a divergence. Could it be that this terrible disease brings about what referenda and 300 years since the Union of the Crowns could not—the re-emergence of an independent Scotland? Scotland is so dependent on England for so much, particularly sponge cakes, that this is unlikely and not desirable. But it has not escaped my notice that Nicola Sturgeon, the Scottish first minister, is a woman, and female leaders have a better track record around the world at this moment.

1270 Tatlow Avenue's first minister is also a woman. The man in the house may assert his independence at some point today by going for a walk, but he is dependent on direction regarding so many tasks that require foresight and planning so that any belief he has of his own independence is on a false foundation. And he wouldn't have it any other way.

Sun shining again, mes amis

Versatile Principles

R obespierre coined the term "Versatile principles" during the French Revolution. I don't know the context so shouldn't really comment, but here was a man who believed in the concept of virtue, and in the process of creating a virtuous society sent people to their deaths. It is a shibboleth that most people who aspire to work in politics do so out of a belief that they can promote the common good. Either that, or they are on a power trip or their ego leads them to believe they are the only person capable of doing what needs to be done. If having versatile principles means one is going to have to compromise, then I think I understand the meaning of the phrase.

What I *am* failing to understand at the moment is how people are suddenly realizing stuff. Suddenly, knowing that a statue of a famous person is a representation of an idea and a human being who was inherently evil is the new virtue. There is something unwritten here that has an undercurrent I don't much like. There is an inference that I, as a sixty-eight-year-old middle-class white male, am guilty of something. I am unsure where my guilt lies but am prepared to accept it or not should it be pointed out to me. Certainly, growing up in the 1960s I was keen to meet girls but, I have to admit, there was a certain gynophobia that came into play when dealing with the opposite sex. Indeed, in my boys' world and that of my early manhood, I hadn't had much contact with girls or young women. I was extremely shy of them, and my face always reddened at school when I had to talk to one. So, most of them transcended human kind, they rested as goddesses on a pedestal. It took a long time for me to recognize that they were fellow human beings with all of the flaws and frailties men possessed as well.

> *"We see women as concepts rather than flesh and blood."* **John le Carré**

Mr. le Carré understands boarding school boys better than I do!

So I am, or should I say "was," guilty of many misdemeanours in those years that are totally unacceptable today. One thing I was never guilty of, however, was homophobia or racism. I always failed to understand why people might be frightened of somebody who was not a heterosexual. I failed to see how anybody of another persuasion or race was a threat. I will admit to having an antipathy towards certain Americans and white South Africans, the former needing to prove a certain cosmopolitan understanding that their melting-pot history teaching had notoriously failed to do. The latter had to prove to me that they were anti-apartheid before gaining my acceptance. And yes, I am aware that that shows me to be a virtue signaler and a gung-holier-than-thou proselytizer of the worst kind. So indeed, I now come across as a condescending, patronizing bastard. There is no escape for any of us is there??

> *"He found they were all in a single place, a single proving ground for virtues not yet stated."* **John le Carré**

Are we all going to be pilloried in ten years or so for something we are guilty of doing now of which we have no awareness at the moment? I certainly believe that one of the wrongs of our current society is that we have closed all the institutions that provided bed, board and care for the mentally ill. Riverview here in Vancouver is the classic example. There are mental patients who have been killed by police officers because there was no Riverview and they were therefore homeless and off their medication. Organ donations, and this is personal, should all be an opt-out system rather than an opt-in one. One of the things I noticed in my recent hasty retreat from Scotland is that they were about to legislate that organs could be taken from anybody who hadn't opted-out. There is much anguished ringing of hands in Ottawa that Canada did not get a place on the rotation of temporary UN Security Council countries. I don't understand why because both Ireland and Norway are mostly in tune with "our" values. It is not like they are countries notorious for human rights violations. They have also contributed more to the good works of international organizations than we have here in Canada. We should be cheering them home rather than whining our loss. Their win is our win. We have no reason to be jingoistic in our chagrin.

OK, my generation has contributed to climate change and planetary pollution. This is true, but please don't blame this on how we behaved in the 60s. I went through school and life never seeing a plastic fork or bag. Most people owned one car, if any. I did not pass my driving test until I was twenty-three years old. Flights in an aeroplane were rare enough to be an occasion. I would never have contemplated flying to Budapest for a stag weekend, never have thought of driving if there was a convenient bus or train, never owned or used a dishwasher, and I had a bath once per week. Sure and all, if it had been possible for me to be profligate then I would have been. No saint me!

It is true that, at the moment, I am grumpy enough at certain aspects in the current climate that I want to get off my backside, get on my hind legs and become a history teacher again. I want to get out there and tell the world that my ancestors were flung off their land and replaced by sheep; that the Irish who became a diaspora were forced to leave Ireland because the potato crop failed and they were starving; that the South Vietnamese boat people were faced with death at home and hope abroad; that the current batch of Syrian refugees really don't have a choice. Two hundred years ago, people were on the move; in 2020 (COVID permitting), people are on the move. The history of the peoples of the world is one of movement and migration. Please don't castigate me because a fellow European called the Salish Sea, Howe Sound. There are some beautiful indigenous sounding words. Skookumchuk, Sechelt, Squamish all evince a lovely First Nations nuance we should not lose. I was born in Aberdeen, not Deemouth, which would be the anglicized version. I played rugby at school against Cwmtawe Comprehensive School, which used to be Ystalyfera Grammar School. Dear Reader, these two schools are *not* in England!! Let's give the First Nations people their language back as a beginning towards reconciliation.

OK, OK, I am belabouring the point, but in the future let us dig a bit deeper into our past and into the characters of that past before we start throwing stones. Those of us who live in glass houses should be very careful when we chuck pebbles about. Plus, my friends, some clever soul many years ago invented the mirror; it would be wise if, occasionally, we looked into it. We might spot a blemish or two.

Twenty-One Seconds!

hus *didn't* speak Trudeau. Don't know whether you have seen it, but he was asked a question about the stuff going on in the USA at the moment, and for longer than it took Usain Bolt to win gold in the 200 Metres, he said nothing. I have very few heroes as world leaders at the moment, except perhaps Merkel in Germany and Ardern in New Zealand, but that twenty-one seconds gave a respect and a nuance to his leadership that buffed a bit of a better shine on it.

> *"If I broke my silence, the strength would depart from me; but while I held my peace, I held my foe in an invisible mesh."* George MacDonald

Sadly, because he is the prime minister he did have to break his silence. What was he thinking in those twenty-one seconds? I must admit to racism in Canada, I must not be too critical of what is happening south of the border, I must not be too preachy, I must speak honestly. Above all, I must learn from the example of two presidents, Trump and Obama, and I must sound like one of them and not the other.

Our son, Grant, once said that "Silence is nothing's sound." I liked that statement and particularly admired the fact that it came from a ten-year-old. Scientifically, his words are probably true but definitely *not* the case when a person doesn't speak. The greatest lies are often spoken in silence. Silence conveys either wisdom or misunderstanding. Who was it who said:

> **"Better to remain silent and be thought a fool than to speak out and remove all doubt."**

At the moment there are people who are "removing all doubt." They cannot have a pause in the conversation because pauses to them are awkward, they allow too much time for an audience rejoinder, they leave space for thought. It is not good for their image to have people doing rash things like thinking, Dear Reader.

I have had many wonderful "bosses" in my teaching career. The best were always those who did not operate with a rule book but worked using their instincts, their humour and their understanding of humanity. At the beginning of one school year, there was an issue that needed addressing urgently. I considered the absence of a competent math teacher for Grades VIII and IX to be urgent. The term was some three weeks old and still no math teacher had arrived. Eventually, I fixed up an appointment with the headmaster as the problem was not being fixed lower down. I went in well prepared, well versed in the issue with a healthy but respectful dose of righteous indignation. (Shouldn't have needed to do that, it was really as simple as no math teacher, please get one!). I entered the office.

He shook my hand. How is the family? Grant playing some great rugby, I hear. Alison, a bit of a star in class. How is

Irene? Great reports from parents, Pete. Hey, did you watch any of the test match cricket? What did I think of Brian Lara's batting? (Cricket story of his own). Really great to have you on board here. One of my finest acquisitions. Hey, it's late in the day, let's have a beer.

I left his office, smiled at his personal assistant. My chest was puffed, my face was a grin, I felt like the brightest star in the firmament. I sang all the way home in the car, and I couldn't wait to tell Irene. She was home and she listened to my interview experience.

"Soooo, are you getting this much-needed math teacher?"

Silence.

"Well, that's what you went in there for, isn't it?"

Head down, hand through hair, bubble burst, tyre punctured, fall from the headiest of heights to the deepest emotional abyss.

Eventually, a math teacher arrived, and the children received what they needed, so it all had not been in vain. But, Dear Reader, I was snowed, I was bamboozled, I was sucked in by good-natured, well-meaning bafflegab; I felt such a fool. I shouldn't have. That particular head had so much charisma, so much character, such a wonderful command of language that he was able to fundraise like no other person I have ever met. He was kind, good-natured and well-meaning. His ideas were innovative, adventurous and thought-provoking. He had the spirit of an adventurer, the courage of an explorer, and better people than me had been carried along by his gift of charm and bonhomie. Indeed, I should have been honoured that he took the time and *not* chagrined that I failed in my message.

Seumas Heaney had a wish for a person whom he didn't think much of. That:

> *"His tongue to be deadened like the dropped gangplank of a cattle truck."*

Watching the news every night, I hear that mythical gangplank being dropped with almost rhythmic regularity. So, listening to Justin's twenty-one seconds were moments, for once, when the fingernails were not being scraped across the chalkboard; a pleasant relief.

The author John Buchan, who became Lord Tweedsmuir and governor general of Canada, talked passionately about people who had "an extended horizon and a limited opportunity." It seems to me that that sums up minorities everywhere and, particularly at this moment, those in the United States. Also, some ninety years ago he said:

> *"You think that a wall as solid as the Earth separates civilization from barbarism. I tell you the division is a thread, a sheet of glass. A touch here, a push there and you bring back the reign of Saturn."*

> *"There is a very thin line between a warm room and a savage out of doors."*

The optimist in me wants to see the peaceful demonstrations in the United States as a revolution for change, the pessimist walks around a different corner and sees a burning cop car and a store being looted. Decent, upstanding human beings often behave differently in groups, do they not? And not always for the best. This is where real leadership is needed. Yet again I go back to John Buchan for help:

> *"The task of leadership is not to put greatness into humanity but to elicit it, for the greatness is already there."*

Justin Trudeau spent twenty-one seconds searching for the right words, the right tone and the right response. It gave us a taste of real leadership but, before we get too carried away with that, let us not forget that Dr. Bonnie Henry does that every night!

Respect

espect and disillusionment are contrasting emotions. This blog has talked before about heroes and how falling from grace has an impact. Sometimes the person is never the same. It is so easy to be critical and to forget that all humans are human. By inference, this makes us superhuman because we are never so critical of ourselves as we are of others. But, Dear Reader, should we not be harder on ourselves than we are on each other? One of my erstwhile heroes over the past twenty years had been former Secretary of State Colin Powell, but because he supported President Bush with his decision to invade Iraq, I fell away from him. He knew there were no WMD, and he should have voiced that belief and resigned in the process. So now we are hearing from him again. He is reasserting his presence and voicing that he is not a supporter of the current president of the U.S.. It is tempting to say, "Better late than never" and "Where have you been?" and so forth. Nothing to lose at eighty-three years of age, and there are all kinds of criticisms that could be levelled at him. But, Dear Reader, I found this quotation of his that I think is relevant to him at this time:

> *"Tell me what you know. Then tell me what you don't know, and only then can you tell me what you think. Always keep those three separated."*

So, I guess, now that he has come out and stated he will vote for Biden in November and given his reasons for so doing, he is practicing what he has preached. Now I am at least retrieving him from my storage box of fallen idols, dusting him off and, if I am not yet giving him pride of place on our mantelpiece, then I am thinking about it.

When did this man become my hero? Why indeed? It could have been for his obvious physical bravery, the fact that he was tried and tested in battle, his leadership in the first Gulf War, but it was none of those things. It came about when he visited the UK and was guest of honour at a dinner. It fell to Lord Powell to give the welcome and introduction. His namesake is no relation, but he stood up and talked about "We Powells." They were a rum lot over the years. The eldest son became a politician, the next went into the military, the next was found a position in the church. Inevitably there was the black sheep of the family, the wayward offspring for whom nothing worked. Ineluctably what happened was that he was sent to the colonies and given a stipend every month as long as he promised to stay away. For some it was the making of them, and they returned home having milked the poverty and natives of every little ounce of respect and self-worth they had. It was an exploitative, shameful piece of empire building of the worst kind. Other "remittance men" failed, fell off the face of the map and were never heard from again, which was equally fine by the family back home. Lord Powell completed his speech by saying:

"Welcome home, Colin."

Side-splitting laughter from the guest of honour and so forth. The inference could have been that Colonel Powell was a "black sheep," therefore this was racism of the worst kind. Taken out of context, it would read as such. But there was nothing at all racist about it. It was well within the bounds of acceptable humour given the nuances and the style of the telling. I believe, wrongly perhaps, that this was the moment when this wonderful man became a hero of mine. Being self-deprecating and being able to laugh at oneself is always a step towards me liking a person and, I suggest, most of us feel the same way.

Watching with horror the scenes recently in the United States, I am trying to understand why intelligent human beings make judgments on others based on the colour of their skin, indeed, on their gender or sexual orientation. I do not understand it. But then I look within myself and find there are aspects of my character that are racist. I don't like them very much, and I want to eliminate them from my being but, Dear Reader, they are there. No matter, for example, how I try to judge each person on their merits, there is a coldness comes over me when I am confronted by an Englishman who speaks with a plum in his mouth, whose attitude is upper class and the world owes him a living and the rest of us are the "great unwashed." OK, I can get over it and make the effort and befriend and try to learn, but initially, Dear Friends, my class-conscious Britishness wants me to move away and not engage. I have an antipathy towards such people that is more than skin deep. At my age, I should have grown up and away from such prejudice, but the fact is that I haven't. OK, so disliking somebody because they come across as an upper-class twit is not racist per se, but it has the same basic foundation in our inner being, does it not? In reverse, of course, I hear a stranger with a British accent and feel an immediate affinity. That is, perhaps, easier to explain because we will have ***something*** in common. I know they will know things I know whether that be the newspapers, the traffic on the M25, Yorkshire accents, *Monty Python*, cricket, narrow roads and hedgerows in Somerset, the difference between an English pub and a Scottish bar. All of those things have a tendency to draw me towards, and then we discover that our first impressions are right or wrong and go our separate ways or not. Common culture does not make anybody racist, misogynist or homophobic. Standing up for the national anthem means I believe my government is going to take care of me when I need it; taking a knee means I know it won't. If I were American, I would be taking a knee at this moment in history.

I think today I will finally dust off old Colin Powell and put him back in pride of place on my mantelpiece. He has regained my respect.

How to Social Distance in a Riot

First, wash your hands! As one is lining up the bottles for the Molotov cocktails one is going to throw at the police, it is very important that one does so in a sterile environment. It would be devastating if an athletic cop caught a burning cocktail hurled it back and caught coronavirus in the process. Second, wear a mask. The beauty of wearing a protective face covering in a riot is that it serves two purposes. It stops you giving other people your COVID-19, and it prevents you from being identified on CCTY. Thirdly, maintain the six-foot apart rule. This will need some pre-planning. The stick you were going to use as a cop-beating baton may be somewhat shorter. Canadian Tire sells hockey and lacrosse sticks that are well over six feet. Pick handles and baseball bats will not work, but a long-handled shovel may do. Fourthly, if the police turn on the fire hoses, ensure that you are in the firing line. There is nothing like a powerful jet of water to force a lurking bacterium to take cover. Fifthly, if arrested, please ensure that the arresting officer wipes down the handcuffs with the packet of steri-wipes that you have thoughtfully brought along for the purpose. Insist on getting into the paddy wagon with only two other people. When you appear in court, wear gloves and a Perspex mask. Insist that the judge wears the same and with absolutely no orange make-up at all. When you are fined, insist on paying cash. They won't accept this, as paying by card is more hygienic, but it is your right.

You will probably be bound over to keep the peace. You will be required to keep gatherings to fewer than six people. In some cases, you will be under house arrest and forbidden to leave your own home, in which case you will find yourself back in the same boat as the rest of us!

Different rules may apply in different countries. In the USA, for example, it is a lot easier to social distance if one has an AK47. In Canada, it is easier to social distance because we apologise way before we get too close. We are less likely to riot here anyway because at the slightest inkling of unrest, Justin will pay us off with our own money. In the UK, people would like to demonstrate (and possibly riot) but Brits need to understand what they are demonstrating against or for. It takes time to understand what the prime minister is saying and days to work out what Boris means, by which time one has cracked open another bottle of wine and can no longer be bothered. In Scotland, everybody understands what Nicola says and are fearful of a Glasgow Kiss should they take to the streets. No worries in Cardiff because the Welsh are not great demonstrators or rioters because it is hard for them to gather in large crowds without bursting into song. In Northern Ireland they have lots of experience of violence in the streets. Belfast and Derry seem tough places to grow up, and no self-respecting virus would dare appear there for fear that the local branch of the IRA may take them into a disused warehouse and kneecap them.

So, my friends, I do not understand how there can be a peaceful demonstration, a la cities in the USA, during a time when there is a disease that has killed over 100,000 of one's fellow citizens. It seems to me that the trouble in "the land of the great white individual" is there are no "fellow citizens." Such has become the aura of the freedom of one to exploit the resources of the many that there seems to be an America of "haves" and "have nots." But I shouldn't be speaking like this because this is a country I have rarely visited, certainly not in the last twenty-five years, so it is a terra incognita where be dragons to me! Socially distance they must and yet they risk a vigorous exchange of bodily fluids when crowded in a mass or in a sweaty contretemps with an opponent. It is not looking that great for your average American demonstrator or peacekeeper. Experts will tell us that it is the easiest thing in the world for a peaceful crowd to be incited into a riotous assembly. Professional incitement can be manufactured by any group or individual bound on trouble. There is no rhyme or reason why somebody demonstrating against the unlawful killing of a citizen should break a window and loot a shop. But then why would Vancouverites riot when a sporting event has gone the wrong way? There is a market for a peaceful demonstration. It saved the Carmanah Valley and the ancient giants of the rainforest. Hong Kong demonstrators no longer have anything to lose. As a child in the 60s, I noticed there were demonstrations in the UK. There was "Ban the Bomb" and protests against the Vietnam War. I remember the chants of "Dubcek, Svoboda" as Soviet tanks rolled into Czechoslovakia in 1968. I was never tempted to take to the streets for any of these or indeed when other things came to the fore in the 1970s, "Thatcher, Thatcher, milk snatcher," along came the Falklands War and the Miners' Strike in the 1980s. I remained on the fence. But then, Dear Reader, along came CAMRA, and something within me stirred. Here was a subject close to my heart, something that directly impacted me. After all, I had done my time in London drinking Watney's Red

Barrel, aka "Water," and felt I deserved something that has body, has flavour, has strength. So I took some interest in the "Campaign for Real Ale"—even attended some of their events—but I never, ever marched in support of my passion. But then I didn't have to because the country as a whole recognized a worthy cause when they met one. Britain embraced microbreweries with such passion and commitment that the mega breweries were doomed.

OK, Dear Reader, I make light of a serious situation, and I apologise, but despair begats humour. What else can one do when the Civil War was fought and won over 150 years ago and still people are judging others by the colour of their skin? Apart from the fact that it is racial prejudice, it is also very, very silly and defies any credible intelligence in the perpetrators. Everybody needs to sit down, take a deep breath and share a decent beer.

Sun is shining.

Water

As we live in a temperate rainforest, it was inevitable that eventually the subject of water should come up.

As a teacher at Collingwood School, I put myself in charge of deciding whether or not the children were to have an indoor recess. It was a philosophy of mine to get them outside as much as possible. I don't think any of my colleagues liked to have an indoor recess. So, often it would be raining, and they would go out. Only on a persistent downpour of a day would they be allowed in.

Scandinavians believe there is no such thing as bad weather only bad clothing. There was the problem. Ensuring that the children came to school with wet-weather gear so that they were protected from the elements was an issue. Too often, a car-delivered child would arrive without wet-weather gear. I tried to solve this by having the children keep their waterproofs at school but, Dear Reader, there was always one. Of course, there were covered areas outdoors where children could shelter so they could always avoid a soaking.

Assemblies happened once per week, so I met with the person in charge and asked if I could do a wet-weather performance. I explained to my class that I wanted them all to be dressed in rain gear for the Monday assembly. I was forceful and enthused in my delivery. I wanted the children to be excited to perform in front of their peers. I did manage smiles and nodding heads, so I was encouraged.

"Soooo, to recap, I want you all to have your rain gear ready for assembly on Monday morning. Luca, you look confused?"

"Errr, you want us all to come to school dressed as reindeer?"

Children look at me, look at Luca, giggles behind a hand. Confused look on the face of the teacher.

"No, no, no, not reindeer, Luca, rain gear."

Slow dawning on Luca's face, little chuckle, and we were all smiling.

It was September and early in the school year, and suddenly I had my opening for the assembly. I YouTubed and found a version of *Rudolf the Red-Nosed Reindeer,* which was duly played to the gathered throng. Colleagues and children all looked confused, it not being appropriate to the season. It was yet another example of Davidson pulling out a tenuous connection, drawing a weird link in order to get a message across!!??

Back to water. (I suppose I could have dug up *Singing in the Rain* for that assembly!!) A few years ago, I read a book entitled *Water.* I don't remember who wrote it. I do remember that one of the premises was that water was becoming so valuable that it was likely that wars would be fought over its availability. The author painted painted pictures of ranches in drought-bestrewn areas and ones where water is a plenty.

In areas of shortage, the ranch from the air looks like an oasis of green and vegetation while much of the rest of the acreage is dry and struggling. In wetter climates, the opposite is the case. There is a gap in the forest, in the bushy surrounds where sits the farmhouse. I grew up in the UK where I took water for granted except that it was not always hot enough for a shower. But, needing a drink of water I reached for a glass and a tap and was instantly gratified. That is still the case. I am aware, because of media messaging, that there are areas of the world where fresh water is not available, where drinking water is a risk, and where people have to walk miles to obtain it. What I do not understand is why there are First Nations reserves in Canada where fresh water is *not* available.

We have become hyper aware of racism over recent weeks. Because I am of a privileged colour, a privileged class and a privileged gender, it has been difficult for me to understand what it is like to be a visible minority or to walk for a day in a woman's shoes. So, I have to see videos of police harassing people of colour or killing them to have some understanding and belief that this is happening. I have to see phone clips of a woman being harassed to have understanding. I have to experience it vicariously. Because I have a belief in and everyday experience of the niceness of people, I find it hard to take that people can act in threatening ways to others. I have had to adjust my thinking to the fact that, as a nation, Canada may be equally as racist as other countries. So, a cop beating a First Nations chief can be a rogue policeman, one cop does not make a flawed system. Every job has weak links. But, Dear Reader, people who live in this country and have done so for 10,000 years and do *not* have access to fresh water is a national disgrace. I don't know whose fault it is. What I do know is that I arrived here as an immigrant in 1991 and poured myself a glass of water on my first day. How can it be that in an under-populated land of plenty that simple task is not available to all??! Intolerance and prejudice are parts of the characters of individual human beings. There is little that can be done about that except when society shames them for who they are. Systemic racism in institutions is becoming clear and was not something I believed existed. I had a naïve faith. But what really, really confirms it for me that it is there are First Nations reserves that do not have access to fresh water!!?? Surely, in this day and age and in this country, this is an easy fix. There is the expertise, the money, the nous, it just takes the political will. Here in privileged North Vancouver, if we suddenly had a water leak through earthquake, disaster or something else, there are enough people who are articulate and adept enough to put forward a quick solution. I don't believe we would be without this facility for long. After all, we soon regain electrical power after we have had a cut.

Any rate, it is not raining, and I am going for an early morning walk with my friend. Have a good day.

Saracens v. Exeter

T he Saracens and the Exeter Chiefs are the two most powerful rugby clubs in England. Saracens are the current English Premiership and European Champions. On June 1, 2019, as I have mentioned in a previous blog, I was at Twickenham Rugby Ground with about 80,000 others to watch an exciting final. I won't go too much into the history of these clubs, but I will touch on their origins and symbols.

The Saracens were formed in 1876. They were so named for the "endurance, enthusiasm and perceived invincibility of Saladin's desert warriors of the twelfth century." When they were formed, their closest rival was a club called the Crusaders. Of course, they were. Eventually the Crusaders folded and amalgamated, ironically enough, with the Saracens. Today their fans wear a fez, which is a stylized form of cap probably originating from Persia. The badge on their jerseys is a version of a symbol of Islam.

The Exeter Chiefs have a Native American as their badge. He is wearing a full-feathered headdress. The fans, too, wear headdresses at the games. Their chant is modelled after an Indigenous person's perceived chant. It is called the "Tomahawk Chop." Their second team is called "The Braves."

Given this information you will see, Dear Reader, that I was sat down with my brother, George, my friend, Jamie, and his Canadian father-in-law, George Boyce, in a house of ill-repute!! In addition to the 80,000 fans, there were the players, the support staff, the employees and vendors in and around the rugby ground, so we must have numbered over 100,000 people. One hundred thousand examples of political incorrectness! It was competitive on the pitch and extremely friendly off the pitch. It was a day full of banter and bonhomie. Yet it was an act of betrayal of every virtue that was ever signaled!!

I do not know how many Muslims or Native Americans were at the game. I am not Muslim or Native American so I cannot speak to how they might feel if they were a witness to this occasion. Presumably there are citizens who will take offence at such naming and traditions. I do not have the right to gainsay the culture of others. But, dear friends, these two clubs were *not* set up to mock or disparage a race or religion. Far from it, they were both formed in honour of a warrior breed, one that fought with courage, grit, determination and teamwork for their birthrights. The town of Exeter was never going to name its team the The Cream Teas, and the London borough of Hendon was never going to call its team The Milksops. They both wanted symbols of virile manliness and, yes, before you ask, they *do* have strong women's rugby teams as well. So, when public opinion and some law of the land eventually strikes down their current traditions and their mores, it may be time to point out to the powers that be that rural Devon is a long way from North America, physically and culturally. Yet they have regarded the native peoples of that far away land with so much awe and respect that they have named their local rugby team after them. Similarly, the Crusaders of the twelfth century went on their mission to bring back Jerusalem as the centre of their belief in Christianity. They fought against the Saracens and returned to England with an awe and respect for their opponents so much so that their descendants named their rugby team after them.

Of course, I understand how the Confederate and Nazi flags should have no place in a country with the endemic racism of the United States or anywhere else for that matter. A swastika is a symbol of stupid, facile hatred the world over. Of course, I understand how a statue to a man who made his fortune in trading slaves is offensive. What surprises me, I suppose, is that it has taken so long for the debunking of statues and other such emblems to happen. Indeed, I would not be surprised if somebody came along and ripped down Lord Stanley from his place in his park and, while they were at it, ripped away that old womanizer, Robbie Burns, from in front of the rowing club. After all, despite his magnificent poetry he was free and easy with his virtue. So, back in Bristol (the city that should be razed to the ground because it was built on the appalling nefariousness of so many), Colston Hall, a musical venue for so many years, Colston School, producer of outstanding rugby players and scholars for so many years, are, presumably, going to have to rethink their name or otherwise they are going to be cuddling up to the statue of their namesake in the harbour. Nobody in their right mind condones slavery; nobody in their right mind forgives inequality of opportunity; nobody in their right mind looks down on anybody else because of the colour of their skin or their gender or their religion. But, personally,

I would like to have seen a petition formulated based on a history lesson on how Colston created his wealth. I would like to have seen a debate in council. I would like to have seen Colston discussed in schools and universities. I would like people to understand why he needed to be removed from places of honour.

Was Churchill a racist? Probably. Most people were back then. Did he condemn people to death by starvation and poor wartime decisions? Yes; he was partly responsible for Gallipoli and the Bengal famine. Oh, and let's fling in the fact that he did not want India to become independent. Was he a neglectful father, an absent husband, a huge ego and a man with a tendency to ride roughshod over others in pursuit of his goals? Quite possibly. So we can have the debate about his ethics and morality and, if that is too far beyond our Canadian bailiwick, we can bring it home and strike John A. Macdonald from our coinage, a la the City of Victoria and her statue of him.

There are thoroughly bad eggs out there. Pol Pot, Hitler, Mussolini, Ivan the Terrible, Caligula, Nero, Saddam Hussein to name but a few. Most people, however, are a mixture of all of the flaws and foibles of our humanity. Many leaders and captains of industry are giants among humankind. The trouble with being larger than life is that their faults are supersized as well. We petty men and women have to sit and watch and decide which unseemly aspects of their character we are going to ignore considering what they have done "pro bono publico." We need to cut some of our current leaders a bit of slack in light of the current crisis. We need to look back in history and remember that LP Hartley once said:

*"The past is a foreign country. They do
things differently there."*

One does **not** need to be male to climb Everest or sail single-handedly around the world. One does not need to be white and privileged to run a business or reach the height of a profession. White privilege does help, I know, still more in a class-ridden system like the UK, but the laws are in place so anybody can rise if they are given a good start, and sometimes **because** they are given a bad start. There are First World failures in the creation of cultural ghettos that foster tribalism. In the United States, there is that awful legacy of slavery that they cannot seem to move on from. There also seems to be a two-tiered education system that favours the wealthy and inhibits the poor.

We can still make progress, but it doesn't come by expunging an episode of *Fawlty Towers* from the archives!! If we resort to burning the books it is only a short step to burning the people who wrote them. We surely must not deny what was. There are so many people in the world who have suffered prejudice and death because of colour, misogyny, homophobia and religious prejudice. They cannot breathe the heady air so many of us here in North Vancouver have been allowed. I want all of those people to be able to inhale great writing, great knowledge and great works of art. If breathing in great novels and plays means people become exposed to Fagan in *Oliver Twist* and Shylock in *The Merchant of Venice* and all of the anti-Semitism those characters inhabit, then so be it. If *The Taming of the Shrew* is misogynistic, Tom Sawyer uses unfortunate language, *Gone with the Wind* carries unfortunate inferences, then so be it. When we breathe in, not all of the aromas are pleasant. We have to see and hear and read how people think and thought. Denial is not a healthy way of life. Denying that something happened or was written is a scandal. Suck it all in and identify what is bad air and what is good. Talk about the whys and the wherefores. Don't let censorship insult our intelligence. "I can't breathe" is an apt message. We should all have a right to hear and see what we were, to breathe in every word that was ever written or said, otherwise how do we know what we can become?

Since writing this piece, the Exeter Chiefs have been asked to change their name and their logo. They have done away with their mascot but insisted on keeping the rest arguing that it is "respectful" of the First Nations' culture. Saracens have flown under the radar so far. There are other rugby teams out there which are, at least, examples of cultural appropriation. The Highlanders with their Scottish symbol in New Zealand, the Crusaders with their meaning of going on a crusade to promulgate the Christian religion. I am still learning, as we all are. I must admit that something within me does grate when, for example, one sees English people wearing Scottish kilts at an English wedding. It seems somehow incongruous and out of place. Is my Scottish ancestry and pride scarred for life by this example of cultural appropriation? Hardly.

Pyramids

L adies and Gentlemen, I have discovered that the pyramids need to be pulled down. They were built by slave labour to honour a man who was a misogynist, and during the process many of his workforce died. I do not think they should be daubed with anti-pharaoh graffiti, so I am suggesting they be reassembled in a museum and used by students to learn the evils of their history. While the virtue signalers are touring around Egypt, they might consider blocking up the Suez Canal because, after all, it was built by de Lesseps so that the European imperialists could more easily rape and pillage their colonies. Gustav Eiffel and his Parisian tower needs some debate, but there should be no doubt that the Arc de Triomphe should come down because it represents the glorification of war and the oppression of peoples. Samuel Johnson has Imlac say of the pyramids in his book *Rasselas*:

> *"Those who have already all that they can enjoy must enlarge their desires. He that has built for use till use is supplied must begin to build for vanity."*

Seems like a pretty good summing up for me. Johnson went on to say:

"I consider this mighty structure as a monument of the insufficiency of human enjoyments."

I have never seen the wonders of Egypt, but I am sure I would be impressed. They look like the Trump Towers of their day, obviously built to honour a big ego and men who thought they were gods.

It is good that there was a fire in Notre Dame Cathedral. Hopefully when it is rebuilt it will not be labelled as "Our Lady," a hopelessly inappropriate label for our times. It should be called "Notre person who has a menstrual cycle," according to certain virtual signallers. J.K. Rowling has found, to her cost, that calling such people "women" is no longer appropriate. We need to move forward on this quickly. "Maternity hospitals" need to be called "People who give birth hospitals," remembering, of course, that these people no longer give birth to boys and girls. To me, wrongly, I suppose, "women" is not a bad word; I am with J.K. Rowling on this. I guess I am slow to come around to the belief that it is time our language became more complicated, time we used several words where previously one sufficed. So, I am full of ignorance about sexual orientation and have no knowledge about how people can be persecuted because of their sexual proclivities. It is not my area of expertise. But, Dear Reader, surely we take people as we find them. The content of their character has nothing to do with whosoever they choose to share their bodily fluids with. It is none of my business whom or what Joseph or Joanne decides to sleep with. It is a bodily function with an emotional attachment. But if we find common interests or discover we are kindred spirits and enjoy each others' company then why would I be in the least bit interested in which consenting adult has sex with which other consenting adult? It is far too much information to be privy to intimate aspects of anybody else's sex life. Quite simply, it is none of my business and has absolutely no bearing on whether or not I like or dislike them.

Of course, I am old and may need to be retrained. How do I know that I am old? Well, because the receptionist at the doctor's office told me to:

"Sit down over there, Dear."

I have to admit that calling me "Dear" was a bit of a red rag. I was tempted to respond:

"OK, my love/me duck/hen/darlin'/my girl."

Depending on what would have been fine in various regions of the country that I grew up in back in the day. I suppose I find it a bit strange to be called up to an appointment by my first name as well. I always expect to be called formally, **"Mr. Davidson"** when I am in line for something. Indeed, I would much prefer to be called **"You over there, forgotten your name, yes you, the old bastard asleep in the corner pretending to do the crossword, yes you, it's your turn."**

Now *that* I can relate to. Perhaps I should be spray painted with graffiti and thrown into a harbour.

I guess I also have a problem with the language of sexual orientation. I understand why women may wish to be called

"Ms." instead of "Mrs." or "Miss." If one person wants to be called "Zie" or "they," then I will fit in. I am a bit of a language fiend. I do love words so much that some phrases grate, but others amuse. For example, I loved the story about the two wee boys at the back of the class. The teacher used the term "glitch" when there was a problem with the SMART board.

"What's a glitch?" whispered Eric.

The other wee laddie nodded his head wisely, leaned over and said,

"It's a female dog."

"Glitch" is not a word I ever came across in the UK.

I understand language and culture are intrinsically linked. I understand there are dialectical differences, but it grates with me when somebody in Tim Hortons says:

"Can I get a double/double?"

I would not last too long as a server there because I would be answering something along the lines of, "Of course you can, but would you like one?" Thus, would I reply in my classroom to:

"Can I go to the washroom, Mr. Davidson?"
"I don't know, can you?"

Or something that has crept into our language:

"Where are you at?"

Hmmm, surely no need for "at"! Can somebody explain to me how one can have a moment that is not in time? Any rate, I am being a puerile pedant. I make equally as many mistakes, but I do hope the listeners would pick me up on them.

Back to language and culture and, in this case, the movies. Tom Selleck is playing a famous architect who is on holiday in England. Archetypal Englishwoman at the cocktail party has heard about his skill and decides to approach him and make small talk over the mini-sausage rolls and drinks trays.

"I say, I say, I've heard an awful lot about your stunning erections."

I know I am an age-challenged person and white and privileged to boot. I find it difficult to adjust so that changing my terminologies may be a difficult task. I will probably always call my mother "Mum." Irene, my wife, has never, ever been my "partner." How could she be a "partner" to me? That is a word that suggests equality, and I have failed miserably for thirty-plus years to become her equal. I am drooping as I write, so I suppose I could do with a "power nap". I am pretty sure that I can still say 'forty winks' or take a 'wee kip' with impunity.

Back to the pyramids. Were the pharaohs simply intending to build a back-yard barbecue and one brick led to another and voila? One could certainly not have a group of buddies around and stand on the top sharing a beer and the view; there's no room for that. Maybe they were gyms, exercise regimes. Up rises Mr. Pharaoh in the morning, makes Mrs. Pharaoh a cuppa tea in bed, gives her the papyrus to read and announces:

> *"I'm just going to run the pyramid, Dear.*
> *Back in a jiffy."*

> *"How many reps?"*

Maybe there is a gap in our studies here. Maybe several households had gotten together and run lines from the top of the pyramids to their back porches so they could hang their washing out to dry. Maybe a zipline to the ocean?? I guess Gustav Eiffel had a load of spare metal left over from a railway he was building.

> *"Hmmmm, je crois je will build une*
> *grande tour avec toute cette junk et charge*
> *beaucoup de people un sackload de monnaie*
> *a ascender ca."*

Marco Polo to the builders of Venice:

> *"If I were you, I would build it on land.*
> *But you know best."*

A Chinese household back in the day. In walks Dad with a plan under his arm:

> *"What's that you've got there, Dad?"*

> *"It's a plan, son, the emperor wants us to*
> *build a wall."*

"Why?"

"Well, yesterday it was a garden bench, the day before that it was a rockery, previously a little path to the shrubbery. Now he wants a wall, Son."

"How big, how long?"

"Didn't say. Let's make a start."

Nunc est bibendum. Pete

"And now you come in my awakening which is my deeper dream."
Khalil Gibran

CHAPTER 8

REMINISCENCE

The bane in the existence of remembering is rose-tinted spectacles. We exaggerate our memories of the past, their goodness and their badness. It has been said that nobody looks upon art in the same way. We are all the victims of our own individuality or uniqueness. So it must be with memory. Our contemporaries may not remember in the same way. What was, may appear either with exaggeration or understatement. Some, therefore, may question whether these events ever happened at all. So, the following reminiscences fall victim to time and imagination.

Absence and Presence

Back in 1974, my Westminster College rugby team was on an away trip to another local teacher's college, the name of which escapes me for the moment. We were a close-knit bunch of guys who really enjoyed each other's company. We did not have many fans, particularly fans who travelled to our away games. We did, on this occasion, have Eric come along who was meeting a friend after the game. Eric had never played a rugby game in his life; he was short and slightly built. He was a homosexual and was very effeminate to boot. We all loved his wonderful sense of humour, his incredible bantering command of the English language and his open-hearted bonhomie.

It was a muddy field with a possibility of rain. Both teams got changed and were on the field waiting for the referee, but it became obvious after about ten minutes that there was not going to be one. There was no way we were not going to play, so we had to find somebody to ref the game. After much discussion, a committee of three approached Eric and asked him to do it. The colour drained from his face. Both captains spoke to him reassuringly. We didn't care how bad his decisions were, we would not question them, we would not argue, we would support every one of his actions. "Please, please," we pleaded, "without you there will be no game." So, the game began, players nodded and smiled and called him "Sir" at every awful decision—and there were many. It was without doubt the politest rugby game I had ever played in. Twenty minutes before the game ended, however, there was an altercation between several players over a clash of heads. The referee tried to intervene, but all gentlemen's agreements fell apart amidst an unseemly brawl. Frantic blowing of the whistle and passionate pleas from Eric fell on deaf ears until he finally abandoned the game. Somebody heard that mouse-like squeak of finality, and clenched fists and arms raised to strike suddenly became open hands extended for the traditional handshake. Smiles broke out, and the two teams walked off the field together, bantering about the game. In the bar afterwards, Eric was inconsolable. Somebody had told him what a useless referee he was and then bought him a pint. He wasn't a referee, he explained. He never intended to be a referee. He only had a bit of an understanding of the laws of the game and, besides which, there would have been no game but for him! The bus ride back to college was rowdy, and songs were being sung with awful tuneless tenor. Asleep at the back with a blissful smile on his face, happily unaware of the hangover to come, was Eric. And, my friends, he had not bought a drink all night even though his friend never turned up.

Rugby, like many competitions, is a Jekyll and Hyde experience. There is a thundering, competitive presence on the field and a milque toast gentleness off it. (OK, not quite "milk-toast gentleness"—some Davidson iterations are a contrast too far—but you get my drift!) There are two very different presences and two very different absences. Rugby is a sport, but it is also a culture. It is very effective at separating its game face from its human face. It is able to switch very quickly and effectively from one side of its persona to the other. It could teach many groups and organizations a great deal about how to manage their "virtue signaling." They could learn to broach their political and religious differences in a way that gets their arguments across but are able to do so accepting that not all people are all good or all bad. I like Walt Whitman's statement:

> *"Do I contradict myself?*
> *Very well then I contradict myself,*
> *(I am large, I contain multitudes.)"*

The presence of an idea that may seem callously self-serving does not mean the absence of an otherwise altruistic being, does it? I am uncertain about this when hearing, reading and seeing people in action who want to give the benefit of the doubt.

> *"We are all patchwork."* Montaigne

Sky is blue. Off for a walk with an ex-rugby player. Have a day, my friends.

Hope

A friend of mine from my rugby club served in the British military. He fought in the Falklands War and kept the peace in Northern Ireland. When The Troubles were at their most dangerous, he was patrolling the streets. Every corner turned was an excursion into potential death. Every building housed a potential sniper. He recalled being on patrol one day when they were shot at from a building. They knew the marksman was high up, but they could not pinpoint where. After a long period of frustration and pot shots hitting the street, there was no way forward for the patrol. The sergeant asked him to dash across the street, presenting himself as a target so they could establish the enemy's position. Brad replied:

"Sergeant, there are three hopes in this world. Some hope, no hope and Bob Hope. You have no hope of getting me to do that!"

Brad never related how the whole incident panned out, but it was likely a better outcome for the patrol than the gunman. Brad was alive to tell the tale. He was also stuck aboard the *Sir Galahad*, a Royal Navy ship that was about to disembark its soldiers when it was bombed in the Falklands War. Some forty Welsh guards and crewmen lost their lives. Brad survived without a scratch on his body but, no doubt, scratches on his memory and his soul.

I don't know where Brad Herman is now. I do know that he seemed to breeze through life on a wing and a prayer.

When our children were young, we used to car/camp in our summers in BC provincial parks. Inevitably, we travelled east and ineluctably arrived in Hope where we would stop by the river for a picnic lunch. We had milked all of the jokes that will have been a part of your repertoire as well, dear BC-ers. To reiterate them here would be trite. But we always breathed a sigh when we reached this small town because we felt we had finally left the city and were really on holiday. Our hopes were of a lake lazing, loon-listening lounge by an evening glow from a campfire and a sinking sun. We hoped for sun and dry, blue skies and fishing and swimming. Occasionally we did have rain, and when we reminisce about those days we forget there were flies. I don't know what it is about human beings, but when nostalgia beckons it does so with rose-coloured spectacles. There were NO flies on our BC trips; there were NO midges in my Scottish childhood?? But there were, Dear Reader, there really were.

Speaking of Scotland, Irene and I had two small tents when the children were but bairns. We were on the Black Isle a short drive north of Inverness. We pitched our tents on a beach side campsite. We ate our suppers, walked on the beach, kicked a ball and returned to snuggle in for the night. The wind got up and the rain came in, changing quickly from vertical to horizontal. So, Irene and Alison bedded themselves down with neat, feminine efficiency in their tent. Grant and I crawled into our scruffier bedspace. I found my flashlight under a sock, pyjamas appeared from deep in the bottom of my pack. *Hairy Maclary from Donaldson's Dairy* was the book of choice at that time. Grant knew the words by heart. So we puffed up our clothes as pillows, arranged the book and the light and settled down for story time. But, dear friends, there is a short square of linen cut from an old sheet that was a little bit bigger than a handkerchief (we still have it somewhere). It was Grant's "sheetie." Every night he wrapped it into a sausage, unwrapped it, re-rolled it, cuddled on it, drooled on it and slept with it. Outside the tent, the wind blew and a cacophony of rain battered the canvas, yet we were warm and dry and reading the story:

"Bitzer Maloney, all skinny and bony."

"Daddy?"

"Yes, Grant."

"Where's my sheetie?"

"Around here somewhere, and 'Hercules Morse as big as a horse.' Which of all the doggies in this story is your favourite, Grant?"

And the storm without blew harder.

"I need my sheetie, Daddy."

"Oh look, Scarface Claw the toughest cat in the world. Isn't she fierce, Grant?"

"Sheetie, Daddy?"

"Shall I read it again, which is your best dog?"

"Where's my sheetie, Daddy?"

"It's in the car, Son."

Slow boyish rumination, thoughtful look, search for the right words. Finally, "Get it Daddy."

And the wind blew, and the rain drove, and I got dressed with difficulty, found my car keys, pulled on waterproofs, managed to get my shoes on, unzipped the tent, stepped into the night, dashed for the car, fumbled with the lock, found the sheetie and repeated the process to get back into the tent, gave him his sheetie and snuggled back into my sleeping bag.

"Daddy."

"Yes, Grant?"

"Read the story again."

I guess I could have been hard and pleaded the "No, Some, Bob" trilogy of hopes to avoid leaving the tent. But then I would have had little hope of sleep myself because of guilt, let alone much-postured pleading from our son. Truly it was my fault. He was a child. I was responsible for his belongings. I should have been better prepared. I did notice, in the flurry of dashing back and forth to the car, that the lights were out in the other tent and all was at peace.

Eccentricities

Apparently, the Marquis de Sade was a prisoner in the Bastille until a week before it fell at the beginning of the French Revolution. He was released because he had adapted his slop funnel into a megaphone and was using it to harangue the people both within the prison and outside of it. He had browbeaten the prison authorities and the local Parisians with his orations so much that everyone had had enough. They had no ear protectors in those days! There is something inevitably appealing about harmless eccentrics, is there not? People who do not fit the mould, who think outside the box and cock a snook at the norms of society, produce a smile and a nod of approval from me.

Sometimes!

Back in 1973, there was a campaign in the UK for everybody to plant a tree. "Plant A Tree in '73" tripped glibly off the tongue. Some ten years or so later, a TV camera crew was sent to accompany a gentleman who had planted a tree in 1973. The goal was to film him returning to the tree to see how it had grown and progressed in the ensuing years. So, they filmed him as he was leaving his house, followed him through the village, commenting and talking all the way with the tree being the ultimate destination. It became obvious, however, as they proceeded that he had no idea where he had planted his tree. They were outside the churchyard.

Not there. At the village green. Nope. In the pub garden. Hmmm! Eventually the camera angle wilted, and chuckles rose from interviewer and film crew as the villager rustled through the bushes determined to find his tree. It was an abject failure but a very funny piece of television.

I played rugby with a guy called Dick Best back in the day. He related the sorry tale of a failed job interview. He breezed into the interview room to be confronted by who he assumed to be his future boss engrossed and ignoring him from behind a newspaper. He was unsure whether to introduce himself forcefully, remain standing or sit down. After a long delay a face appeared from behind the paper and said, "Try to attract my attention."

Well, Dick had had enough of these silly games and, being a smoker, pulled out his lighter, lit the bottom of the paper, turned and left the room. He heard the flurry of activity and the language as he left but did not turn around. Was that the meeting of two eccentrics or was one perfectly normal? An urban legend, possibly.

Then there was the middle-aged woman who came to Kingweston House in Somerset to talk to eighty teenage boys about sex. It was an event held in the dining room. She was, as I remember, in a tweed suit with sensible shoes. She climbed onto the dining room table and continued talking while on her hands and knees and explained that this was the position that Peruvian women adopted when they were giving birth! This wasn't very exciting for teenage boys for whom interest was sparked by Diana Rigg in her leather suit starring as Emma Peel in *The Avengers* on Saturday night. The biology teacher had tried to give us the sex talk but was quite categorical in that he could talk about "the plumbing," as he called it, but not about the emotional side of things. The "emotional side" for us could be summed up in one word: "lust." It was all about Raquel Welch in an animal skin, a Bond girl appearing from the ocean. It really didn't have much to do with South American mothers and a pipe-smoking man telling us about how things worked. As I remember we already knew how things worked.

Any rate, sex education has moved along, and now it is admitted—even in boarding schools in the UK!—that our parents did that. This was a fact I thought impossible at the time.

Going for a walk with a friend. Have a good day.

One Memorable Day

What with three months of lockdown, isolation and social distancing, the adjustment has been difficult for all of us. We have all likely sought some form of escapism. Last week I decided to find one day in my past that was extra special to me. Irene, my wife, I think will forgive me if it is not our wedding day, memorable and joyful though that was. Alison, our daughter, will forgive me if I do not touch on her first place in the 100km Cotswold Way Ultra race. There have been many fantastic days in my life.

Back in the late 1990s and early 2000s, Collingwood School had kindly involved me in the rugby programme. Thus, every June the senior rugby team would decamp to the University of British Columbia (UBC) over the other side of town for the Provincial Rugby Championships. Collingwood School have won the AA championship on numerous occasions thanks to their coaches David Speirs, Roger Hatch, Peter Brampton, Scott Rickard and Ian Kennedy, who have built excellence over thirty years. However, in the years 2004, 2005, 2006, my eyes were more firmly focused on Carson Graham School where our son, Grant, was playing.

2004 and 2005 were bronze medal, third place playoff years for The Eagles, as the team is known. On both occasions, Shawnigan Lake School had seen them off in the semi-final. 2006 was graduation year for so many, including our son.

It was the last chance to win for that cadre of Grade XII players.

Thunderbird Stadium is an idyllic venue. There is one large set of stands on one side in which to sit and a welcoming fenced-in grassy bank on the other. The teams played both semi-finals in the stadium. Irene and I watched nervously through a tight semi-final between Carson Graham and Oak Bay from Victoria. 14-12 is a narrow victory in a rugby game and, indeed, a crucial refereeing decision had gone Carson Graham's way, so the victory was not without controversy. Still and all, it was an uphill road to climb because Shawnigan Lake, Carson's bête noir from the previous two semi-finals, was again a powerhouse and firm favourites to win the final.

On the Saturday of the finals, I had watched all day with a total lack of attention. My focus was on the last game of the day, the AAA final. Irene and I took our seats in the stands and watched the teams come out to warm up, go back into the changing room, then come out again to begin the game. Cowardly as I am, I could watch from my seat no more, and I told Irene I had to watch from elsewhere, that she was on her own. So, I moved to the back of the stands where I could watch and pace with no other distractions. I walked miles back and forth that afternoon, I sweated over every yard gained, agonized over every inch lost. I white-knuckled my way through every kick against, I closed my eyes through every kick for. Every point scored by the opposition was a year off my life, every score for The Eagles was an anguished joy. A neutral will tell you it was not a great game to watch; it was a grind and a grope, every blade of grass was fought over, every margin of error threatened loss and disappointment.

Such was my emotional involvement that I did not care whether I was entertained or not. Such was the trauma of the game that I have no memory of the details. But, the Carson Graham Eagles had a surprising lead at half-time, and nearing the end of the game they were 18-5 points ahead.

Never counting one's chickens before they are hatched has almost always been my modus operandi. So with five minutes to go there was no way that I was going to make my way down to the side of the field and give a premature shake of the hand to the Carson coaches. With two minutes to go, however, I started to move from the back of the stands and, with determined slowness, came to a spot behind one set of posts where Ramsay, one of the coaches was standing. I found myself stood next to him. He nodded a brief greeting before giving his attention back to the game. The clock ticked down so, so slowly. There was still too much time left, too many fraught possibilities. What if Shawnigan were to score now? How much injury time would there be? Could it be that, having come so close, Carson could still lose it? Success and failure still hung in the balance. But I was suddenly conscious of a hand in mine, a firm grip and a wide grin. Our boys were about to win the game. After three years of preparation, Carson Graham had banked their first-place gold medal with an 18-5 victory.

So, June 3, 2006. Game over. Gold medal won. A moment and a nod of appreciation to Head Coach Tom Larisch, who had done so much for the team and the individual players throughout his tenure. Ho hum! Nothing to do but go home. Irene and I joined in the back slapping, congratulated boys and coaches, watched the presentations and drove home. End of story. Not quite!

Irene and I were at home. Suddenly, Grant turned up still in his sweaty, dirty rugby gear but with his gold medal around his neck. He had had to leave his battered old truck at UBC because I had inadvertently taken his keys home with me. So there was no alternative but for us to make the long drive back through the city and out the other side to the UBC endowment lands and the student residences. I had the school mini-bus, so he piled into the passenger seat and we drove off. There was very little conversation on that journey. I remember the day as blue sky and sunny. There was a synchronicity about that companionable silence between father and son that is never likely to be repeated. The deep sigh of relaxed calm, the gentle smile of contented peace, the quiet realization of a battle won, the slow satisfied heartbeat of physical exhaustion were almost palpable. A stranger with us in the bus could have reached out and touched the mood, the heady once-in-a-lifetime atmosphere, the dawning that this was a private moment between father and son, and that we were oblivious to the wider world around us. It was a memorable day. It was Saturday, June 3, 2006. And that long ride back through the city was far, far too short.

I do hope, Dear Reader, that you have all had such wonderful days in your lives and that you are able to take as much pleasure in remembering them as I have in writing this down. Maybe you can find your own memorable day and, if you can be bothered, share it with me. I would love to hear from you.

Life and Deaf

When I was playing rugby for Highland RFC in Inverness in 1971, Cliff Parr befriended me. He was a couple of years older than me and therefore wiser. Well, actually he considered himself wiser, and I was prepared to go along with his version of his character because he was older than me. We had an away trip to Glasgow to play Strathclyde University. It was a long journey, so we were billeted by our host rugby club overnight. As we met early on the Saturday morning, Cliff was rubbing his hands.

"Concert tonight, Pete. Great place to pick up burds."

So, early on Saturday morning I suddenly became wide-eyed and bushy-tailed. If Cliff said it was so then it was so. We were destined for a game of rugby, a couple of beers and an evening of music and female company. Even with my faith in Cliff, I only really saw that two parts of the plan were likely and the third was one of life's forlorn hopes. We played our game, had our pints and trekked off to the concert hall to discover that the night's entertainment was a band called Black Sabbath. They eventually became famous, but at that point they were a sort of cult and relatively unknown.

Looking around the crowd, the third part of the plan looked eminently possible. University students thronged into the hall eager for the music to start. The time came for the entertainment to begin. The band strutted onto the stage, guitars and drums at the ready and struck up a chord. The whole place resonated, the loudness was beyond belief. I had never heard anything quite like it and ***never*** anything so loud. We were immediately a part of a jumping, thumping mass of youth and energy. Such was the cacophony that the close proximity of Cliff and me meant hand signals of communication only. There was not a chance of any verbal communication. Ready wit and repartee were lost amidst it all, and all chances to impress the opposite sex were drowned under rhythmic drumbeat, harsh vocal and twanging guitar. It quickly became a life-and-deaf situation when all that was left of the evening was an attempt to enjoy the music. By the end, my ears were ringing, my head was throbbing, and Cliff's quest had failed. We returned to our billets alone having learnt something, but we weren't sure what.

I don't know about you, Dear Reader, but I have never been very good in large groups at parties. Too many conversations at once mean that every oral or aural participation is tangential. I tend to touch on this verbiage here, that loquaciousness there. I hear the beginning of the joke but not the punchline. I am in on the end of the story but do not hear the meat in the middle. So, in the past, if I was standing at a drinks party or a special occasion, I would be reaching for the passing sausage rolls and the free glasses of fizz as the waiter did his rounds. I always thought there was something wrong with me. I struggled to be an active part of the group but always seemed to end up apart from the conversation. I wondered how others were able to do the same as me with the finger food and the drinks and be perfectly at their ease.

Years of unease passed until I finally attended an occasion and resolved to find somebody with whom I could engage as an individual without too many others around. I was interested to listen to whomever it was. Whenever there was a lull in the chat, I would find something else to ask and was quite happy that I was receiving the story of their life and they were learning nothing about me. It all became a bit one-sided, but it was a great deal more pleasant only being with a couple of people rather than half a dozen. It was my way of managing my life-and-deaf situation. I was always genuinely interested in others and, finally in a smaller group, I was able to hear more and appreciate more. I soon found myself immersed in their tales and fascinated by what made them tick. This, Dear Reader, gave me a flashback to my time at boarding school.

You see, friends, in my last year at Millfield School I was made prefect in charge of church. I boarded with seventy-nine other boys in Kingweston House, an old English manor house with accompanying church. We all had to attend the 11:00 a.m. Sunday service. It was my job to find a boy to read one of the lessons. Nobody wanted to do this. So, more often than not it ended up being me. But, Dear Reader, there was Sammy Ashamu. Sammy was a wonderful Nigerian lad, always smiling, always happy, always energetic. Sammy wanted to read the lessons. He had come to England and the school relatively late in his education, and his English was not great. He mispronounced words willy-nilly, which would have caused embarrassment to a lesser mortal. Sammy didn't care. He mispronounced them with panache, he mispronounced them with aplomb, he mispronounced them loudly. The boys were a large part of the congregation, but locals made up the rest. The attending villagers were a mixture of peasant farm workers and upper- class worthies. Neither group was able to understand Sammy. The former spoke with accent and dialect, the latter with plum in the mouth snobbishness So my job became easier. Every week, one of the biblical lessons began with Sammy and there was quiet satisfaction when he reached "Here endeth the lesson" and sat down. I was able to sit back and observe. It would be wrong to say I did not notice many of the locals craning to hear Sammy speak, several cupping their ears in their hands to seek a better understanding. The deeper the frown, the more determined was the effort to fathom what he was saying. Of course, my contemporaries in their Sunday best uniforms struggled to muster the serious attitude befitting of the occasion as Sammy spoke. Spluttering giggles emanated from shimmering jackets throughout the back rows of the little church. After a few weeks of Sammy's stimulating presentations, the vicar approached me and delicately asked if I could vary things a bit and find other readers to do the Sunday readings. I said I would try. I approached Sammy and told him he was going to be "rested." He accepted this with his usual equanimity. So, off I went to comb the halls and seek out new readers. Word had got around, and I became a pariah. People would see me coming and turn about. Boys would speed from their saunter suddenly having found a purpose to sprint towards. I failed miserably to find another reader, so I became the lesson reader for the next few Sundays. And, Dear Reader, it might as well have continued to be Sammy because those who had struggled to understand him, struggled to understand me. They would have struggled to understand the pope!!You see, friends, most of them had been too close to noisy farming machinery for too many years, and some had had too much rough cider over the years, which cannot have helped. No ear plugs then. They were effectively deaf.

My advice to those of you who think you are going deaf is that maybe you are not. Not every failure to hear is a hearing problem, it is often an ambient noise getting in the way. If you think you have a life-and-deaf problem, then eliminate ambient noise first. That's my excuse, and I'm sticking to it.

June 1, 2019

J une 1, 2019 was a wonderful day. I was staying in an
Airbnb in Nelson Gardens in the West London Borough
of Hounslow where I had my first teaching post back
in 1976. I woke early. The day shone with heat and blue
and sun. I walked towards Whitton High Street. I found a
breakfast "greasy spoon" and drank too many cups of coffee.
As I was leaving, I ran into Martin Johnson, who captained
England for many successful years and led the British and
Irish Lions. For those of you not au fait with rugby, Martin
Johnson is an icon. I respected his privacy by not catching
his eye, by not approaching him, by not coming up to him
to shake him by the hand. Icons should be allowed to sit on
the mantelpiece undusted, unnoticed and untouched; they
should only be there for us if that is their wish, don't you
think, Dear Reader?

Well breakfasted and with an anticipatory spring in my step, I
began to walk towards Twickenham rugby grounds, the home
of English rugby. I was walking through neighbourhoods
where the gardens were busy setting themselves up as food
stalls, favour shops, and terraced rose gardens were becoming
businesses. Fans were arriving from all directions. It was a
slow, steady coming together. I walked past the grounds
with its iconic lineout statue, its towering stands. I continued
towards Twickenham High Street where I had arranged to
meet my brother, George, in a local bookshop. As I walked

over the railway bridge, I ran into two very well-dressed men of about my age who were wearing straw hats and bow ties. A brief vignette of a conversation revealed them as Sale supporters down from Lancashire for the game—a game in which their team was not a participant. That did not matter, for such occasions are bigger than the game. As I proceeded to the bookshop, I found a Costa coffee shop, walked in and found myself a window seat. So, I had the newspapers, the crossword, a book, a coffee and, most importantly, a people-watching seat par excellence. I texted George with a change of plan. He was now to meet me there. I sat and watched fans in the street, locals in the street, strangers in the street. A gentleman arrived in the coffee shop off his bike (God knows why he had biked from the rural southeast to urban crowdedness). George arrived and immediately disappeared into the toilet to put on his shorts. We supped coffee, had a bite and then walked back to the ground amidst gathering throngs, gathering heat and gathering excitement. I stopped to buy my friend, Nigel, an Exeter Chiefs baseball hat, and then we walked on. Soon we were taking our seats in the grounds. Suddenly, I received a tap on the shoulder and my friend, Jamie, was there along with his father-in-law, George, whom I had heard so much about but had never met. It was a joy to put a face to a name, to try to link stories to reality. We shook hands and settled in to watch Saracens v. Exeter in the English Premier League Rugby Union Final. It was a high-scoring, exciting game in which the wrong side won! 80,000 people exited the grounds, smiled across a fan divide and made their ways home by train, bus, walk or car. We said farewell to Jamie and George, and brother and I fought a desperate and losing battle to find a pub that was not full and was showing the European Football final between the two English clubs, Liverpool and Tottenham Hotspur. We failed in London but caught a train back to Cambridge where George lives and caught the second half of a lousy game in a local pub. The day was over, but the memory has lingered.

I was staying in the village of Little Shelford for a further two days with George and his wonderful wife, Jo. George is very well-read, very quick witted and has a marvelous sense of humour. He kindly took the Monday off work and took time to show me the sights and sounds of Cambridge, including a wonderfully eclectic barbers' shop.

So, Dear Reader, that 1st of June, fantastic as it was at the time, has now assumed iconic status in the Davidson memory. We have all moved from that freedom of movement that we in the western world have taken so much for granted to a different world. So, in reflective moments throughout the year, I sat with a wonderful memory of June 1, 2019. Now, my friends, a year later, in a world of trauma and change, a glorious day of happiness and pleasure has assumed a stature and grandeur of mythical proportions, way, way beyond where it stood in my memory as recently as March of this year.

These are *my* memories. But I know that all of you are sitting back and looking at highlights of your lives last year and thinking the same thing. There is so much that is right and wrong with the past. Nostalgia is a deceitful friend. But great occasions *then* are even greater occasions *now*, are they not? A long weekend in Norfolk or Sun Peaks, a reunion of old friends, a seasonal celebration, a Friday night in the pub after a long week in the office that may have been part of our comfortable existence previously are not possible again. Yee Haa! I am so grateful I had June the 1, 2019. I am so lucky to be here to look forward to another date, another occasion, another memory at some time down this difficult road.

Father's Day

I have an image of what a Father's Day should look like, and it doesn't involve a Hallmark card and a Denny's brunch. Nor does it involve a host of special events like waterskiing or fishing or monster truck rallies or—please no!—NASCAR. I have never understood why fathers have to appear macho and, therefore, do macho things on Father's Day. I am not saying we should go to the ballet or sit in the back garden writing poetry, but please no Neanderthal grunting or loud expressions of machismo or driving fast in noisy cars or antisocial motor bikes. It is wrong to say that men are not nuanced; that they have to search through the dusty shelves in the garage to find their sensitivity. We may not often be found wandering through the daffodils beside the lake or dallying over a dainty cuppa tea. But we do notice when our wives have been to the barber and had themselves a haircut; we view the new hair shape and added tinctures of colour with a subdued joy, but a joy none the less. We express unmitigated delight at the arrival of a new colour scheme in the front room. We cannot wait to put together the IKEA bed for the out-of-town visitor, although we do hope they are Swedish enough to appreciate the effort.

I never understood why the day I became a father was such a surprise to me. After all, there had been warning signs. The fact that Irene was pregnant was a significant suggestion that we were going to have a child. Then I had been dispatched to antenatal classes despite my desperate pleas that I had nothing against natals per se! What did I learn there? I learned we should have a bag packed when the day was closing in on us. I was told that when Irene was in labour I was to try to distract her. So, I bought a joke book and had a copy of the *Sunday Express General Knowledge Crossword* handy. Indeed, Alison Margaret Davidson arrived on Monday, 14th October at 5:30 a.m. We were in England, but it was Canadian Thanksgiving. Irene had spent the whole day in the maternity ward on the Sunday, and I had cooked us a turkey. I was much chagrined when she refused to eat it, was not interested in my jokes and had no idea what the capital city of Albania was. Alison arrived. Irene had been through the mill that night. I had to leave to go to work. In hindsight, I could probably have taken the day off, but nobody thought to offer it, and I never thought to ask.

Grant arrived in the middle of the school summer holidays. Yet again, I was surprised. I think he was easier on arrival on Irene, but I am full of admiration for what women have to go through in this traumatic process.

Lois is Irene's long-time school friend. When her husband, John, was driving her to hospital when their fourth child was about to be born, he pulled into a gas station and stopped.

"We have plenty of gas, why are we stopping?" she groaned from the passenger seat.

"I know, I know, but I can't stand hospital coffee."

There was the mother with her two young children on the nine-hour flight from Vancouver to London. A middle-aged gentleman on a business trip was sat next to them. The children would not settle, so the man spent large portions of the flight entertaining them, soothing the crying, calming the eating crisis, and so forth. He had started to be a bit frayed around the edges as they came in to land but asked kindly if her husband was meeting her at the airport.

"No," she said, "he's three rows behind us."

We all know that fathering and mothering are not exact sciences. Despite thousands of years of putting babies on the planet, we have not perfected the art of ideal parenting. Irene seemed to understand and be well prepared for the sleep deprivation. I, however, was not so. Strolling around the front room with our baby boy at 3:00 a.m. and knowing I would be setting off to work in four hours was a time when I felt I actually did do some proper parenting. But Irene took the brunt. It was she who was practical and realistic, she who planned as much as anybody could plan, she who understood we were in this for the long haul.

So when Father's Day comes along every year, I sit back and take the plaudits, but really and truly I feel a bit of a fraud. I won't admit I was an innocent bystander in the raising of our children, but my role was hardly one of "I lead, the rest follow." On some occasions, I think Irene believed that when I arrived home from work fit for not very much, that she was in the process of raising three children and not just two. But, Dear Reader, I did leave a café hungry on Saturday morning because our son threw a tantrum and there was no way we were going to subject other customers to that. Neither of us ate, and Alison was delighted to see us go and have her mum and her breakfast to herself. So *that* one moment of self-sacrifice, Dear Reader, justifies me having this day—the longest day of the year—in my honour.

Happy Father's Day to all of you who are, but I, for one, will be tipping my hat, raising my glass, planting a big kiss on the cheek of the one who really did all of the heavy lifting over the years.

Advice

I s it our fate as adults to give advice? Is it our destiny as teachers to be forever advising? How many times in our lives have we heard what we should do or, worse, what we should *have* done? Advice is inevitably a mixed bag, is it not? I guess I should know about that classic piece of advice which is, of course, asking for directions when one is lost en route. But, Dear Reader, I wouldn't know about that. I am a man, and part of signing up to become one was to promise *never* to ask for directions. It's a solemn oath. So, I have wasted thousands of miles worth of gasoline because my destination has always been around the next corner, down this lovely B road and so forth. The virile promise I made is for life!

It seems that the more power we are given in our lives, the more we feel we can dish out our thoughts freely on things way beyond our expertise. We find film stars pontificating on pandemics, footballers spouting off about politics and journalists giving medical advice. I do, however, love reading what the rich and the famous have spoken about over the years. Here is a selection:

"Calling me 'Sir' is like putting an elevator in an outhouse. It don't belong." Abe Lincoln

"Beware the serpent's eye that charms to destroy." Abe Lincoln

"Watch. When the tide goes out, you can see who has been swimming naked." Warren Buffet

"Try to see what everyone has seen and then think what nobody has thought." Lester Sinclair

"We should be even more cautious than we were in the past because the power we have to make big mistakes is now greater." John Gray

"Will level must exceed skill level."

OK, so not all of these quotations are examples of advice, they are more aphorisms or witticisms. But here at least is some advice:

"Don't chase two rabbits, you'll end up losing them both."

"Take rest. A field that has rested gives a beautiful crop." Ovid

"Sometimes it is better to trust great friendship rather than great wisdom." J.R.R. Tolkien

"Think in the morning. Act in the noon.
Eat in the evening. Sleep in the night."
William Blake

In my latter years at Collingwood, I remember a particularly good speaker delivering a speech in the gym as part of professional development. I cannot remember the theme of his speech, but I can remember this particular vignette. When the American poet and icon, Robert Frost, was lecturing at one of his many universities, he had a visit from one of his students. This confident young man breezed in and explained briefly and arrogantly that Mr. Frost and he had a lot in common because they were both poets! Hmmm! That's a bit like a man sitting down with a woolly mammoth, patting him patronizingly on the tusk and announcing that he and the beast have so much in common because they are both hairy! It seems to be an unfortunate part of our society that if we want to succeed, we have to sing our own praises, brag about our own achievements. If we make claims to be a so-and-so, then we have to be careful. Don't get me wrong, if it states on our documentation what our profession is, then that is written, that is stated, that is what we are. If, however, we say we are the best in our chosen field, the statement becomes arrogant braggadocio. It has a tendency to annoy the listener. Robert Frost's response to the young "poet" was to say he cannot make that claim, that it is for somebody else to laud him as a poet or not. The following advice would seem to be wise and supportive of that idea:

"When your work speaks for itself, don't
interrupt." Henry Kaiser

I used to have a colleague who is Polish. She came to this country after completing her education in Poland. She speaks Russian, German, French and a bit of Italian. She did not reveal this, so her students were unaware when they were speaking Russian in the back of her class that she knew what they were saying. She was too nice a person ever to use this. My point is that she is an extremely well-educated history and geography teacher. She very forcefully spoke to me one day and exclaimed that she believed that if she went quietly about her business in her own country then her contribution would be recognized. Doing so in North America meant she had to climb a rooftop with a megaphone and announce her achievements to the world. We all know men in suits who make sure they have sprayed the breath freshener, bragged about their MBA, talked a good line but have *no* substance. That is not to say they will not attain it, but knowing everything at twenty-five years old is not possible. A bit of humility and an opening of one's ears is possible if one allows it to be. They should perhaps try to learn from Goethe that:

> *"A talent is formed in stillness, a character in the world's torrent."*

As I sled down the hill of my life, I hope I am still a bit away from the snow bank at the bottom, and I hope I have learned that the main ingredient in stardom is the rest of the team. We cannot expect an institution to deliver our perfect utopias, and that one hint is worth two bushels of advice. Thus saith Ron MacLean, John le Carré and the Farmers' Almanac.

But then, Dear Friends, in the words of Washington Irving:

> *"I am always at a loss to know how much to believe of my own stories."*

So, Dear Friends, grab a pinch of salt and take it!

Do It Yourself

When I was a young man, I occasionally worked in the construction industry. Actually, that is a lie. I will rethink this statement. When I was a young man, I occasionally worked in the *destruction* industry. I was called upon to fetch and carry, to pass the tool from the toolbox, to barrow the concrete to be levelled. In the old days when there was such a thing as a pay packet, Duncan Smith and Sons used to pay us on a Friday afternoon, usually when we had finished the day's work. Sadly, on one Friday for reasons best known to themselves, they paid us at noon. We decided to pop off to the pub to have lunch and celebrate this early windfall. The pub led to a carry-out of beer and the arrival back at the job site at knocking off time. Blinking through the haze of alcohol, we saw that the concrete company had dumped its load in a pile on the driveway. We had forgotten about that. At this point, it was not solid. It was setting but saveable. We looked at our watches and went home. There is something spectacular about the anger of a construction company boss when he hears from a homeowner that there is a solid pile of concrete blocking her driveway. Our heads bowed down shamefully on that heated exchange, that tremendous tirade on the Monday morning. We made no excuses, we maintained our silence, we rode out the storm. Duncan had said his piece so there was a pause, and then he smiled ruefully. "I guess it was a mistake to pay you bastards in the middle of the day."

Duncan was a nice guy. We never let him down again.

I think I understand the pleasure and satisfaction people get from doing things themselves, and I try desperately to find that enthusiasm in myself. Our first house was a two up, two down terraced house on a main street in the City of Lincoln, just seventy-four paces from the Roaring Meg Pub. It needed rewiring. I bought the book. Irene was out one day, so I took up the floorboards to find the wires. I found them. They were there. I then put the floorboards back down, repositioned the carpets and began saving the money for an electrician. You see, Dear Reader, that has been the story of my life: try something practical, make a mess of it, phone somebody expensive to fix it. Now some of you will say that showing a bit more guts, determination and persistence would lead to success. Some have rudely asked if I can read, inferring that I should be able to read a step-by-step process on Google as well as anybody. All of this may be true, but it requires I notice things and steps and ally myself to a confidence and practicality that defies my limited dexterity.

Rob Moser will remember the excellent attempt to unblock the drain in front of the garage door. It was an awkward angle, parallel to the surface of the ground. I decided that Irene's hoe would be the best tool with which to tackle it. I put it in handle first and then drove it farther in with the sledge hammer. It was a tough battle to get it in, but I succeeded so that there was really only the head appearing, no longer a working hoe by the look of its mangle, but the drain would be free. I wiggled and manipulated, pulled and pushed but it was wedged solid. Finally, I enlisted the practical help of our excellent neighbour, Rob. Plan was to drive my car onto the lawn and, using a tow rope, hitch the hoe to the tow hitch on the car. Thank goodness for Rob because he rigged up a safety rope so that if and when the hoe was set free it would not become a missile potentially killing our southern neighbour or an innocent dog walker. A few hefty doses of horsepower and I received the shout from Rob that it was free. Thank goodness for his kindness and safety-conscious practicality. I went into the house and Googled how to unblock a drain.

"Step One: Call in a plumber."

"Step Two: Buy your wife a new hoe."

"Step Three: Give your neighbour a six pack."

So, I did call the plumber, ladies and gentlemen, I did.

Is it fair to say that most of us have unpacked the IKEA piece of furniture, put it together and, upon completion, been left with a package of screws?? Is it right to suggest that the art of construction does not involve a sledge hammer? Is it fair on the provincial medical system for me to turn up at the clinic with PCR on the end of my fist and a Canon inkjet printer wrapped around my foot? Was it wise of Irene to accept me as her husband all those many years ago when she could have had somebody handy and handsome? In mitigation, I do like digging, I do a bit of cooking and washing-up. I don't mind shredding documents, although deciding that the shredder was too slow and putting them in the composter and setting fire to them was not the wisest plan. Apparently plastic melts. Next time you give me a composter, Nigel, I will sue if it does not come with advice about fire and what not to burn.

I have two wonderful friends who begin a day in their summer holidays with a task around house or garden. They become so immersed in their job that time flies. They start at dawn and five minutes later it is twilight, so involved do they become. I understand passion and becoming so involved that one is in a state of flow. Indeed, yesterday with the strimmer I was very happy destroying buttercups and tufts of weedy grass. Suddenly, the plastic strip container at the bottom flew off into the bushes. I gave a less than determined search for it and then went and got out the lawn mower. Irene happened by, found the bit and fixed it while I fulminated my frustrations on innocent blades of grass. I guess, Dear Friends, DIY is like everything else in life: it's about attitude.

"We have a system of beliefs that is so successful we don't understand that it's belief any more. We think of it as knowledge."
John Gray

CHAPTER 9

CONCLUSION

Now that I have come to the end of *Pete's Pandemic*, it has been over four months of learning, a time of casting about trying to hear news that is good and wise and shows us a way forward. There has been much febrile floundering from our world leaders, and there has also been much conflicting evidence from the scientists. One has had to shift through a maze of beliefs that are often based too much on the nature of the presenter and are either too optimistic or too pessimistic. One has to find the pragmatist and stick with her. One has to dismiss the buffoon and the liar. One has to sift the word salads and find the nuances. One has to look at the experts and demand proof of their expertise. Finally, one has to realize that nobody really knows the outcome of this disease and, having done so, have had to become comfortable not with governments, scientists, pundits, celebrities, our heroes and our heroines, but with ourselves. We have to find our own place in our new world, dig deep into our own reserves, find joy in our own realms and be our own person, Dear Reader.

This pandemic diary is over from me, but the disease continues for us all. Stay safe, my friends.

100 Declared

For those of you who are cricketers (and I know at least one of you is), the aim of every batter is to score 100 runs every time he or she goes out to bat. A century is the goal. It can take hours to get there. Every bowl balled at you is a risk. You could be out with a duck (zero) first ball, which would be a "golden duck," or you could fall one short at 99. If ever there was a fickle finger of fate, then cricket will supply it whether one is a batsman or bowler or fielder. It is a game of soporific somnolence much of the time that suddenly demands split-second timing and the most athletic of muscle twitches. If the team for which you are playing is already sitting on a high score, then they will be eager to declare their innings over to get a chance to bowl at their opposition. If, however, their batter is approaching 100 runs in that innings, it is the gentlemanly thing to stay batting until he has failed or succeeded in reaching it. Then he is "Not out 100" and his team is 541 for 5 declared or some such score. The innings is over.

Well, Dear Reader, I have reached 100 of my COIVD blogs and am declaring these daily diatribes over for the time being. You will have no doubt sensed I have struggled for subject matter recently, battling for clear ways to fulfil the commitment. You will have noted that recent scribblings are drivelling more than usual. So, unless something world-shattering comes across the news, local or otherwise, then these musings are terminated for the time being. What could return me to the air waves?

Hmmmm!

Headline:

"Greenland Buys New York"

"In a surprising development today, the prime minister of Denmark, Mette Frederiksen, announced that the Danish government had helped Greenland purchase New York from the Americans. She announced the move along with sweeping changes for New York society. There is to be a revisionist history of the sinking of the *Titanic* with a massive campaign to rehabilitate the iceberg. T-shirts with "The Iceberg was Innocent" and "All Icebergs Matter" are already on sale. The Statue of Liberty is to be renamed. It will now be called "A whale of a statue." The New York Marathon is to be replaced by kayak races up the Hudson River. The new government is scheduled to take over as soon as the ice breaks up and they are able to travel there."

"Boris Johnson Dyes Hair"

"In a remarkable move, the prime minister of Great Britain and Northern Ireland has—(sorry, I'll start that again)." "In a remarkable move, the prime minister of what used to be Great Britain and Northern Ireland, minus Scotland, Wales and Northern Ireland, under the new name "England," has decided to reopen pubs. Mr. Johnson, with hair now coloured purple, made the announcement today while posing by the statue of Winston Churchill. He has encouraged common sense and social distancing but realizes common sense often disappears after two pints and social distancing calls it a day at some point between the third and fourth. George Flatley, the publican of The COVID Inn in Leicester, said, "We are just happy to be back in business. We've changed our name from The Royal Oak to The COVID to give it a more modern feel. As an opening gesture to pull in customers, we have created a new beer in honour of the virus. It is called The 19 and after the nineteenth pint you get a free necktie decorated with pictures of the coronavirus, red on a blue background. Of course, you can still buy a Corona if that is to your taste. Ha! Ha! For the non-beer drinkers, we have created a special cocktail called *The Bournemouth Beach,* which comes in a variety of flavours."

"Prince Harry and Megan Spotted in Iceland"

"In a remarkable turn around, the Royal Family has announced that Prince Harry has decided to resettle in Iceland. He was asked why he had chosen Iceland. He said that he had grown up in the Royal Family, so he was used to geophysical disturbances. An erupting volcano held no fear for him.

"Bard on Beach Banned from Vancouver"

A debate in council has agreed to ban all Shakespeare's plays from being performed in the downtown area of Vancouver. A spokesman for the council, reading from a prepared text, stated:

"The following are the reasons why the plays of Shakespeare are no longer going to be performed within the city limits:

1) *Macbeth*, "The Scottish Play," is an example of cultural appropriation.

2) Shylock in *The Merchant of Venice* is an example of anti-Semitism.

3) *The Taming of the Shrew* is misogynistic as well as a philologist slur.

4) Falstaff is portrayed as obese, i.e., horizontally challenged.

5) Caliban is portrayed as a monster.

6) There have been cases where a white, privileged male has played Othello.

7) Most of his plays glorify heterosexuality.

The council would like to add that banning these plays is an unfortunate curtailment of some of the greatest works in English literature. But we've deemed the words of the past inappropriate in a society that wants to move forward in a spirit of reconciliation and sensitivity towards visible minorities. We realize that the vast majority of people will be upset at this decision. But we were elected to represent you, which means we know better than you do, we matter more than you do, we are obviously more responsible than you are. We are in the know and you aren't. So in the spirit of true democracy we expect you to suck it up.

Signed: The mayor of Vancouver

"Working for a more inclusive and apologetic tomorrow."

"Sixty-Eight-Year-Old Man Trims Nose Hairs"

In a remarkable moment of temporary sanity, Peter Davidson, a retired teacher, trimmed his nose hairs today. When asked why he had done so, Davidson explained that he was rummaging in his medicine cupboard for his toenail clippers when he stumbled on his electric nose hair trimmer.

"It was a remarkable moment," said Davidson. "I suddenly realized what was important in life and acted upon it immediately."

Davidson is now writing a letter to the British medical journal, *The Lancet*, titled "Why do ears grow hair?"

"Since I turned sixty, I have realized that hair is growing in all sorts of unusual places. Having read about Charles Darwin's theories on the survival of the fittest, I have wondered what use hair in orifices is, believing that there must be one."

Davidson's wife, Irene, has threatened to take the garden strimmer to ears and nose unless he "gets a life," as she so succinctly puts it.

Epilogue

Thanks for taking the time to read these writings. If you are of a conscientious nature you will have realized that my claim that I wrote 100 blogs is not reflected here. There are five short of the century because the other five are missing in the ether. I lost them. Sure and all, I could have written five replacements, but they would have been outside the context of the time, a false representation from a different motive.

All that remains, Dear Reader, is to thank you so much for your time and patience. If you have felt duty-bound to read these issues, then I apologise and thank you for your kindness and patience. If they have given you an unfortunate insight into the inner Davidson, then I am truly sorry. If they have brightened your day, then I am pleased. Thanks so much for being part of the solution to my COVID stress. May the new normal be more like the old normal very soon. Stay safe. Peter Davidson.

Pete's Pandemic Bibliography

Ackroyd, Peter. "Dickens." Published by Sinclair Stevenson Ltd in 1990.

Bakewell, Sarah. "How to Live: Or a Life of Montaigne in One Question and Twenty Attempts at an answer." Published by Chatto and Windus in 2010.

Barnes, Simon. "The Meaning of Sport." Published by Short Books in 2006.

Boswell, James. "The Life of Samuel Johnson, LL.D (1791)." Published by Henry Baldwin.

Bryson, Bill. "Notes from a Small Island." Published by Reed Books (Canada) in 1995.

Buchan, Ursula. "A Life of John Buchan: Beyond the Thirty-Nine Steps." Published by Bloomsbury Publishing in 2019.

Bulfinch, Thomas. "Bulfinch's Mythology." Published by The Modern Library in 1998.

Burns, Robert. "The Poetical Works of Robert Burns." Published by Frederick Warne and Co. in 1787.

Chatwin, Bruce. "The Songlines." Published by Franklin Press in 1987.

Cleese, John. "So Anyway." Published by Arrow Books in 2014.

Dalrymple, Theodore. "Not with a Bang but a Whimper: The Politics and Culture of Decline." Published by Ivan R. Dee in 2008.

Diamond, Jared. "Guns, Germs and Steel." Published by W.W. Norton in 1997.

Douthat, Ross. "The Decadent Society: How We Became the Victims of Our Own Success." Published by Avid Reader Press in 2020.

Frazier, Charles. "Cold Mountain." Published by Atlantic Monthly Press in 1997.

Fry, Stephen. "Mythos: The Greek Myths Retold." Published by Penguin Random House UK in 2017.

Gladwell, Malcolm. "Blink: The Power of Thinking Without." Published by Back Bang Books in 2005.

Gladwell, Malcolm. "Talking to Strangers." Published by Little, Brown and Company in 2019.

Goodwin, Doris Kearns. "Team of Rivals. The Political Genius of Abraham Lincoln." Published by Simon & Schuster in 2005.

Gewen, Barry. "The Inevitability of Tragedy: Henry Kissinger and His World." Published by W.W. Norton and Company Inc in 2020.

Heller, Joseph. "Catch 22." Published by Simon & Schuster in 1961.

Hitchens, Christopher. "God Is Not Great." Published by the Hachette Book Group in 2007.

Hitchens, Christopher. "Hitch 22: A Memoir." Published by McClelland & Stewart in 2010.

Hitchens, Christopher. "And Yet…." Published by McClelland & Stewart in 2015.

Isaacson, Walter. "Kissinger: A Biography." Published by Simon & Schuster in 1992.

Johnson, Samuel. "Rasselas." (1759).

Keane, John. "The Life and Death of Democracy." Published by W.W. Norton & Company in 2009.

Kipling, Rudyard. "Kim." Published by MacMillan & Co in 1901.

Le Carré, John. "A Perfect Spy." Published by Hodder & Stoughton in 1986.

Le Carré, John. "Our Kind of Traitor." Published by Viking Press in 2010.

Le Carré, John. "Agent Running in the Field." Published by Viking in 2019.

Le Carré, John. "Absolute Friends." Published by Hodder & Stoughton in 2003.

Mantel, Hilary. "Wolf Hall." Published by HarperCollins in 2009.

Mantel, Hilary. "Bring up the Bodies." Published by HarperCollins in 2012.

Mantel, Hilary. "The Mirror and the Light." Published by HarperCollins in 2020.

Martel, Yann. "Life of Pi." Published by Knopf Canada in 2001.

McIntyre, Ian. "Dirt and Deity: A Life of Robert Burns." Published by Harper Collins in 1995.

Murphy, Michael. "Golf in the Kingdom." Published by Penguin in 1997.

Macfarlane, Robert. "The Old Ways." Published by Penguin in 2013.

Macfarlane, Robert. "Mountains of the Mind." Published by Vintage Books in 2004.

Pasternak, Boris. "Doctor Zhivago." Translated by Richard Pevear and Larissa Voloknonsky, 2011. First published, 1957.

Paterson, Banjo. "The Man from Ironbark." Published in "The Bulletin" in 1892.

Quammen, David. "Spillover: Animal Infections and the Next Human Pandemic." Published by W.W. Norton & Company in 2012.

Rankin, Ian. "Let it Bleed." Published by Orion in 1995.

Shakespeare, William. "The Complete Works of William Shakespeare." Published by Collins in 1971.

Shepherd, Nan. "The Living Mountain." First published by the Aberdeen University Press in 1977.

Tolkien, J.R.R. "The Lord of the Rings." Published by Allen and Unwin in 1954.

Tomalin, Claire. "Charles Dickens: A Life." Published by the Penguin Group in 2011.

Twain, Mark. "The Original Illustrated Mark Twain." Published by Castle Books in 2001.

White Jr., Ronald C. "A. Lincoln: A Biography." Published by Random House in 2009.

Willink, Jocko and Rabin, Leif. "Extreme Ownership: How Navy Seals Lead and Win." Published by St. Martin's Press in 2015.

Wolfe, Linnie Marsh. "John of the Mountains: The Unpublished Journals of John Muir." Published by

University of Wisconsin Press. Copyright Wanda Muir Hanna, 1938.

Woods, Randall B. "LBJ: Architect of American Ambition." Published by Free Press in 2006.

Woodward, Bob. "State of Denial." Published by Simon & Schuster in 2006.

"The Farmers' Almanac." First published by the Almanac Publishing Company in 1818.

"Nae Bad Ava: Mair Doric Poems compiled by The Reading Bus" Published by The Reading Bus Press in 2009.